THREE MEN IN TEXAS
Bedichek, Webb, and Dobie

Three Men in Texas

BEDICHEK, WEBB, and DOBIE

ESSAYS BY THEIR FRIENDS IN THE *Texas Observer*

Edited by Ronnie Dugger

Introduction by Ralph W. Yarborough

UNIVERSITY OF TEXAS PRESS

AUSTIN & LONDON

To what they stood for

PREFACE

"And so now all three of them are gone from us: Roy Bedichek, Walter Webb, and Frank Dobie," Hubert Mewhinney wrote.

"Their influence on modern Texas is beyond measure.

"They never won an election; they never ran for office with a hillbilly band playing imitation folk tunes; their influence was on intelligent men; and we might as well face it: intelligent men are in the minority."

They were, said Frank Wardlaw at Dobie's funeral, "an incomparable triumvirate who were at once the conscience and the directing force of many aspects of the intellectual life of Texas."

"The three of them," Angus Cameron wrote, "make a formidable trio of Americans who have reflected a universal wisdom by knowing more about their home region than anyone else knows."

They were teachers, and they were writers. What they knew they wanted to share, what they did not know they wanted to learn, and each of them wanted to make and leave behind him something that was not here until he passed here. One was a naturalist, one a historian, and one a chronicler, but each of them was each of these. The manly love between them, a handsome thing in times and places blighted by great ugliness and banality, shone from them into their friends and contemporaries, and they shared themselves freely with those younger than they who went to them wanting to learn from them. They lived out their lives doing their work, and they did not leave here, but died here.

I was close to only one of them, and to him not long. There was no special reason why I should edit the issues of the *Observer* about them, except that I was editor of the *Observer*. To write about them I chose people who knew them. Since I undertook to elicit whatever the contributors wanted to say about these their friends and did not tell them they had this or that facet assigned to them, what they wrote was not preconceived as literary criticism or as scholarly consideration of these three men within the areas of learning where they worked; what we have here is what their friends said about them, about Bedichek and Webb soon after they died, about Dobie while he was still alive. This, then, is not a thing to please those who seek evaluations free of emotion and friendship, nor certain academics, but still it is a valuable thing, for these were good men, and here they are remembered.

R. D.

Austin, Texas

ACKNOWLEDGMENTS

Acknowledgment and thanks are extended to Mrs. Lillian Bedichek, Mrs. Terrell Webb, and Mrs. Bertha Dobie for their generous help and cooperation and to each of the contributors for patience and forbearance with the editor. Edgar Kincaid's article on Bedichek first appeared in the newsletter of the Texas Ornithological Society, Jack Fischer's on Webb in the *Graduate Journal* of The University of Texas, and Archer Fullingim's on Dobie in the *Kountze News*; each was subsequently published in the *Texas Observer* of Austin, Texas. Harry Ransom's article on Dobie first appeared in the *Austin American,* and Dr. Edmund Heinsohn's remarks at final services also appeared in the local daily. Duncan Robinson on Bedichek, Tom Sutherland on Webb, and J. E. Reynolds on Dobie are published in this book for the first time. The rest of the articles first appeared in the special editions of the *Observer* devoted to these three men, or, in a few cases, in other issues of the *Observer.*

CONTENTS

CONTENTS

J. FRANK DOBIE

CONTENTS

ILLUSTRATIONS

Following page 152

INTRODUCTION

Bedichek, Dobie, and Webb—names to stir a Texan's blood and pride, but names to sober him, too. For these are the names which, in this generation, evoke thoughts of freedom—free men, free thought, and free expression. In past generations, these were thoughts evoked by names such as Austin, Houston, Hogg, and Reagan—the names of Texas' politicians and statesmen. But strangely absent from the Texas scene this past third of a century have been politicians and statesmen whose names could stir the hearts of Texans. In an age of conformity and uniformity, politicians adopted a pattern of dull blandness to get elected in a world where ghosts held the greatest glory. But the vacancy on the political front was filled on the academic front, and the greatness of a proud people was carried on by Roy Bedichek, J. Frank Dobie, and Walter Prescott Webb.

In my undergraduate days at The University of Texas, I was never so fortunate as to draw a class taught by Dobie or Webb, but I was a participant in another way, as practically all the students were. Each night at the boarding house, or in old B Hall, or at a frat house (I lived in all three), we would gather in a room and listen to the narrations of those who studied under the provocateurs, to hear the day's jokes, admire their wisdom, discuss their philosophy—and wonder why Frank Dobie went to jail rather than pay a parking ticket.

My greatest personal pleasure and gain from these three men came years later, after World War II, from the hours spent in their presence at the Austin Town and Gown Club, which they adorned and illuminated. We enjoyed their fine and lively books, but nothing inanimate could compare with the men, themselves.

Still alive in many men's memories today are Dobie's defense of the sit-down strikers in Detroit, his championing of the rights of Mexican pecan shellers in San Antonio, and his call to a shocked state for the admission of Negro students to The University of Texas, years before it happened. (The Regents in 1947 struck his name from the rolls of The University of Texas because of his noncomformity.)

Webb stunned his fellow Texans by reminding them, in the pages of *Harper's*, that a portion of his beloved Texas was a true desert—and he sought to get water for it by his shock treatment. Bedichek discomfited many stuffed shirts in many ways—throwing barbs at pale eggs and fat steaks produced by implanted, artificial growth-stimulating chemicals.

These men of great ideas gave hope and encouragement to some of us out on the hustings and to millions who found their own thoughts expressed for them by "Mister Bedi," Don Pancho, and Dr. Webb.

Practically all of the articles written about them are concerned with their literary attainments, but each of them worked in far broader fields in their common search for a better environment and life for man. Each encouraged political action: Bedichek in man-to-man talks, Webb as an adviser and a writer of speeches, Dobie as a political essayist, a broadside composer, a writer of polemics, a political satirist. There was something of a Tom Paine in Frank Dobie.

Each of them aided and encouraged me, personally and through the courage and the integrity of purpose that they together represented. I read and enjoyed their books, but it was the words they spoke that helped me most. I owe all of them a lasting debt, something higher than gratitude for something deeper than encouragement. The "mystic chords" keep their memory green.

They are gone now—all gone. Who will take their place? Some say the breed was Old Texan, and is gone forever. Free voices have been in short supply in most of the generations of man's history, but such men do not die out. It is from the very struggle for freedom that men take strength. Among the free-lance writers and the editors of small papers and small independent journals, I see that fight carried on today, at high cost. As they struggle for the survival of free expression—their struggle for freedom making survival difficult—the struggle makes them. The yearning of Texans for men in the tradition of Bedichek, Dobie, and Webb will not be quenched short of fulfillment.

Ralph W. Yarborough
United States Senator from Texas

Austin, Texas

PHOTOGRAPH BY BILL SHROUT

ROY BEDICHEK

J. FRANK DOBIE

My friend, Roy Bedichek

Nature is the complex of all complexities. One part of a man may be as simple and serene as the cow chewing her cud in the noonday shade of a tree a thousand miles and a hundred years away from any milking machine; and yet the whole of this same man may be as complex as the genius of Shakespeare—that is to say, the greatest genius in the world—ever penetrated. It will be a great deal easier to show Roy Bedichek in the simplicities of naturalness than to express him in the naturalness of the highest intellectual and emotional complexities.

His going to bed with the chickens in summertime and not too much later in the wintertime and getting up with the morning star at all times made his friends smile. He favored several kinds of independence common to the country . . . He liked to cook outdoors, eat outdoors, sleep outdoors, look and listen outdoors, be at one with the unexplaining wind from the south, with the swing of the Great Dipper around the North Star, and with the first bob-whiting at dawn. He preferred camping on a hill so that he could watch the firmament, rather than down in a shady valley by water.

The last car he bought, in 1951, was a Dodge pickup truck in which he could carry enough water to make his camp on a hill comfortable for a day or two. This pickup was for camp purposes, but he used it to run about in also, his wife owning a sedan. He got an immense satisfaction out of trucking in cow manure, also occasionally chicken manure, for his compost pile, with which he annually fertilized his garden. He got a satisfaction out of hauling his own wood

1

in from the country; he liked especially cedar stumps that he wouldn't have to cut for the fireplace. He had complete camp equipment, including a tent-fly to go with the truck. Part of the equipment was a field guide to the flora of the country and a field guide to the birds. He always took along something to read as well as to consult; above all, he took along the most richly and variously stored mind I have known. Not for him the dream of retiring to some private land and mating with "some savage woman" to rear his dusky race. For him back to nature was not back to the primitive, there to be saved from "poring over miserable books."

His father, James Madison Bedichek, an ex-Confederate soldier, quoted philosophers and talked philosophy at the family dining table. He proved up on a quarter-section of land near the village of Eddy, not far from Waco in central Texas. Here he and his wife ran what they called the Eddy Scientific and Literary Institute, dubbed the Bedichek School by the public. Mrs. Bedichek boarded and roomed some of the pupils. Roy's aptitude for books was as congenital as that for milk. The atmosphere of literature and of thought was as natural to him as the atmosphere in which a lone buzzard soars over a cedar-covered hill or in which a coyote trots through the mesquite, sniffing for a woodrat's trail. I would not call his taste exactly austere. He took pleasure in witty limericks, even though bawdy; he could talk for hours with some cedar-chopper whose literary vocabulary was limited to the printing on a bottle of Levi Garrett's Snuff. I've heard him say a dozen times that he could no longer read American fiction because it is so pallid and insipid compared to the great Russian fiction rammed to the breech with vitality: Turgenev, Dostoevsky, Tolstoy. He admitted Balzac into their company. During a long span of his life he read the greater part of Shakespeare about once every two years.

The Walt Whitman that he knew by heart and had absorbed into his very marrow was not the sentimentalized "good grey poet" but the tough poet of democracy. "He is our greatest exponent of Democracy among the poets," Bedi wrote me in a letter. "The reached hand, bringing up the laggards—could there be a more expressive phrase of the true inwardness of Democracy than that?" Along with Whitman, his favorite American writer was Thoreau, acid, with the wild taste, a rebel. Bedichek gloried in the influence that Thoreau's

"Civil Disobedience" had on Gandhi and India and is still having over the world.

While he was writing *Adventures with a Texas Naturalist,* or maybe it was *Karankaway Country,* he made a habit of reading pages of Plato with his pre-dawn coffee. Plato helped start the day for him on a noble plane and put him into a creative mood. At this time he would not wilt the freshest part of the day with the littleness and banalities of a morning newspaper. For no man writing a book has morning ever been, to quote a 1945 note from Bedichek, a time to "stoke the furnace of indignation against numerous manifestations of Fascism in this country." He never learned the Greek language, but his ideal of a balanced life, of a just proportion of the elements that make up a human being, was essentially Greek. In reading Homer, he compared several translations. As hundreds of quotations and allusions in his books and letters would show, the immortal essence of the Greeks was in his veins.

It seemed to me that the philosophy of Henry George had a more determining effect upon his economic views than any other writing. Henry George advocated a single tax and did not consider it just that an individual owner of real estate should collect the unearned increment given to it by population and labor. Bedichek believed in the single tax but would justify buying a piece of land by saying, "It's better to run with the hounds for your dinner than with the hare for your life."

Immanuel Kant's categorical imperative was his golden rule: Do only as you would have others do; or, act only as if you would have the act become universal law. The categorical imperative is contrary to the ways of greed and lust; so was Bedichek. He was as unenvying and as free from greed and jealousy as any man could be. Anybody who knew him would as soon expect apples to fall up instead of down as for him to misrepresent a fact.

In the early 1920's he suffered from a rash caused, he was told, from eating too much of high proteins, especially eggs. He became for the rest of his life what Sam Houston called "a damned vegetarian." He was not too rigid, however, to enjoy latitude upon occasion. As a guest he ate of the meat set before him. He took the lead many a time in getting a few men friends to go out in the country for a meal and talk. There was always a steak, and Bedi always insisted

3

on cooking the steak over coals. Nobody could cook it better, and he was no slacker in eating his part of it. Cooking meat over an open fire mitigated in his mind any "protein poison" it might have; at a hotel table I've seen him dispose of an untouched steak to somebody else who could eat a double one. He had a theory that the deeper down into the earth a plant puts its roots, the richer its fruit is. He positively gloated in dilating on the mineral and other virtues of pecans. He loved to mix a green or a fruit salad and would linger long and lovingly in detailing his recipe for such.

In theory he was against doctors; I think he wrote considerably on a book intended to expose at least several sides of the medical profession—though he believed very much in his doctor daughter, Mary Virginia Carroll. He would quote an old proverb: "A man's either a fool or his own physician after forty." He said that a sick man should have as much sense as a sick cow: she quits eating and goes off and lies down.

Sometimes it didn't seem at all natural to me that Bedi should be practical. He was a productive gardener, as his table, his deep freeze, and many a mess of vegetables he gave to friends showed. Yet he put a kind of ritualism into gardening that farmer folks wouldn't and couldn't bother with. When I drove with him in his pickup I constantly wondered how he made it through the streets—but he always made it.

He liked raw milk, believed in its virtues for himself and his family. He had a contempt for boiled and chemically treated milk, something taken out and something else put in. For years he milked his own cow. There were vacant lots not far distant from the Bedichek home on East Twenty-third Street in Austin, where a cow could graze. The last cow he had, about 1932 or 1933, was a four-gallon milker. She was very gentle and very much devoted to the Bedicheks, but keeping a cow and milking her became too much of a burden, and Bedi sold her to a man out near Deep Eddy on West Sixth Street. This man saw the cow being milked. Bedi told him that she wouldn't give milk unless she was treated gently and fed well. He got up at two o'clock in the morning to lead her to the purchaser, thus avoiding the traffic. The purchaser hadn't had her more than two or three days before he complained that the cow wasn't giving the milk claimed for her. He wanted his money back. Bedi went out there. The cow was shrunken and showed abuse. While the man was away for a minute,

4

his wife told Bedi that her husband had beaten the cow. Bedi felt like beating the man, but he left. He didn't give him his money back either.

In the vigor of early manhood Bedi drank some whiskey—maybe not too much—although after he married any drinking was bad economically. I don't think he ever loved any man quite so much as he loved his college friend Harry Steger, with whom he went to Europe and who died young. He cried all day long, so Mrs. Bedichek has told me, after receiving word of Steger's death. One of his favorite anecdotes was of meeting Steger on Congress Avenue in Austin one day. They both wanted a drink but before entering a saloon swore to each other that they would take only one and then get out. They took the drink, and it was good. "Well, let's go," said Bedi. "That drink makes me feel like a new man," Steger said, and "now the new man has to have a drink." I never did ask Bedi if he joined the new man.

By the time I got to know him, he wasn't smoking the pipe or cigar he had once smoked. He took real solace in a bottle of beer along in the evening or with a Mexican meal—but virtually never more than one. Along about 1954 or 1955 in the middle of a terrible drouth devastating much of Texas, I brought back about a dozen cases of Carta Blanca beer from Monterrey, Mexico. I had a devil of a time getting them past the customs ignoramuses at Laredo. I had to prove my right to pay duty on beer just as beer dealers pay it. I hadn't more than got to Austin and got a few bottles cooled than I called up Bedi. For awhile I shared that Carta Blanca beer with other people, especially when Bedi was around. When only two cases were left, I cut off everybody, including myself, and saved it especially for Bedichek. Occasionally there might be two or three or half a dozen other men; I'd offer them what they wanted to drink, and if they wanted beer they had to take Schlitz (Bedi's second choice) or something else. Then I'd bring out Bedi's bottle of Carta Blanca. He enjoyed that sort of petting.

As newspaperman, chamber of commerce exponent, and director of the Interscholastic League of Texas, Bedichek had done a vast amount of hack work. Anybody who works for a living spends the majority of his energies in hack work. But though Bedi was a university man, specializing in the humanities, he had never been deflected by the Ph.D. system into the inferiorities of literature. He had spent a lifetime reading the best before he turned author with seventy just

5

over the hill for him. While H. Y. Benedict was President of The University of Texas, I heard him say that Bedichek should be teaching literature. "Why not put him to teaching it?" I asked. "Because every Ph.D. professor of English would have a colt if I did," he replied. That was the truth! Sawdust never yearns toward vitality.

We all learn with wonder of the feats in memory performed by the Macaulays of history, but I've never known anyone else in the flesh who held in memory so precisely so much of what he had read as Roy Bedichek. He could have produced a magnificent anthology of English poetry solely out of his memory—as rich as Lord Wavell drew from his memory in *Other Men's Flowers*. He had the added faculty, perhaps of a higher order, of always being able to draw from memory anything related to a subject brought up by conversation or in his own flow of thought. Sometimes he had to restrain himself from clogging his writing with allusions and "decisions that had from the time of King William come down."

Early in the summer of 1953 Jess Akin of Austin decided to paint the portraits of Bedichek, Walter Webb, and myself. He had painted mine unsatisfactorily and wanted to make another attempt. If a person is being portrayed for his significance, every effort should be made to make that significance appear on his countenance while he is sitting for the painter. I volunteered to do my best to keep Bedi's features illuminated while he was being painted. I knew that he would do more talking than I, for he was just naturally a better talker. I illuminated him for four half-days. After Akin was through with Bedi, he took me on, and Bedi came to brighten me. We had eight conversations amounting to perhaps thirty hours in less than two weeks. I can say of Bedichek as Johnson said of Burke: "That man draws out all my powers." Neither he nor I was empty or exhausted when the sittings came to an end. Sitting and talking had become a kind of occupation with us. Several times I thought I would make notes on the subjects of our talk. I did not. Naturally, we recurred occasionally to the same themes—but without repeating. Now I cannot recall a hundredth part of what either said; if I could recall all, a book would be required to hold it. Little of it was trivial. It interested us, and that was sufficient.

Will Burges, lawyer of El Paso, John Lomax, of cowboy song fame, and Roy Bedichek were the pithiest and vividest relators of anecdotes about human beings they had encountered that I have known. De-

6

spite his rich stores out of books, Bedichek in the course of conversations with his peers drew more often from actual experience. He could make any character that interested him fascinating.

He told few stories except to reveal character, to bring out some point, or to complement something else. Lots of times one merry tale would call up another.

Boswell's life of Johnson is the greatest biography in the world because it records the best talk that has ever been recorded. Bedichek often talked as well as Johnson talked—but he had no Boswell to record more than a few snatches of his talk.

As President of the Texas Institute of Letters, I had notice from judges of books published during the year 1956 that Bedichek had won the Carr P. Collins $1,000 award, to be presented at the Institute's annual dinner in Dallas, February 1, 1957. On the evening of January 20, I went to his home, finding him alone. I had telephoned him that I had a letter to confront him with. He was eating a salad of tomatoes, lettuce, cheese, and a little mayonnaise, moistening it down with a glass of buttermilk. He thought I should take a little something and spooned out yogurt into a bowl and put honey on it. We were both honey hounds, honey being the highest form of sweetness—natural. I could not remember having tasted yogurt before. He told me how monks in a Hungarian monastery had cultivated the yogurt germ hundreds of years ago, keeping it secret; how one escaped with the process to Canada, whence it was brought to California, where yogurt is now made and sold. "I get the yeast in a container every three weeks by air mail," Bedi said, "and make six quarts." He described in detail the sanitary processes for making yogurt and its bodily virtues. "Not the same thing at all," he said, "that you buy in grocery stores." I found it delicious.

After the yogurt, I *confronted* him with the letter. He read it aloud slowly. When he came to the point—the $1000 award to Roy Bedichek for his book *Educational Competition*, he stopped, joy on his face. We talked a little and then he said:

Dobie, you'll go away and I'll think that I dreamed you were here with this announcement.

About three thousand years ago a disciple of one of the Chinese philosophers came to him one morning and said, "Master, I dreamed last night that I was a butterfly." The philosopher looked at him hard and said, "Sir,

7

are you sure now that you are not a butterfly dreaming that you are a man?"

That word *confront* you used over the telephone had me puzzled [Bedi continued]. You are somewhat of a precisionist, and *confront* bears the connotation of something unpleasant. I was wondering what sort of blackguard had been denouncing me and what you could have against me.

Thousands of words had special connotations for him. About the time I carried the good news of the thousand-dollar prize, the secretary of the Town and Gown Club, to which we both belonged, sent out an announcement of a paper to be read by Bedichek at the fortnightly dinner. His subject was "Water and Soil Conservation in Texas." I noticed the use of that word "confront" in a quotation from Bedi on what he was going to say:

That which I shall write will be down—I fear *far* down—on the lay level. The authorities bristle with statistics which I only vaguely understand and speak in a jargon that I don't savvy except in spots. Hence my modesty may be compared to that of the Negro in the folk rhyme who was confronted with a medical emergency:

> "Ah ain't no doctor nor no doctor's son
> But Ah kin hol' de patient till de doctor come."

One time on Conversation Rock, at Barton Springs where we swam daily, Fred Thompson was with us when I set out anathematizing the pasteurized, homogenized, vitaminized and otherwise bowdlerized milk now sold in pasteboard cartons, this stuff having driven natural (raw) milk out of the market. I knew Bedi would respond. . . . He never was the kind of person to think all virtue resides in the past and that the world is going to hell. However, the loss of natural things was a frequent theme with him. He was a confirmed believer in the country way of squatting to defecate. The squatting position presses up muscles to aid ejection, he held.

Squatting on the rim of a commode will not do. The rim is too slippery, and a squatter could fall and break a hip. I remarked on how high the seats of old-time privies were. Yes, Bedi said, he had sat on them so high that his feet could hardly touch the ground. But he could, without danger of falling, squat on the plank in which the holes were cut—and squat he did.

I shall die regretting that I did not set down on paper a thousand

8

passages of Bedichek talk before they faded from my mind. Here is a brief note I typed on the night of September 6, 1957. It illustrates the mobility, and homeliness too, characteristic of Bedichek's mind:

Bill Owens, writer and teacher in Columbia College, New York, and Bedichek's friend, came to town and this evening after a swim we sat down under the big elm in our back yard to drink beer and talk. When I brought out three cans in two hands, Bedi told this story, which, he said, came to him from an income-tax man.

In Minnesota, it seems, there is some kind of income-tax law whereby a higher percentage is charged on income made by a joint furnishing entertainment with beer than from one that does not. Anyhow, a Swedish woman opened up a beer tavern in Minnesota and it was soon notorious for the patronage it drew. A tax man went to inspect it.

He saw the place crowded with men. There were other beer places not far away with only small crowds. All sold the same beer. What was the attraction here? The inspector could see no dance girls, no entertainer of any kind, not even a television set. Then he saw the proprietress emerging from behind the counter carrying four bottles of beer. She had one in each hand and one sitting on each breast, where they stood steady while she moved with energy and did not touch them. Was this entertainment?

I keep referring to talk at Barton Springs. One day while we were sunning after a dip in the cold water, Bedi remarked that a "farm-type of woman" he had encountered that morning reminded him of a wise old mare.

"After an old mare has had eight to ten colts," he said, "she gets a look of wisdom hardly seen in the eyes of the wisest philosopher."

On August 7, 1957, after a cold, cold swim in Barton Springs, we sat down about dusk to double hotness in a Mexican restaurant. (This is one of the few uses of the word "Mexican" remaining active. Mexican restaurants in Texas are no longer run by Mexicans but by Latin-Americans.) With Bedichek and me was our younger friend Wilson Hudson.

After much good talk, Bedichek told this story:

One time out in Amarillo they were having a prohibition election. The pros imported a high-powered speaker to convert the heathen and packed the biggest gathering place in town with an audience. This speaker quoted poetry and displayed all sorts of diagrams showing the effects of alcohol on the human organs. Then he unrolled a long linen chart and hung it up on

9

the wall to demonstrate the waste of money on alcohol. The figures and letters on this chart were box-car size so that they could be read half a block away.

But the speaker was adding emphasis by reading them out in a loud voice. Up at the top were so many millions and billions spent each year in America for food, so many for clothes, so many on churches, so many on education, and on through the catalogue. The figures were soaring and the speaker's voice soared to a climax as he read out the billions and millions spent on whiskey.

"And, by God, it's worth it," a mighty voice rang out. It was the voice of Buttermilk Jones. The announcement of his sense of values came in a way that absolutely killed the speaker's facts and figures.

"Why," Wilson Hudson now asked, "did they call him Buttermilk Jones?"

"Because he never drank buttermilk, I guess," Bedi answered.

This putting a high value on whiskey makes me think of an incident during prohibition days [I said]. Not long after the end of World War I, an Englishman and a Texan were partners trading in oil leases and royalties out in the Burkburnett field. Some bootleggers were making more than owners of oil wells. One day a big well came in on land controlled by the partners; within fifteen minutes they cleared a hundred thousand dollars by selling just a fraction of what they owned, and they decided right there to celebrate the occasion.

The Englishman rustled around and found a fifth of Canadian Club whiskey for sale at $50. He bought it and took it to their room. He opened it and poured the contents over ice. Raising his glass, he said, "Here's to whiskey!—the only time in my life I ever paid what it's worth."

Two evenings after this—and a lot of other—talk, we three met again, this time on a shady lawn. I read aloud what I had written, received a few corrections, and saw about three dozen words, sentence structures, and idea combinations to work on. Two evenings later we met again, in a darkening, air-conditioned room, fresh again from Barton Springs with fresh thirst. As we were raising our beer cans, Bedi quoted:

"A chiel's amang you taking notes,
And faith he'll prent it."

I despair at getting into print the felicity and fitness with which Bedichek was forever drawing out of his storehouse. Many writers, perhaps most, read in order to suck in something that they can feed out. During most of his life Bedi read to delight and enlarge his own mind. Now how in the devil had he come to remember those lines from Burn's "On the Late Captain Grose's Peregrinations thro' Scotland"? (He had to tell me the source.) And how in the devil could they lie down there in the cellar of his memory for a generation or two and then, just as occasion arose for their application, jump to the surface like an empty corked bottle released at the bottom of a pool?

On February 24, 1957, I paid Bedi a visit in his shack, taking with me for him a paperbound copy of A. E. Taylor's *Socrates, the Man and His Thought.* On the fly leaf I had written:

Dear Bedi, I give you this book because I would be as bereft if you went away as Crito and the others were when Socrates went. As one of them said of him, I can say of you, my friend, "the wisest and justest and best man that I have ever known."—Dobie, 24 February 1957.

Two days later I received this letter:

Dear, dear Dobie—

After I had been about an hour at work this morning, I glanced up and saw the volume "Socrates" you gave me yesterday. I remembered that I had seen some writing on the fly-leaf which I didn't take time to read while you were here. I had dismissed it momentarily as a "good wishes" inscription and so had let it escape my attention.

I reached up and got the volume in my hand "just to see." I was affected to tears, and I don't mean metaphorical tears but a real secretion from the lachrymose glands. One got loose from the inner corner of my left eye and it felt wet and warm, so I know they were real.

The old Greeks (bless them) were not ashamed of tears. That shame was a part of the sentimentalism and masculine assumption of superiority of that romanticism which assigned tears to women. I am profoundly affected, (stirred emotionally in that nervous plexus situated in the abdomen) by your placing me in a unique position in your affections. Truly, I have felt towards you a friendship I never felt for anyone else except for Harry Steger, who died 44 years ago.

Bless you for recording this where I can turn to it when sometimes: "the world is dark and I a wanderer who has lost his way."

Yours,

Bedi

February 25, 1957

11

Two or three years before this, standing in a group of friends, I said to Bedi, "You are as good as grass."

"Don Quixote," he said, "once told Sancho Panza, 'You are as good as bread. Nothing but the sexton and his spade will ever part us'."

Now the sexton and his spade have come. Something has been sheared off of me.

RONNIE DUGGER*

"Authentic tidings of invisible things"

When I met him, Roy Bedichek was seventy-six years old, and I was twenty-five. He was enjoying his career as a writer the last twelve years of his life, twelve years in which he wrote four books. I was one year into my career as a reformer journalist on a weekly paper, a zealous youth who might have steeped himself in the talk of a Texas Socrates but spent his energy instead crusading for a better Texas. Still, intermittently his last years, Bedichek tolerated my occasional intrusions. Perhaps he thought I was a young man worth encouraging, but also he took pleasure in youth because it illuminated his memories and meant to him life that would go on after him, shaped by his ways; for he was an emulable man.

"Mr. Bedichek," I always called him when I was talking to him; yet, when his name came up among others, he was "Bedichek." He was earthy and humble, and was given to pixie humors, but he was venerable in spite of himself. One spoke about him as one speaks, by objective reference, of a well known person, for he was one of the three old men of Texas letters, Bedichek, Walter Prescott Webb, and J. Frank Dobie, the naturalist, the historian, and the chronicler of the early Southwest. Bedichek knew nature, and how to take care of himself in it; he cited an ancient Greek, or recited verse copiously, at the drop of a happy context; he could spin tales to transfix the very leaves around. There are not many men like him among us now.

He was born in Illinois in 1878. For fifteen years after college he bummed around the country and the world. He picked cotton in the

* Editor-at-large of *The Texas Observer*.

South, peeled potatoes on a river boat, gathered berries in New Jersey, washed dishes in a Chinese cafe in New York City, tramped over the English, French, and German countrysides, assisted a fake divine in Boston, dug coal and explored rivers in West Virginia, cut off hogs' heads in a Chicago slaughterhouse, and homesteaded in Oklahoma. His wife says that when he was young he had "lots of yella hair, and green eyes with lots of spots in them."

A family to support, he edited for papers in New Mexico and San Antonio. Then, as director of the University Interscholastic League of Texas, he affected the lives of millions of Texas school children as the chief designer of our competitions in sports, public speaking, music, and writing. Hold before the young, he said and did, "the great theme of superior performance and the vision of greatness it inspires."

In his late sixties, his chest by then concave, his mane quite white, he began to write, timing his work and rest to "the rhythm of the natural day." Rising at three or four in the morning, he spent an hour or two in his "devotional," the reading of a good book "while slowly sipping a cup of weak coffee." Then he stepped out of his white frame, two-story home and shuffled down an alley a half block to his hideout, a grayboard shed backed by a garage.

On cold mornings he started his wood fire in the pot-bellied iron stove in the center of the only room. He sat in a hard-back wood chair at his plain table; on his aged Oliver the keys looped up and landed on the cylinder like overhead haymakers. The walls were books, from the floor to the ceiling. I did not keep, in notes, the gifts he gave me when I went there those few mornings, recitations of verse, ideas from the past, his own ideas and his enrichments of mine, but had there been nothing but his telling me, "A young man who needs solitude must get a place physically apart from his family, a place altogether his own. If only I had realized that sooner!"—still he would have strengthened my life.

He grew vegetables for his family in a garden by the shed, but I never saw him there. One morning we greeted on a corner of The University of Texas campus and sat for a while on a bench underneath an ancient spreading oak tree, considering the subject of writing style, toward which I, aware that I had none, was vigorously venting my contempt. "Style," I pronounced, "is the man." He warmly

14

agreed, and a little later in the conversation told me who had said so a few thousand years ago.

Later in a review of his book on the history of the Interscholastic League, I disastrously misused a word. He wrote me a two-page letter appreciating the review, not mentioning the mistake (which came to my attention in a nightmare I had); when I went over to apologize, he hardly let me finish and said laughing: "Don't admit it—blame it on the printer! All printers are liars anyway. Whenever I made a mistake on my paper in New Mexico, it was always a typographical error." Once he wrote me to help me with my remorse that I had neglected a gifted, eccentric young Austin writer who had died before I had decided whether to publish a story he had given me. "I have more cause for conscience concerning this man than you have," Bedichek said, "but I don't let my derelictions, real or fancied, dog me around."

The last summer of the drouth of the fifties he took me into the caliche hills southwest of Austin and taught me how to camp. We set up in a small grove of oak trees on a broken meadow. With a grubbing hoe he dug a trench in the ground a foot deep and several feet long and built down inside it a strong fire. After we opened the bedding, he began methodically preparing supper. He liked to linger, he said, over "scaring up a good meal of vittles." (Yet how little of all this I can remember.) Supper was my introduction to sardines on lettuce with a cold beer, to his savory celery soup, and to potatoes and apples carefully washed by hand in a bowl of water, wrapped in wetted brown paper and then again in wetted tinfoil, dipped in water again, and steamed in the coals. He put the brown paper on first because he believed that tinfoil next to the skins might impart harmful chemicals to the food in the baking. In just such details as these, with a patience to do one thing at a time that was as natural as the alternating sounds and silences of camp talk, he wordlessly reproached the clocks, traffic, appointments, modern kitchens, vibrating appliances, elaborate foods—all the assorted urgencies of work and relaxation by which we mostly live.

As the night came into camp and the stars appeared we settled into steady talk across the fire. Women; the struggle for existence; psychiatry, in which he had a deliberately naive curiosity; public men; the contamination of fruits and vegetables by sprays in the fields and on the supermarket counters; books; his early days. Sometime before we went to bed we walked out from under the trees to a higher place and he named stars. I see us as though I was not one of us, an old man and a young man standing together on that rocky incline, looking into the night and wondering.

In the mornings of the several days we were out, he took me around a rock wall, past some kitchen middens grown over since the scientists had been there, to a draw where a spring still ran. He had brought us here because of this, the only fresh water for many miles around and therefore an attraction for birds and animals, as well as us. The rancher who owned the land had built a small stone tank, about eight feet across and chest high, just below the spring, which trickled over the ground, blackening it, but reached the tank and replaced the evaporation. Mr. Bedi and I saw the tracks of deer and squirrels in the mud from the night before, and we drank from the spring ourselves. He stationed us behind brush and trees across the draw, from where we spied on birds that came into the oaks and the sapling sycamore that was growing beside the tank. After a time we went down the ravine to a pebbled arroyo and, walking up and down it, lizards scurrying away from us, we looked at the plants. Daubs of color I would have called weed flowers, bloomless bushes with dramatic futures, Bedichek named and noted. When something stumped him he drew out one of his naturalist's key books and tried to figure it out. In all this I was overwhelmed by my ignorance, but my silence spared him its catalogue.

The heat rising toward noon, we returned to the spring, stripped off our clothes, and lowered ourselves into the icy water and the fallen, mottled leaves in the water tank. Invigorated, again we talked, of our state's most certain hero, Sam Houston, of ancient Greece, of the creative process—all the marvels, and women. I remember his old naked body, and his wet white hair. We lay out to dry on the cement rim of the tank, once a robin came into the sycamore over my head, and we lay still in the shade, the only sounds its rustling in the leaves.

I find now, in some of my letters from him, fragments of what he taught me. He had recited to me a Persian verse, "Do as thy manhood bids thee do, from none but self expect applause,/He noblest lives and noblest dies who makes and keeps his selfmade laws./All other life is living death, a realm where none but phantoms dwell—/

16

A wind, a breath, a sign, a voice, a tinkling of a camel's bell." Responsively I sent him a remark by Thoreau in 1848: "In what concerns you much do not think that you have companions: know that you are alone in the world." He replied: ". . . every man has and must have contacts, but there are some areas, there are sacred places: 'in what concerns you much' you are alone."

"As to camping, Ronnie," ran the note from him one Christmas season, "I have selected a summit with a positively Pisgah lookout from which with night closing in and the stars bobbing up over the horizon we might gain authentic tidings of invisible things." We camped on the hill at a place where it splayed onto a small plateau. Our fire was enclosed, but not closely, by mottes on two sides, Bedichek's pickup on a third, and on the fourth, a distance off, a windmill and tank. The first afternoon a steel bar that extended forehead-high between the mill and the tank malignantly knocked me on my back. Bedichek was alarmed, and I confessed a pain in my forehead. When, the next morning as we walked toward the firesite from our cots, the same bar smote Bedi and he fell on his back as violently as I had, he cursed, laughed, and didn't confess a pain.

A drizzle set in and soaked us, gently but effectively. We were obliged then to hug the fire, toasting towels and wrapping them around our heads, structuring the wood against the morning wind, making the best of things under the unfriendly grey sky. What we lost in nature study we gained in what Bedichek called "animal enjoyment," the smells and warmth of the fire, the talk and hot food, the comradeship drawn closer against the weather. The large pot of celery and potato soup he made that night kept us warm and full deliciously. Serving it up from the fire he said, "Well, boy, if you don't like this mess, you can at least know it's perfectly good for you." He was seventy-eight by then, and I was twenty-seven.

The oak, mesquite, and cedar burned pungently into the fresh washed air. He was thinking then about his last book, *The Sense of Smell.* "I love these smokes. That's a choice smoke," he said. That evening and the next day the wind agitated the windmill; its soft whinnying and whining kept our minds stirred. Staring into the fire, sipping coffee from hot tin cups, rising to stretch, we shared our enthusiasms for Russian novelists, he instructed me in Matthew Arnold and George Meredith and many other of my ignorances, he drew from me my knowledge of modern things he had not given time to.

17

For lunch in the drizzle we had more of the soup, dry barbecued beef, toast, and beer. He did not eat much meat; he said of animals, "We are associates in this brief adventure of life, and we should feel for them, as we do our kind." He said to the fire, to me, to the place we were: "O life is so wonderful if you just look at it right. How wonderful to be able to sit out in the open and eat a wholesome meal." With sureness and lyric feeling he recited:

> Ah! my Beloved, fill the Cup that clears
> Today of past Regrets and future Fears—
> *To-morrow?*—Why, To-morrow I may be
> Myself with Yesterday's Sev'n Thousand Years.

> Lo, some we loved, the loveliest and the best
> That time and Fate of all their Vintage prest,
> Have drunk their Cup a Round or two before
> And one by one crept silently to Rest.

> And we, that now make merry in the Room
> They left, and Summer dresses in new Bloom,
> Ourselves must we beneath the Couch of Earth
> Descend, ourselves to make a Couch—for whom?

A May morning in 1959, he asked Mrs. Bedichek for his lunch a little early, as he was driving Dobie and Wilson Hudson to the country. "I've got some corn bread almost done, you want to wait?" she asked. "Oh I'll wait," he said, sitting back on a kitchen stool. "I need Southern corn bread."

"Six breaths it was over," Mrs. Bedichek says. "How could he die in seconds when he had been so strong?"

I was alone in the woods one day when Bedichek came back to me. Several times since, when I have been alone in the woods, I have felt him near me so simply that all I think is, "Bedichek." It is as though he is not dead.

H. MEWHINNEY*

There is at least one full man

Two things are inextricably mixed: Bedichek himself and Bedichek as a symbol.

Some of us who never spent much time with him still more or less realized ourselves in him. He was what we tried to be: Artist, scholar, and primitive all in one. He must have been well aware of this. There is a letter on the table from my old-time roommate and blood brother Ted Thompson—

> Tam lo'ed him like a vera brither;
> They had been fou for weeks thegither!—

telling of a debate that he and Mr. Bedi were having on a familiar theme. Ted was contending that although there was a real Socrates— a stonecutter who went barefoot in the streets of Athens and disputed philosophy with all corners and perhaps even drank all the others under the table at Agathon's banquet—the Socrates of the Dialogues is Plato's idealized image of man as the lover of wisdom.

But it does not really matter. Maybe Plato overidealized Socrates and maybe we have overidealized Mr. Bedi. Even so, we shall do better for loving the myth we ourselves have helped to make no less than the man himself.

I knew Mr. Bedi for years but because of time and chance I knew him better through Ted than by being with him myself. Only once did I spend a full day with him. That happened when I went to Austin to write a rather trivial newspaper story about Frank Dobie.

The three of us went out to a little ranch that Mr. Frank had in

* A member of the staff of the *Houston Post*.

19

Burnet County. He had offered to bet that one of the wild cherry trees growing along the creek was at least a foot in diameter. For Dobie, the claim was astonishingly modest. The three of us measured his tree and found that it was more than two feet in diameter. We hunted for flint chips on the creek flat—one bunch of Indians or another left flakes on nearly every creek flat in the whole Edwards Plateau country—but we found only two chips of flint and one spent .30-30 bullet.

We watched two birds having a fight. Mr. Frank and I knew that one of them was a scissor-tailed flycatcher but Mr. Bedi had to explain that the other one was a cowbird and she was trying to lay an egg in the flycatcher's nest. And I blew a dog-calling horn that was hanging on the back porch of the house, just to see if it would really blow. It would.

But the thing I remember best is watching Mr. Bedi wash the dishes after we ate dinner and took a nap. This is a simple act. Millions of people, mostly women, wash the dishes every day. But it is not often that you see an artist, a scholar, a naturalist, and a teacher of young men wash the dishes.

Knowing how to do the simple things has got to be a sort of desperate, lost-soul cult with me in the past few years: How to use an axe, a shovel, and a hoe; how to call the dogs with a blowing horn; how to climb the tree and kick the coon out; how to build a fire with one match in the middle of a thunderstorm.

So I watched Mr. Bedi wash the dishes and I thought, without ever saying so: There is at least one full man left in the world. He writes books, he reads Plato, he can name all the birds without a gun, he loves poetry, and he loves the woods, the prairies, the seashore; the hawk in the wind; the blue, blue gentians blooming at the foot of the slope; the Pointers and the Pole Star and Orion, that have shown the way at night for so many thousands of hunters and seafarers; the campfire, with its light flickering on the leaves of the trees.

"For we are lovers of the beautiful," Pericles said in the most famous of funeral speeches, "and yet with no loss of manliness."

BERTHA McKEE DOBIE*

His kindly nature

Those of us who saw Mr. Bedichek often knew his opinions, independently formed and independently expressed, on a great variety of subjects. The futility of trying to recapture his words or the curves of his extraordinarily mobile mouth as he spoke is downright humiliating. I recall very few instances of which I can report, "Bedi said . . ."

It could never be judged of Mr. Bedichek that "he wrote like an angel but talked like poor Poll." He wrote well; he talked as well over a wide expanse of reading, experience, and reflection. One time he admitted us to a secret of his good talk. "I always try," he said, "to turn a conversation to a subject I know something about." I can see now just how he looked when he said that. Afterward it was fun to watch him turn a conversation gently and adroitly, to a subject that interested him—to bulldozing trees out of sites they had held for centuries; to the superiority in appeal of wild flowers over cultivated ones, all except roses; to the importance to health of food grown with organic fertilizer; to the martins living in a box he put up for them; to the arrival and departure times of the swifts that fill our summer skies with sound and movement; to the advantages of a vegetable diet; to the dull ordeal of watching home movies; to Voltaire, some of whose ideas he cherished in a little Haldeman-Julius blue book; to the letters exchanged between George Bernard Shaw and Mrs. Patrick Campbell; to Thucydides; to getting up at three in the morning; to friends whose humor or gaiety he enjoyed; to the shallow or the profound over the range of human intercourse.

He was as often called philosopher as naturalist. "Philosopher of

* Mrs. J. Frank Dobie.

life," I think when I remember these words: "Many things that are true should never be said." His philosophy had a homely quality, as in this, recollected by Edgar Kincaid: "There is hope for a nation that eats corn on the cob and thereby exercises its teeth."

When Mr. Bedichek was to be along on a picnic I always made potato salad. Always, that is, after the first time, when he told me, "All you need to do to get into Heaven is to take along a bowl of potato salad and then when Saint Peter opens the gate hold out a spoonful for him to sample and promise him the whole bowl if he lets you in." Next to the last time I saw Mr. Bedichek was at the Town and Gown spring picnic. From down one of the long tables a scrap of talk drifted up to me. Someone said of the caterer's potato salad, "It's very good." "Nothing like so good as Mrs. Dobie's," Mr. Bedichek assured her. Actually my potato salad is only "pretty good." But it suited Mr. Bedichek, and it suited his kindly nature to bestow praise.

B. C. THARP*

This group of three, seated about the evening fire

My first contact with Roy Bedichek came in the early twenties when I was put on the executive committee of the University Interscholastic League, of which he was the director. Our common interest in the out-of-doors drew us together; he had an omnivorous, insatiable appetite for anything natural, and I was fortunate enough to be able to contribute to his diet some vegetational crumbs now and then.

There was a third—and potent—personality involved: H. Y. Benedict. After he was made president of The University of Texas, he allowed himself no real vacation, but occasionally he did take off for a few days' trip to the coast to indulge his hobby of watching shore birds and collecting their eggs.

Our camping equipment was simple. The only "luxury-piece" was a folding grill which, in use, stood on four legs pressed into the ground. Bedi was Chief Cook. Concerning this he brooked no argument—nor, after the first camp, was there any effort to give him any! He was justly proud of his cooking prowess. Other members of the party could gather firewood, peel potatoes or onions, wash dishes, or set up cots, but Bedi bossed the cooking.

Benny and Bedi ranged up and down the beach environs armed only with binoculars. There was never a gun in the outfit, and I am quite certain neither of them ever shot a bird, though Benny robbed their nests. In this he was assisted on occasion by the others, but I mostly engaged in "weed-chasing." Benny's "catch" was put to dry in

* Late professor emeritus of botany at The University of Texas at Austin.

a plant press in preparation for incorporation in The University of Texas Herbarium.

We usually came back to camp in the evening in time to finish supper and dishwashing well before sunset. This gave time for Bedi and me to take lessons in egg-blowing while assisting Benny in performing this messy but meticulous chore. Visualize this group of three, seated about the evening fire, each with a pan in which to catch the omelet, assiduously blowing the contents from eggs.

We bedded down for the night on folding cots that were equipped, if necessary, with mosquito bars. Benny, whose professional training had been in mathematics and astronomy, would point out whatever constellations and galaxies were visible, explaining differences between them and suggesting the comparative magnitude, temperature, and density of red, white, and blue stars, the infinity of interstellar space, and the incredible speed with which the whole known Universe is hurtling through the infinity of space—and has been since the Beginning—without the prospect of a foreseeable end. In these matters my knowledge was limited to recognition of the Big Dipper, the North Star, the Milky Way, and a few others, including Orion; Bedi's, while much broader, was by no means profound. Of magnitude, one of the most impressive revelations, to me, was the diameter of Betelgeuse. The largest (dull red) star in the constellation of Orion, it is approximately 350,000,000 miles wide—almost twice the diameter of the orbit of the earth around the sun! From such contemplations it was but a logical step to the philosophical implications of the vastness and the orderly arrangement of the physical universe. While the facts do not lend themselves readily to the support of a concept of the Deity anthropomorphic in attributes, neither do they support an attitude of atheism. That was the reasoning, at least, of Benny. With its logical soundness, Bedi was in agreement—and so was I.

Within recent years Bedi's interest in nature included plants more and more. He learned by name all those with which he was commonly associated and equipped himself to key out a great many unfamiliar ones, particularly those that invaded his lawn and garden. Two years ago it was a brome grass newcomer; this year it was a thistle, *Silybum marianum*, with leaves eighteen inches long—the last plant, I think, to attract his attention.

24

T. H. SHELBY*

The desire to excel

Bedichek distinguished himself after retirement as a writer, a philosopher, and a naturalist, but his most important and distinguished service was as administrator of the University Interscholastic League. He enlarged the scale of the league contests year after year with particular reference to the needs of the pupils in the rural and small town schools, and especially in literary and academic contests. He constantly endeavored to guarantee fair and honest competition. He believed with the ancient Greeks that competitive activities stimulate one to his best effort, if they are honestly and fairly conducted. In an effort to meet the needs of all the pupils in the public schools, he increased the number of contests to more than fifty different events, counting divisions and classes. Every type of school, from the one-room rural to the largest city school, had a place in the program. The public school faculties and the faculties of colleges and universities were drawn into the ever-growing plan.

Bedichek's interest in the program was entirely educational. In athletic activities, as such, he had little or no interest, and he seldom attended games or other contests to enjoy the spectacle.

In dealing with those who broke rules, whether contestants or school officials, Bedi never wavered in applying the rules of the league. He might be sympathetic with those who received penalties for rule infractions, but he was never "soft."

His book, *Educational Competition: The Story of the University Interscholastic League*, answers completely the criticisms of those

* Late dean emeritus of Division of Extension, The University of Texas at Austin.

25

educators who fear competitions as a motivating influence in learning and in character development.

The fundamental honesty of the director of the program and his insistence on the contestants' own efforts, unassisted, has shown up in the results of the league over a period of nearly fifty years. Literally thousands, yea hundreds of thousands of young people have profited by this insistence on honest and effective effort, motivated by the desire to excel. The leaders of the state who have thus been discovered and developed can be counted by the thousands. The University Interscholastic League is indeed the lengthening shadow of Roy Bedichek and associates.

RODNEY J. KIDD[*]

Our out-of-doors hotel

Mr. Bedichek had many friends and varied interests, from cultural circles to the ranks of the skilled worker and the laborer. He wanted to know individuals; he could and did talk to the farmer or the rancher in the field, the worker in the garage, the high school coach on the diamond, the school children on the campus, the academician in the halls of learning. In his frequent and extensive travels throughout the state, he always sounded out opinions of people on politics and national or international issues, on stories that are the folklore, on the names the people gave certain flowers, trees, or animals.

I knew Mr. Bedichek as few had the opportunity to know him, for we camped together for days and weeks at a time over a period of twenty years. We camped on the banks of the Rio Grande and the Sabine. We slept by Caddo Lake, and roamed the plains of West Texas. We explored the sand dunes around Big Spring and the big thicket of East Texas. We travelled in the Davis Mountains and through the brush and fields of Central, South, and East Texas. We always preferred campsites to hotels, streams and lakes to bath tubs, and Dutch ovens to the finest restaurants.

When it was necessary for us to make an overnight business trip to any area in the state, he knew exactly where to go, for he had camping spots located all through the state. After the night's camping we were always in the office of the superintendent or the principal early the next morning.

During the years of my association with Mr. Bedichek, we per-

* Director, Bureau of Public School Service, Division of Extension, The University of Texas at Austin.

fected this "catch-as-catch-can" camping to a science—an outdoor ritual that became second nature to both of us. We removed the back seat from the car and substituted two small mattresses. (Mr. Bedichek had an air-mattress.) We had cooking equipment, a nature library, and other items we found essential for "our out-of-doors hotel." One was a five-gallon can of water, for bathing and shaving, and cooking; this was filled at the close of each working day.

After finding the camp site, we had a regular routine worked out. Mr. Bedichek gathered the firewood and cooked the evening meal, which he liked to do. My job was to get out the cots, put up the beds and the mosquito bars, and unload the car. Our meals were good. Sleeping was better than in an air-conditioned hotel. Mr. Bedichek was a terrific snorer, a fact which forced me to set up my cot some distance from his.

After the evening meal, we would lie on our cots and watch the birds through field glasses until dark. Then Mr. Bedichek would look for the evening star, and try to estimate where the morning star would be at 4:00 A.M.

Sounds at night are varied and fascinating. Often birds in season were taking their long flights from north to south, from south to north, to nest or spend a season in another part of the world. Bedichek would expound on these and how they all fit into the beautiful pattern of life; how man often disturbed the balance that Nature had provided; how humanity wasted its great natural resources. Many were privileged to hear these discourses on natural resources, and I heard them under ideal surroundings—under open skies, with all the things he loved about him. To Bedichek, the world was a miracle; even the rotting leaf in his compost bed which, crumbling, brought forth new life to his growing tomato plants and other garden vegetables.

Shortly before Mr. Bedichek retired as director of the Interscholastic League, we decided to make one more attempt to see the "crazy quail" of the Davis Mountains. We went to our usual campspot, near Bloy's camp meeting grounds. We followed our established routine; Mr. Bedichek got up at his usual hour of 4:00 A.M. and made coffee and, after he had had his first cup, I got up. I always waited until he had had that first cup of coffee, because until then he was not in too good a humor. One cup started the conversation, which lasted from about four-thirty until daylight. The topic for the day could be almost anything: the "New Deal," Republicans, educational theories, church projects, government problems.

At that time of year, the quail, if any were around, would be on top of the mountains. After breakfast Mr. Bedichek said I should go to the top of the mountain to find the "crazy quail." "I don't think I can make it," he said. "My mountain-climbing days are over." Our camp elevation was about five thousand feet and, with exercise, breathing was a little difficult. So I prepared a small lunch (as the trip to the top would take all day), put on my jacket, and started the climb to the seven-thousand-foot-high plateau where Mr. Bedichek said I would find the birds.

It was a fine day, and I drifted along. After a slow and easy climb, I finally reached the top. I "jumped" several large mule deer, which momentarily held my attention. In a few minutes up jumped the "crazy quail." I watched the bird perform the antics from which it gets its name and are partly responsible for its near-extinction. It was the thrill of a lifetime to a bird-lover.

Suddenly the bird flew over and down the mountain.

Behind me, shattering the stillness of the mountain heights, a voice said, "You will never forget that demonstration, will you?" Here Bedichek was on top of the mountain, though he was about seventy years old. You could never think of him as an "old man."

Every trip we took was an educational adventure. He always carried his notebook for recording observations on nature and remarks people made on folklore, on soil conditions, on the weather. When he was alone he was writing or he was reading some book that was a hundred years old or more. (He thought it was a waste of time to read a book which had not stood the test of time.)

The will to survive, the competition for living, helped shape a philosophy he carried over from his observations of the natural world to the field of education. His philosophy formed the backbone of the Texas Interscholastic League and gave the League a meaning that extended beyond local "entertaining," "county meets," and "end-of-school" meets. This understanding, this belief that life was basically a matter of survival, enabled him to withstand the attacks of those who opposed competition.

Mr. Bedichek told me he was sure many people would be disappointed in his history of the League, because they would be expecting case stories about League champions, about people who made specific rules, about incidents that resulted in the adoption of certain regulations. "That is not what I am interested in," he said. "I want to write about this basic philosophy of learning, of achievement. I want to show the advantage of directing this competitive urge, this impulse to win, this instinct to excel."

DUNCAN ROBINSON*

801 East Twenty-third Street

It was only by a whim of fortune some thirty years ago that I noticed a sign "Apartment to Rent" on the lawn of a comfortable two-story white house set among towering post-oak trees at 801 East Twenty-third Street in Austin. I wanted to spend the summer studying literature at The University of Texas, with my wife and our small sons with me. Most people who had places to rent close to the University didn't want children.

I rang the doorbell, and a man named Roy Bedichek appeared, took one quick look at my boys and wife, learned that I was an English teacher at North Texas Agricultural College, and said that we could have the apartment. "I love children," he said, "and so does my wife."

Then followed the happiest summer I have ever spent away from Arlington. My youngest son was soon eagerly following Mr. Bedichek's wife, Lillian, around the flower garden, learning Spanish words from her, and the oldest fell in with the sons of Rodney Kidd, who lived next door.

It was a very hot summer, and after supper several times a week we sat out under the oaks waiting for the breeze and talking with Mr. Bedichek, who was the greatest conversationalist I have ever known. He was interested in everything, knew by heart long passages of the *Iliad* and the *Odyssey*, had read deeply in Tolstoy and Dostoevsky, Plato, Greek tragedies, Shakespeare, Wordsworth, Whitman. His mind was a storehouse of all this, but he wasn't the least bit

---

* Chairman of the Department of English, The University of Texas at Arlington.

bookish, for with his own eyes and mind he observed everything about him; he reflected deeply on his own experience, and those who listened to him gained understanding of many things about them that they had only half-way seen before.

What a zest for life! He was up before dawn to get a fresh view of the habits of sparrows and the mockingbirds. He talked with wood choppers, Negroes who raised chickens, farmers—everyone who might have a story of nature to tell him—as well as scholars and others who were facile mainly about what is compressed within the covers of books.

Thus it was not from mere courtesy but rather from ingrained habit that Mr. Bedichek was interested in my opinions, which I then regarded with gravity but think back on now with embarrassment. He sought out my verdicts on the greatness of certain American and English poets, listening as if he were being entrusted with revelations beyond the ken of ordinary mortals. Wordsworth, I contended, was not fit to sit in the same room with Byron or Keats; Tennyson much superior to Browning; Kipling a mere journalist; Bryant, Longfellow, Whittier, and Lowell very mediocre—all of this and much else, none of which makes sense to me now. I did tell him I believed Frost to be a greater poet than Sandburg, and that of the moderns—then—probably William Faulkner might someday turn out something as vital as *Huckleberry Finn*, and this I think is all I ever told him worthy of consideration.

Too soon, the summer soon went by, and I was never again to be intimately associated with him, or to hear anyone else who might point out that the first labor agitator in history could be found in the *Iliad* and that Whitman was one of the first major poets who had a really adequate conception of the importance of women.

Until his death I visited him occasionally when I was in Austin, and we exchanged letters once or twice a year. I am glad I had the sense to save his letters. They compare favorably with Mark Twain's, and I am certain that someday someone will collect and edit the hundreds he sent to his friends,[1] and that they will constitute his greatest book.

He knew that I had once been tutored in the prosaic art of book reviewing by the late John McGinnis of Southern Methodist University, and I suppose it was for this reason that he asked me to review

---

[1] William A. Owens, of Columbia University, is doing this.—Ed.

for newspapers in Dallas three of his books as they appeared late in his life. After I praised *Adventures with a Texas Naturalist* without straining myself in the slightest, he wrote: "Loyalty in friendship, even to lying a little, appeals to me as a form of beauty, dearer because it is on the human level. Only after we are angels is beauty truth and truth beauty."

Later I sent him a carbon copy of what I had submitted to the Dallas *Times Herald* on his *Karankaway Country,* and he promptly replied, "My heart was in my throat with expectation as I tore the cover off your Ms review; and it came goddamn near crawling out of my mouth as I read . . ." He said this was because he was getting old, and that when a man gets old, "he is reminded that no matter what kind of a soul he has, his body is a machine that wears out and when this conclusion comes home to him he becomes avid for praise even if he does feel it is inspired in some degree by friendship."

But he held no exalted opinion of his literary prowess. When I sent him a little note assuring him that he had the finest prose style of any Texan I knew, he wrote back:

I have just been pondering what an ignoramus I am: I know but one language, English; no mathematics to speak of; I can't make the simplest drawing; no music whatever—can't even play a Jew's harp, and these three are the universal languages—still I make a pretense of communicating with my fellow human beings . . . [Again he wrote to inform me,] I don't have much mind any more . . . I got in bed last night with my hat on.

Usually I tried to perk him up, telling him that surely he would be remembered by every civilized Texan, but once, in a mood of pessimism about the space age, I expressed to him the opinion that if man ever got on the moon, he would probably find there a superior race and that man would subdue it and build his filthy prisons for those who resisted him. He replied immediately:

If we get to the moon I think it will be in pieces adhering as blobs of flesh and guts smeared on fragments of the earth that man will finally learn how to blow to pieces. Serve us right, too. Why should God keep the earth we have so messed up, whole. Why should He not give us the ingenuity and finally the power to blow the goddam thing to pieces—no regrets—"the eternal Saki has poured millions of bubbles like us and will pour" including the world we live on. But, of course, He may get tired of us and start a new breed. I would. I am somewhat comforted to know that the fish in the

33

sea will be the last to succumb to hydrogen fall-out. Maybe from the sea's vast womb will issue another and more successful experiment.

The last time I ever saw him I was in company with one of his long-time friends, Dr. E. C. Barksdale, Arlington State College's great history professor. Mr. Bedichek sat out in his barn, which he had converted into a study, and he was pecking out on an old Oliver typewriter the manuscript for his last book, *The Sense of Smell*. We were late keeping our appointment, because before driving to 801 East Twenty-third Street we had called on Frank Dobie at his home. Dobie had been ill and we had meant to stay only a minute, but he had reached under his bed and pulled out a bottle of whiskey someone had given him before the war. Mr. Bedichek was a little irritated at our tardiness, but soon started telling us what he was attempting in *The Sense of Smell*. I pressed him to get through with it and start writing his autobiography. He brushed this suggestion aside, and I told him he ought to have someone arrange his letters for publication. He said, "I don't want to get into them. They would bring back too many memories. And there isn't time, for at my back I always hear 'Time's wingèd chariot hurrying near.'"

I hope there is some sort of personal immortality and that I may someday, upon arriving in his celestial neighborhood, intercede with Boswell to arrange a dinner so that Mr. Bedichek can talk with Dr. Johnson. I fancy that after the conversation, Dr. Johnson might say to Boswell: "Sir, I first thought you had imposed upon me. I did not think that any American could be so wise and so illuminating. I must revise my opinion of those people."

WILLIAM A. OWENS*

On top of Tallman Mountain

When I first saw Roy Bedichek, in January, 1941, I was reporting to him at the Interscholastic League office on the Little Campus at The University of Texas. I had been appointed to do research in folklore and to direct folk festivals. He was to supervise my work because of his work with the Interscholastic League and, as I learned later, his wide knowledge of Texas life and lore.

From where I stood I could see him bent over his typewriter, intent on whatever he was putting down on the yellow copy paper. When Miss Willie Thompson took me in and announced me, he stood up and leaned forward to greet me. His old brown suit did not declare the man, but his face and manner did. So did the clutter of books, files, and mementos of an avid collector of all kinds of information. I felt that I was being brought into the openness of his life and mind, and that at the same time I was being tested on my right to be there.

He put aside the copy for the issue of "Interscholastic Leaguer" he was working on and together we tried to define the job I had. But talk about work kept getting lost in talk about bird lore and folklore and English poetry. At one point he leaned back with his hands clasped behind his head and recited William Morris's "Defence of Guenevere."

In the nine months I was on the job, Roy Bedichek put me through an education that was superior to anything I had ever encountered, in college or out. The course covered the whole range of human experience. His mind never failed him when he needed a quotation

* Novelist, director of the summer school at Columbia University, and Roy Bedichek's literary executor.

from literature or philosophy to expand an idea or support an argument. For variety he turned to anecdotes about birds and animals, and occasionally to Texas ballads and songs. The education never stopped. When we were on hikes, or on long trips to Interscholastic League meetings, he always had something new to bring up. Whatever we heard or saw brought forth at least a lively comment, and at times a synthesis that was illuminating because it was unexpected. He was a lecturer, a talker rather, who never ran dry because of this ability to relate.

Over the years after I left Texas, in letters and in whatever meetings we could arrange, the discussions went on. One of the rarest of these occasions for me was a trip to the Big Thicket in 1956. I went to collect historical information about the oil fields, and learned a great deal. I learned much more listening to Roy Bedichek and Lance Rosier talk about the ways of birds and snakes and alligators. For three days we were completely removed from consciousness of the foibles of people.

The last time I saw Bedi he stayed overnight at my home, which is on top of Tallman Mountain, the last of the Palisades. This time he broadened his audience enough to include my two children. He kept us entertained all evening with talk of birds he had seen on walks in Westchester and Central Park. We were up at dawn for a walk along the Palisades. At seventy-nine, he set a pace difficult to keep up with. Though it was April and a cold wind was blowing from the north, he stood for an hour on a high bluff, determined to get a glimpse of an American eagle.

He set down the names of other birds he saw, but the eagle was uppermost in his mind. When we could no longer stand the cold we came back to the house and warmed ourselves with hot coffee before the living-room fire. As if driven, away we went again, this time into the woods along the rim of the mountain, where I knew the eagle had nested the year before.

This time we were more fortunate. Through an opening in the branches overhead we saw a great bird soaring high against the blue sky. I was sure it was an eagle. He had to be convinced. We observed what characteristics we could and rushed back to the fireplace to study the bird books. I will never forget the pleasure he showed when he wrote in his notebook that on that day he had seen an American eagle on Tallman Mountain.

36

EDGAR KINCAID*

"Look ye also while life lasts"

Mr. Bedichek did not favor the present fashionable practice of bird-
ing in large groups, because such thundering herds trample down
wild flowers and scare birds away. Usually his maximum number of
hiking companions was two. Nevertheless, he took so many bird
walks that by 1940 virtually every interested person in Texas and
many from other states had been in the field with him.

Mr. Bedichek believed in identifying all the birds without a gun.
In a letter to a Professor Brandis, now of North Carolina, he wrote:

> So, it's a 4-page job to distinguish these two species (House and Purple
> Finches), whereas with a gun it's no job at all. The gunman doesn't get the
> very flower of nature experiences, that is, dealing with natural objects in
> their proper environment with life in them, but with the husks and leavings
> of life. I much prefer the 4-page method.

He had a way with known or suspected specimen collectors. To
those who came to Austin looking for the Golden-cheeked Warbler,
whose world nesting range is confined to the eastern Edwards
Plateau, he would say:"Well, I'll tell you. There used to be lots of
Golden-cheeks around here, but the collectors and cedar cutters have
pretty well cleaned them out. I don't think you'll have much luck
finding them." But to anyone who just wanted to enjoy these beautiful birds alive, he would say: "I'll be happy to show you some.
When can you go?"

Mr. Bedichek showed me my first Golden-cheeks. He took me out
to a cedar brake that was alive with them. Thin clouds raced by that

* An Austin ornithologist.

early morning, so that the sun seemed a great ball rolling along just above the horizon. In memory it seems that almost every other cedar was crowned by a singing male, each with his brilliant black, white, and golden plumage in the perfection of early morning and early spring.

His fellow naturalists will no longer hear Mr. Bedichek relating his experiences with Whooping Cranes, Attwater's Prairie Chickens, Golden Eagles, Vermilion Flycatchers, Golden-cheeked Warblers, cedars, cedar cutters, Mexican Primroses, Cenizas after a rain, water, soil, Rusty Lizards, frogs, and almost every other natural thing under the Texas sun. He practiced the inscription placed beside the fireplace of another naturalist, Olaus Murie:

The wonder of the world, the beauty and the power, the shapes of things, their colors, lights, and shades; these I saw. Look ye also while life lasts.

JOHN HALLER*

"Worse . . . Football."

The first time I met Roy Bedichek I was working on the trees at Dr. Walter Prescott Webb's Friday Mountain Ranch, and the first subject we talked about was birds. Bedichek was then over seventy and I was not yet thirty, but he seemed the younger.

At more or less regular intervals he would emerge from the house, stroll over to the place we were working, and chat with us about the trees and the birds. Being new to Austin and to Texas, I knew nothing of him. No reputation intervened to distort my judgment, and I was left free to respond to him on merit and merit alone. At first I thought he was the caretaker; after we had exchanged a few words I began to think he was a retired professor. As we continued to talk through the four or five days of our work there, I came to see in him the simplicity and vigor of a Cincinnatus and the mental acuity of a George Bernard Shaw.

"You boys chisel away at those trees like woodpeckers," were his first words.

"We are after the same thing," I replied. "Borers. Some of these have burrowed so far into the wood that I don't believe the woodpeckers could find them."

You know [he said] it's remarkable how far into the tunnels the birds can penetrate. The woodpecker's tongue is hinged at the front, instead of at the back like ours. It lies in his mouth pointing backwards and is so long that its tip is kept rolled up in a special cavity formed in the bone of the head. When he wants to dig out a borer, he uncoils that long tongue, shoots it

---

* A tree surgeon and author of a book on the care of trees.

out of his bill, and impales its barbed point in the insect, like an Indian throwing a lance.

Only a year or so later did I learn that Bedichek was being held in benignant captivity at Friday Mountain Ranch by Webb and others of his friends so that he might write *Adventures with a Texas Naturalist*. His chats with us and his strolls about the place were rests from his task.

Later Bedichek called me to work on the trees at his home on Oldham Street. This time we became better acquainted, and as I rested between trees, he took me into his study and showed me his library. His interest at this moment was centered on a book someone had written about the human digestive processes.

The thesis is that meat is digested in one part of the intestine and vegetables and fruit in another part and that the two things should not be eaten together. By drawing on anatomy, physiology, and evolution, the author makes a good case for his beliefs. Whether you agree with him or not, it's a good book to read.

Several times afterward I was called back to his house in a professional capacity. Many other times I went by for a social visit. Always I found the man with the same vitality, the same alertness, the same wide-ranging interests, and the same progressive outlook. Frequently I found him in his garden, and each time the memory of Cincinnatus at his plow returned to my fancy.

One summer I left Austin to tour Canada and, having no place to leave my car, took the liberty of asking Bedichek if I might leave it in his side yard.

"O course you can!" he said. "Going to Canada? Don't be in a hurry to come back. Take your time. When I was a young man, I traveled all over this country like a hobo, tramping and working my way. Those were the best times of all! Will they ever come again?"

The book I took with me across Canada was Balzac's *Droll Stories*. When I returned to Austin forty days later and went by Oldham Street to pick up my car, Bedichek and I talked for about an hour about Balzac. "The greatest of writers," he said. "None better anywhere." It turned out that he knew the *Droll Stories* intimately. He quoted long passages from memory almost verbatim. "The Succubus" had impressed him in particular. He called it the world's greatest short story, and I was inclined to agree with him.

One time when I called on him he was working in the garden with a handkerchief tied over both ears.

"Earache?" I asked.

"Worse," he said, shaking his fist passionately at the University. "Football." The speakers at the stadium were going at full blast.

"Did you ever read Schopenhauer's essay 'On Noise'?" he asked. "Nobody has ever stated the case against it more strongly. But the din then couldn't have been half what it is now. You know, I think I'll sit down and bring that essay up to date." And his lip curled with scorn as he began to name off all the intrusions on his privacy: the loudspeakers, the automoblies that raced screaming by, the honking, the shouting, and the general raucousness of modern life.

"I go to bed at 8:00 at night and get up at 3:00 in the morning. Nobody comes around to bother me at 3:00 a.m. It's the only way I can get any work done."

Bedichek's capacity for satire was pronounced. I think he could have been a kind of minor Swift, and I've always been sorry that he did not devote more time to the development of that characteristic.

His learning was immense; he was very broadly read in the literature of all nations. He had a strong feeling for nature, a marked talent for close observation of her, and a gift that was frequently almost poetic for her delineation. He had a penetrating and original way of looking at life and men and books; he was fettered by no tradition, bound by no conventions. His mind worked acutely over a broad range of subjects. He was one of the most broadly cultured and luminously intellectual of modern Texans. How shall we replace him?

CHARLES RAMSDELL*

Freedom from pretense

When the subject is Roy Bedichek, there is a temptation to write about the man rather than his work. Even for me, who can not claim to have been a close friend (although my father was his close friend), the temptation is strong. I had hoped to know him better. I last saw him when he stopped the light truck he was driving near his home, seeing me afoot (I was going only a few paces); he put out his hand, gave me a hearty clasp, said he was glad I had moved to Austin. That was like him: no questions; no "why had I moved; what did I propose to do." He was simply glad. A little later I passed by his house and saw how green his garden was, with a row of tall corn in it. And I commenced to spin a scheme. "He must work certain hours in his garden," I thought. "I could ask him to let me come then: I would not be encroaching on his time and energy. He loves to talk, and this way he could talk without the interruptions that are always forthcoming in a group of people."

The scheme was never more than half spun. I console myself with the reflection that Bedichek did, after all, succeed in conveying his rich and spacious mind on the printed page, where it is more eloquent than it could ever have been in talk. For he was not merely (among other things) a minute observer and a large thinker, he was, I think, the finest artist in prose that has written in Texas, about Texas.

By the restriction "in Texas about Texas" I mean to limit the field so as to exclude a very few stylists who, like Katherine Anne Porter, have not been especially concerned with the region. Miss Porter said, in a recent interview in Austin (*Texas Observer*, Oct. 31, 1958), that

* A writer who lives in Austin and Mexico.

42

she is the only "serious" writer to come out of Texas. What she should have said, I believe, is that she is the only serious writer of *imaginative* works to come out of Texas. There could be no cavil against that statement.

Adventures with a Texas Naturalist, written when Bedichek was seventy, is a work of art, if there ever was one. It is also what I would call "a classic of Texas literature," if such a tired and tarnished word as "classic" did not seem more incongruous than usual when applied to writing as fresh and unstilted as Bedichek's. Teachers of English, who, of course, do not generally know good English when they see it, should prescribe the *Adventures* to all young people with ambition to write. There are not many books in which the language is treated so lovingly, and yet with respect.

Let us dwell for a moment on the theme of Bedichek as Artist. The difficulty here will be to refrain from quoting.

Bedichek's style is a reflection of his character, in that there is an absolute freedom from pretense. There is not a pompous or a parroted phrase in all his work. There is an easy naturalness, the buoyancy of an open but positive mind, that enabled him to pass without self-consciousness from the most glowing descriptive color to the thin grey abstraction. Like one of his beloved birds, he could look very close at the life about him, savoring every bit of it, caressing the texture, or he could soar far above it and generalize.

In the chapters on "Fields and Fences" he gives us the feel of the Texas hill country, something more than just a picture, without ever resorting to the deadly method commonly known as description. Elsewhere, by subtle suggestion, he contrives to give us the feel of the egret's courting dance. And here we must insist on a quotation, for this is the substance of the whole Bedichek philosophy, of his Yea to life:

"I came to the conviction that some eighteen-million centuries after the nebula cohered into an orb, something new entered, not at all controlled but destined eventually to dominate physical laws or at least to adapt and use them for its own purposes. Under this seaside spell I repudiate mechanism and all its thin and shivering conceptions."

And then, there is the chapter on the mockingbird's song, which is also a chapter on the appreciation of Walt Whitman, "the most contemptible old hog that ever rooted in the mire of his own imagina-

43

tion,"—so the professors dismissed him when Bedichek was a boy. Bedichek formed his own opinion.

And there is the last chapter, which deals with the theme of time, in much the same manner that Johann Sebastian Bach deals with a theme, taking it through modulations and changes of pace, coming back to it at the end. We start with the shadow of an ancient oak; we come to the ancient cedar-chopper on the hillside; suddenly we are in ancient Rome and on the islands in the Pacific; then we are back in the Texas hills with the cedar-chopper again.

I have passed by the garden, and it is withered and streaked with yellow, a sad reminder of mortality and of schemes that come to nothing.

I console myself by remembering the words that we have, that are the essence of a rich life, and think of the vermilion fly-catcher: "Poised high in the crystal-clear air that morning, he seemed to me to be a star of the first magnitude which the vanishing darkness had failed to take with it from the daylight sky."

LETTERS TO EUGENE GEORGE, JR.

"My generation is daubed with blood"

Selections from Bedichek's letters to architecture professor Eugene George, Jr.:

1951

Dear Mr. George:

. . . I am still a widower, an independence I don't especially care for. My wife is having such a fine time in New York that she will probably stay another month. Meantime, I am gardening and having, also, a hell of a fine time. I'm even preserving some of my garden-truck in a deep freeze I purchased the other day. Also some cocktail parties at which I drink only fruit punch, but find quite enjoyable, even though a friend or so gets a little loud now and then. I sympathize with and greatly admire the French poet, who, reproached for not participating in a drinking bout, and asked how he could get the inspiration to write poetry without stimulants, replied, "A bowl of soup intoxicates me sufficiently." That is, to *live* is to be sufficiently *stimulated*.

Don't fail to give me a ring whenever you happen to be in Austin, and maybe we can arrange another little stroll in the woods.

Yours truly,

Roy Bedichek

May 30, 1951

P.S.—Likely the bird that looks like a scissor tail but without the

45

tail is really a scissortail without a tail—Young birds are now coming off, and don't get their tails for some little time after leaving the nest. *Walden* is one of the great books of the world, "driving life into a corner" as it proposes to do, and *does do*. Did you ever read Thoreau's "The Duty of Civil Disobedience?" R. B.

[In a letter to Eugene George on June 29, 1951, Bedichek said that a letter from George had moved him to write a paragraph into a speech on the "non-fiction book." Bedichek then quoted from this writing of his, including this portion.]

"In a certain sense, the publication of a book is the grain leaving the sower's hand—seed scattered to the four winds, on a venture. And, like in the sacred parable, the great reward comes from that which falls into good ground and brings forth the divine fruit of sympathy and good will and appreciative understanding, "some an hundredfold, some sixtyfold, some thirtyfold." ...

This surely is not to belittle monetary rewards, but to point out the source of inspiration which is responsible for nine-tenths of all creative writing; and, for that matter, for nine-tenths of all worthwhile artistic endeavor. From this source comes the comforting assurance that the strange world lying beyond one's everyday associations is not an unfriendly world. The same Greek word stands for *stranger* and for *enemy*. Other human beings are traveling the same paths though out of sight. ...

The world is full of people, often massed and driven together by the requirements of institutional and social order, but for each individual, it is a lonely world. We are all lonely, with a loneliness which mere physical proximity does not satisfy. We yearn for that deeper, more fundamental association with our own species. Our souls are gregarious, like seeking like, forever and always ...

Dear Gene:

... Do you suppose Condorcet would have been so optimistic had he lived ten years longer? Russia of 1917 was full of optimism. So was our own American Revolution. The eighteenth century was a wonderful century, more wonderful, in my opinion, than the 19th, which Alfred Russell Wallace calls "The Wonderful Century." The human spirit really went forward and up in those hundred years. Only in 500–400 B.C. in Athens did man come nearer become man than in the 18th century. Condorcet's life span lay inside it. He witnessed the ascent but did not live to experience the fall. Naturally, he was optimistic. Living my whole life side by side with Voltaire would have been enough to make me optimistic. Diderot and Rousseau would have helped me, too. Alas! mechanization was just taking command in good earnest the year I was born. In 1878 the "mechanization of murder" in the meat industry was just coming into its evil flower.

My generation is daubed with blood.

But let's talk it over.

Bedichek

Sept. 20, 1951

Dear Gene:

... The rage for wholesale slaughter of all life, including our own, possesses like a demon this generation. It is an age of devastation, senseless devastation in which we live, and this terrible possession will finally give our age its name in history, if, indeed, any language on earth can supply a sufficiently sinister word or phrase. The gentle gardener poisons his soil to kill pill bugs and in so doing annihilates great numbers of beneficient creatures, including the lowly and lovely earthworm. An airplane spreads the deadly DDT over a square mile of cotton field to kill worms or weevils and in so doing kills honeybees which fertilize the cotton, and birds which have been attracted there to feed on these very pests ...

A month ago a leaf-eater attacked my lima beans, the most luxuriant growth of them I ever saw. They were cutting the leaf-surface into lacework and my neighbors were urging me to spray. The vines hadn't until that time produced a single bean-pod the whole summer. They supported leaves and blooms and nothing more. Shortly after this insect had trimmed the vines of their excess foliage, the beans began to put on, and now they're loaded. It may have been the cool weather that started them to fruiting, and it may have been that they were getting thru an extravagant leaf-surface a daily overdose of sun-

47

light. I don't know. Anyway I refused to spray, the insects continued to devour the leaves, and now I have more beans than we can eat . . .

Yours,

Bedichek

October 26, 1951

November 6, 1951

Dean Gene: Thanks for your paragraph on the chair. You say something there that is worth repeating. "One problem in this world is to try to keep manmade ugliness from spreading." That has widespread application. Advertising, of which America is so proud, would be something really to be proud of if it were held within the limits your statement so admirably sets. As I listen to radio, glance through newspapers and magazines, glimpse ghastly billboards as I motor along highways—indeed, nearly every waking moment that I am not shut up in my study with my nose in a good book or hammering this typewriter—nearly every waking moment I am subjected to the Hitlerian repetitions of advertising, perhaps 75 percent of which spreads ugliness either of material things corrupting taste or, far worse, disseminating and lodging in the minds of millions ugly thoughts and emotions,—more's the pity in the souls of the young. The old and even the middle-aged are already corrupted.

The best end to attack the Big Thicket is near Liberty, that is the south end. That is about five hours away, as *you* drive, about six as *I* drive. The next place is north and near Livingston, about the same driving-time away. Next, the heart of it at or near Silsbee. Here I have a standing invitation to occupy a comfortable camp-house with all equipment which might be just what one would like in dead of winter. It is on railroad right-of-way, an old section-house.

Perhaps the most educative period would be early spring, when birds are busy mating and nesting, flowers are blooming, and the swamp-creatures are awakening to new life. I can imagine a fine outing in any one of these locations for two observant and appreciative individuals with about a week to spare.

Maybe we'd better let this idea incubate . . .

[Not signed]

48

December 12, 1951

Dear Gene:

I am working fairly well but am lonesome for the woods. Got another nature book from *News* to review—more than I bargained for, but guess I'll do it, as it seems to be a pretty good book by Edwin Way Teale. He gave me quite a boost in New York *Herald-Tribune* and one good turn deserves another; but, if I find I have to say anything harsh, I'll return book to *News* to get another reviewer for it. Much hyprocrisy about reviewing books and I don't like it a bit.

Yours,

Bedichek

1952

January 6, 1952—Head of Bull Creek, Travis County.

Observers: B. G. Bedichek, Eugene George, Jr., Roy Bedichek
Weather: still, cold (35 degrees) sunny

Robins—thousands
Cardinal—several
Bluebirds—hundreds
Lark Sparrow—few
Slate-colored junco—dozens
Arctic towhee—several
Phoebe
Carolina wren—four
House finch—several
Chipping sparrow
Arkansas Goldfinch—several
Turkey Vulture
Ruby-crowned kinglet
Golden-crowned kinglet
Cactus Woodpecker
Chickadee—several
Western Mourning Dove—several
Mockingbird

Myrtle Warbler
Flicker
Black Vulture
     amateur

Dear Gene:
Yesterday I got what you say I deserve for living a long and virtuous life—viz., a pair of B&L 9x35's. Ever since taking this magic contrivance into my hands yesterday about noon, my heart has warmly nursed a secret joy. And besides, I'm about ready to take off to the mountains!

Yours,

Roy

May 22, 1952

Dear Gene:
I hail the good news as only cheering item in my news-budget in some time, except birth of another granddaughter, which gives me (undeserving oaf that I am) five beautiful girls and five splendid boys—ten in all.
Am just returned from two months camping. Not a night in a house nor a meal in a commercial eating house the whole time. Don't you envy me, you bug, nosing around under chips you call houses?
Expecting you, I am Sincerely,

R. B.

July 29, 1952

1954

Dear Eugene—
If indeed you do go up Cimmoron Canyon, over the divide at Eagle Nest's Lake and on down into the Red River Valley, I want you and your chosen one to do me a favor. Select some morning, bright and

early to visit Costillo Canyon and there look for and find the water ouzel. If Costillo is closed, any other canyon around there with running and plunging water will do as well. But before you make this excursion read "The Water Ouzel" in John Muir's *The Mountains of California,* for it is the most glorious biography of a bird in the English language. I see a volume of Muir is coming out edited by Edwin Way Teale on September 21, copy of which I mean to give you and the lady as a wedding gift, but not in time to take with you. *The Mountains of California* is in the Library. Please read the chapter on the WO before you leave.

R. B.

September 5, 1954

1 9 5 6

Dear Eugene:

I have run on to an excellent key to the flora of the country east of here but it is a key based on internal characters. So I have a project for us to start on—that is the insides of flowers. You being an architect will be interested in structure and stresses and strains which nature devises, and I being curious about the ways of God will take much delight in unravelling the ingenuity of these devices. We shall need magnifiers and I have it in mind to buy a microscope but maybe we can get along with less high-powered and high-priced equipment. We shall see . . .

R. B.

March 19, 1956

1 9 5 9

Roy Bedichek
801 East 23rd St.
Austin 5, Texas

April 14, 1959

Dear Eugene:

Remembering (seems years ago) your professional interest in, as well as your aesthetic enjoyment of, patterns in Nature, I want to call your attention to a design and the wonderous harmonious coloration of a strange thistle which has made its appearance this spring on the vacant lot just north of the old garage in which I have my "study," so-called.

I first noticed this growth on account of its ravenous demand for space. From the root-crown it sent out menacing leaves all 'round the compass until a circular area about a yard in diameter was pre-empted. Every spring [*sprig?—Ed*] of rival vegetation in this circle was promptly smothered. Having thus assured itself of lebensraum, the stalk rose about an inch above the root-crown and threw out a second tier of magnificent, threatening, long-spear shaped leaves in every direction. As if aware that something very precious was soon to appear at its center, a third round of terrific leaves was projected from the slowly growing central stalk; not as the other in the plane of the ground, this tier was tilted up a bit. Then another higher tier, also up-tilted came out, so that the plant now presents from above such a phalanx of needle-like daggers that hardly an insect can thread the mazes of its leaves. No tough-lipped goat or other browser could manage a nip or a nibble from it without severe punishment, and certainly no bird could alight among its barbarous thorns and prickles. ~~Finally, a rather insignificant fourth round of leaves appeared.~~ No, I've already counted this one. Truly, this plant must have evolved in a habitat simply swarming with deadly enemies; for, armed cap-a-pie, there's not a loose or neglected point or joint anywhere.

Having completed these elaborate preparations, swelling buds as big as guinea-eggs appear in the top of the defensive cone, carefully nested in a forest of thorns, while the buds themselves, as if mistrusting the fortifications so "thoughtfully" prepared for them, have armed themselves each with three tiers of the most fearsome prickles of them all. Three mornings ago I discovered that the central bud had opened a little, but it has proceeded so cautiously that even now it shows a spot of glorious reddish purple no bigger than a bean.

From the first I knew that this plant was something new in thistles for this area, so I called my friend, Tharp, who is supposed to know the vegetation of Texas better than anyone else. It stumped him and he said he would have to wait until the bloom came before the plant could be identified. I am going to call him over as soon as the bloom is unfolded.

Meantime I am telling you that there is awaiting your inspection a perfectly ravishing pattern of leaves; broken lines of dingy white on a background of ashy green. I believe you would like to see the coloration, the defensive devices, and most of all, perhaps, the leaf-pattern, so complicated and yet so seemingly simple that I get lost in trying to trace it.

Selah.

Bedichek

GILBERT McALLISTER*

No affectation, no defense

Among Bedichek's many admirable characteristics I remember primarily his unpretentiousness, his humility, his unaffectedness.

I recall a visit last summer when he was over at my house checking data pertaining to physical anthropology for his new book. While showing him around the yard before he left, I thought of the cristate rainbow cactus my wife and I had found on a hike earlier in the spring. To my surprise these monstrous forms were new to him.

"And you pass yourself off as a naturalist," I said, "and have never heard of these? *Texas* naturalist? You don't even know cactus."

"Listen," he said, "hear that call? It's a cuckoo. You see, I know birds."

"Then call yourself an ornithologist and not a naturalist. Texas naturalist! I believe you're a fake."

Seriously and very quietly he said, "Don't tell anybody. I've got by for a long time and few know I'm a fraud."

Whereupon we both had a good laugh.

This is so typical of his sense of humor, his delight in teasing. With all of his tremendous knowledge there was no affectation, no defense of this ignorance, if it could be called that. Immediately his mind became alert. Why do these forms get this way? Is their genetic mechanism changed; does it go haywire? How commonly do they occur? And a dozen other questions I couldn't answer.

* Professor of anthropology at The University of Texas at Austin.

A LETTER TO ONEITA HILDEBRAND

"Whitman constantly exposed his soul"

When a teacher sent Bedichek her paper on Walt Whitman, Bedichek was moved to write her a letter on Whitman. He also gave a copy of the letter to Dobie:

Box H, University Station
Austin, Texas
December 4, 1945

Dear Miss Hildebrand:

Your letter and the Whitman paper have interested and pleased me very much. I think you did a good job with the Whitman material, and I thank you sincerely for letting me see the finished product.

I note that you make considerable use of Holloway, and quite properly, since no one can deny that his is a scholarly work. I never met him although he was here at the University for several years. I get the impression from reading his book that he is a prude and I am therefore puzzled that he was interested in Whitman at all. His two- or three-page disquisition on the poet's New Orleans love-affair resolves itself into a sort of apology, setting forth that *if* the woman was a prostitute she was not of the *lowest order* of prostitutes; and that *if* she was dark, she was not so *very* dark. This is what one may call a hair-line, color-line defense, and an appeal for clemency on the grounds of *degrees* of prostitution, neither of which, I think, Whitman himself would have undertaken to plead in any court of morals to which he might have been summoned.

Whitman constantly exposed his soul, while carefully concealing and even lying about the ordinary details of his life with which the biographer has to do. Where he went and when; how many trips he made and in what directions; what women he loved and where, and whether black, white, or chocolate-colored or to what degrees of prostitution they were severally addicted; how many, if any, children he had (he once boasted of having five)—all are disputed points and no one has yet dug up authentic records in any way conclusive concerning them. As to his private life he has given us, indeed, "only a few faint hints and indirections."

What he stood for, however, in the great world of thought, how he reacted emotionally and intellectually to the art, music, politics, morals, social organization, economics, events and contracts of the stirring times in which he lived are all set down with great clarity in his poems and elaborated in his prose.

I have never myself accepted as valid the European interpretations of *Calamus*. In my opinion he speaks there of pure brotherly affection, the Damon-and-Pythias relationship, comradeship, "manly" love, which he called curiously "athletic love," a term apparently of his own coining, since it cannot be found anywhere else in literature. I am familiar with the passages hard to reconcile with this view; but, on the other hand, there are ten times as many passages which cannot be reconciled with any other view.

The companion piece, *Children of Adam*, dealing with love between the sexes, represents a revolt against the really ridiculous reticences of the Victorians, and is certainly quite beyond anything in English in giving uninhibited but, nevertheless, idealized expression to this phase of human experience. We feel here that Nature speaks "without check and with original energy."

I am returning your excellent paper herewith, and thanks very much for dispensing my regards around the college.

Yours truly,

Roy Bedichek

Miss Oneita Hildebrand,
No. 1205 West Mulberry,
Denton, Texas

P.S. Since you are an English teacher, I shall have to apologize for the typing of this letter. Since none of our stenographic force is inured to the language of literary criticism, and since help is too scarce to risk any resignations, I have had to do this letter with my own fair hands on my thirty-year-old Oliver typewriter.

R.B.

JOHN HENRY FAULK[*]

Nature purges, "like great drama"

Mr. Bedichek's unusual mind had as many sparkling facets as a well-cut diamond. I attempt no more than a few impressions from conversations with him and letters from him.

There was a near-mysticism about his devotion to Nature. He wrote to me ten years ago:

Only Nature is normal, no matter how eloquently Oscar Wilde and his aesthetes argue the contrary. The aseptic sea cleanses all the filth the land dumps into it from ten thousand gorged and retching rivers. Nature does the same for those souls who understand and practice the occult rite of immersion in her. But no Methodist sprinkling will do. It must be a thorough-going Baptist immersion. It purges, in the Aristotleian sense, like great drama.

When I went to live in New York City after World War II, nearly every letter that he wrote to me contained a warning against what he called "the city's fetid atmosphere" and an admonition never to accept its values. Then, while he was visiting with us a couple of years ago in New York, I remarked to him that I had been having a series of dreams involving sights and sounds of my youth in Travis County; swimming naked up on Barton Creek, roosters crowing, whip-poor-wills calling in the woods. He nodded eagerly and psychoanalyzed me on the spot.

Why those dreams are simple, Johnny. It is nothing more than your body and soul crying out against the unnatural environment of this terrible city. Your body is an animal's body, my boy, and your organs, every fiber in

[*] Noted entertainer and writer.

you, must have contact with Nature. Your skin needs the natural heat of summer, the natural cold of winter; your ears need to hear the natural sounds of the earth; your eyes must behold the natural beauty of the land; your soul must have exposure to the eternal drama of the changing seasons.

Then followed a resounding denunciation of air-conditioning and central heating as creators of unnatural environment that would have panicked our appliance manufacturers. In the garage study where he spent so much time, Mr. Bedichek had only a wood stove for heat in the winter (fueled by wood he fetched in from pastures and sawed himself) and shaded windows for coolness in the summer. It was a comfortable place any season.

He delighted in observing all the flora and fauna of the earth, though the behavior of some of Nature's creatures and plants distressed him. Not long ago he acted out, with grimaces and hostile gestures, the aggressive nature of a certain thistle, explaining how the species choked out and destroyed all plant life in its vicinity. Some years ago, in answer to a letter that I had written him observing that the bluejay was the bully-boy of the bird world, he wrote,

Yes, the jay is really a terrible bird. He is an Ishmaelite, his bill is against every bird. The other morning I started across the back yard and a headless Inca dove fell at my feet, the dove that really summarizes all the gentleness and peace-lovingness attributed in our folklore to the species. Following the headless dove and reaching the ground almost at the same time was a ravenous blue jay. I had to kick him off his prey. But after I had identified the specimen, I put it up in the tree so that he might have it back again. Jays assault my fig trees, ruining half a dozen figs at each visit of one, for they peck a bite out of one and then another, too impatient to sit down and eat one fig clear up. The devils do me a lot of damage, but I wouldn't kill one. I would sorely miss him if he were gone. He is the most colorful permanent resident on my little hill of Post Oaks, and while his scream is raucous, his lovenote I find quite musical. So far as his own species is concerned, he is a very generous bird. If he finds something good to eat, he calls in all his fellows at once.

With the species Homo Sapiens Mr. Bedichek took greatest delight, and, at times, found severest fault. His enlightened, searching mind had roamed freely through history, and he had achieved a position of wisdom and insight from which to observe the behavior of his own species. On matters political and social he had firm and liberal convictions, but when friends of his, men he had known in his younger years, became opposed to him in their opinions, he maintained a warm affection for them. Politicians and public servants who betrayed the faith of the people most infuriated him. He once wrote me that he was preparing a paper comparing Homo Sapiens with Rhattus Norveingus—mankind with the brown rat, "the most imperialistic of his species." In 1951, he wrote,

Don't get too discouraged over the state of the nation and of the world. We are launching out on an imperialist policy . . . that is the state of the public mind, or rather the public's passion. To reason with it at present would be like petting a mad dog.

And further on in the letter he commented,

Men, my boy, are demons in disguise . . . ay, and women, too. . . . more so, and more demoniacal than men. Our breed, among all the animals in the world, is most cursed . . . and still, I would not, if I could, do as Whitman wanted to do—"go and live with the animals; they are so placid and uncontained." These terrible contradictions in the soul of a decent man will run him crazy if he dwells too much upon them. Better garden and read Gandhi, dine on vegetables, sup on yogurt and black bread, and sleep anights.

Of a politician who had sacrificed principle for political expediency, and who, in Mr. Bedichek's opinion, was power-drunk, he wrote me: "Did you ever notice that Homo Sonuvabichicus is one species that can never disguise itself?" Last year he wrote to me: "My wife and I simply choke up when we get to talking about the inarticulate inbecilities of Eisenhower."

Mr. Bedichek's gray hairs were testament to his many days here on earth. In spite of this, the atmosphere of youth hovered about him always, even to the moment he came to "shuffle off this mortal coil." This phenomenon is best expressed in a letter he wrote me a few years ago:

I go to Barton's every afternoon and have a delightful cooling off. What a poem that place is! Do you not sometimes dream of its great towering pecan trees over sparkling waters? The Apaches knew a good thing. Did you know that the whole south bank of Barton Creek from springs to mouth is one solid kitchen-midden built up through ages of occupation by Apaches and their predecessors? I used to get relics by digging almost anywhere along the bank. In a former incarnation I was an Apache, living on pecans and deer meat, working the excellent flint that protrudes here and there from the limestone ledges, and chasing my fleet-footed love over cliffs and down creek-beds. Her voice was ventriloquial and often led me like an echo far astray where I found many flowers and forgot all about the little vixen. I know all this must have happened or I wouldn't have such a longing to get back into living in the wild. My next incarnation is impending, and I'm hoping.

WILSON M. HUDSON[*]

Bedichek's rock

"These boys are having such a devil of a good time that I hate to get them out." These were the last words that I heard him speak. Mr. Bedichek was watching his grandson John and a friend of his dive into the deep, clear water of Barton Springs. With his grandfather's help John was practicing getting his head down and straightening his body out. It was six o'clock and Mr. Bedichek was afraid that Mrs. Bedichek would be worried; he had told her he would be home at about five.

My wife and I had come out at about four-thirty. We had been much surprised to see Mr. Bedichek sitting on the concrete across the creek. It was too early in the season for him—May 20—and he was not in his usual place. Once he had begun coming out in July, he would be at Barton's every day until the first norther had struck. He was in the habit of sitting on a rock down by the big spring that comes out of the fissure in the limestone. Just behind this rock was a small sycamore tree that had managed to get a start and hold on by thrusting its roots between the layers of stone. Mr. Bedichek did not sit under the tree for shade. It was the sun that he wanted, and he got plenty of it directly as it slanted to the west and indirectly as its rays were reflected from the water. When he had had enough he had to take but a few steps in shallow water to enter what he called the "bathtub," a spot about two feet deep just where the cold water rushes out through the fault. He had a special way of getting into the

* Author, professor of English at The University of Texas at Austin, and secretary-editor of the Texas Folklore Society.

bathtub, which is overhung by the slanting fault face on one side and bounded on the other by sharp rocks just under the water. He would stand with the overhang on his right and then let himself fall backwards into the spring. I have seen him do this many times, but whenever I tried to do it myself, I grazed the rocks on the way down. He would sit in the spring and throw a double handful of water over his head, each time exclaiming, "Woof! woof!" This "woof, woof" was a part of the ceremony.

During July and August from three-thirty till five-thirty every day Mr. Bedichek would sit on his rock and talk to his friends. When he felt himself getting too hot he would interrupt the conversation for a quick dip in the bathtub. In a big flood of two years ago the sycamore tree was snapped off. Its upper branches became filled with driftwood and the force of the water was too much for it. Mr. Bedichek had hopes that the tree would grow out again, and it has sent out new shoots. He thought that if all the shoots but one were trimmed away, the tree might make a comeback.

Once I said to him, "Mr. Bedichek, when you and I are dead and gone, this rock will still be thought of as Bedichek's rock." Everyone seemed to regard the rock as his, and only a stranger would take his place while he was cooling in the bathtub.

In *King Lear* there is an allusion to an old rhyme, "Pillicock sat on Pillicock hill." Taking a hint from this, I made up a couplet for Mr. Bedichek's amusement.

> Bedichek sat on Bedichek's rock,
> The water was cold but Bedi was hot.

One of the most regular visitors to Bedichek's rock was Mr. Dobie. He did not alternate between the rock and the bathtub; he had his own way of cooling off. He would swim around in the deep water until he felt chilled; then he would go up on the hot cement and lie down. He said the heat of the sun above and of the cement below would drive the cold deep down into his bones.

In the course of an afternoon ten or fifteen of Mr. Bedichek's friends might come over at different times for a chat. If there ever was such a thing as a literary salon in Austin, its location was Bedichek's rock. This is not to say, though, that the conversation was limited to literary matters; it ranged far and wide, for Mr. Bedichek was ready to talk to anybody about anything. He had a very large store of information on a great variety of topics and he was willing to acquire more by listening. Every day Virginia Conkle would swim up to Bedichek's rock and sit there awhile. Fred Thompson would always come out too, though he was sometimes rather late. One summer Mary Lasswell was on hand every day. It would not be possible for me to name all those who counted on a visit with Mr. Bedichek at Barton's, because I do not know all of them. Judge James Hart and his wife, old friends of Mr. Bedichek's who were in the University when he was, had a habit of swimming every day too. Mrs. Hart liked to cool off in the bathtub; I have heard her say jokingly, "I wish Mr. Bedichek would get out of the bathtub so that I could use it." On his visits from Houston, George Fuermann always knew where to find Mr. Bedichek and Mr. Dobie.

Almost every afternoon someone was sure to ask Mr. Bedichek a question about birds. "I saw a bird the other day that I've never seen before. It was smaller than a redbird and larger than a wren. It was gray all over and had a topknot. What was it?" Then Mr. Bedichek would consider all the possibilities and arrive at what he thought the best answer. "The only small gray-backed bird with a crest is a titmouse. Yes, it must have been a titmouse." So he told me on that last afternoon. I am only beginning to try to learn something about birds.

Mr. Bedichek surprised me again and again by how much poetry he knew by heart. He quoted freely from the nineteenth century English poets and also from Shakespeare. Browning was one of his favorites; when he first learned that my wife was a student of Browning, he quoted from the middle of "Sordello," an early poem of Browning's remembered today mostly because of the quips about its obscurity. Mr. Bedichek had been a great reader of the Russian novelists, and he knew Tolstoy and Dostoyevsky very well. He said they opened his mind and led him on as no English novelists had ever done. He thought that only Thomas Mann among the Germans was comparable to the Russians; I have heard him say that *The Magic Mountain* is one of the greatest modern novels. What he liked about it was its philosophical cast and its ironic playfulness in the realm of ideas. Once we talked what must have been an hour about the great debate between Settembrini and Naphta.

There was hardly a subject that Mr. Bedichek did not touch upon, and it was always evident that he possessed both information and in-

64

sight. On the shelves of his study at home he had a fine collection of scientific and literary books, including all of Darwin and Jeffrey, most of W. H. Hudson, and many others. One of the last books that I borrowed from him, which I still have, is a copy of Gorky's *Reminiscences* of Tolstoy, Chekhov, Andreyev, and Blok. We were in the habit of lending each other books. Mr. Bedichek did not confine himself to established classics but regularly read a national newspaper, a news magazine, and several scientific periodicals, so that whoever talked to him about current affairs had to be sure of his facts.

Many are the conversations that I have heard between Mr. Bedichek and Mr. Dobie at Barton Springs. With acute, truth-seeking minds, they would throw themselves whole-heartedly into whatever was being discussed at the moment. For the most part they agreed with each other, but when a difference arose they would make no effort to turn aside. They were the best of friends, but sometimes idea would clash with idea or attitude with attitude. Once Mr. Dobie remarked that when traveling in the back country of Mexico he liked to have a *mozo* sleeping at the door. This offended Mr. Bedichek, who immediately took Mr. Dobie up and accused him or reducing a human being to the status of a watchdog. Mr. Dobie tried to explain that it was *la costumbre del pais* and that the relationship between a *mozo* and the man he served could be a very fine one, but Mr. Bedichek was not to be convinced. Sometimes the deadlock could be broken only by Mr. Bedichek's dipping himself in the bathtub or Mr. Dobie's toasting himself on the concrete; but in a few minutes the two would be back together talking about something else.

Sometimes the talk would be so good that they couldn't let the sinking of the sun bring it to an end. One evening I remember in particular. After the sun had begun to weaken, the three of us went to a Mexican restaurant on East First Street, drank ice cold beer, and continued the conversation. We told stories, mostly true ones, each suggesting another in unbroken rotation. Such an evening of perfect conversation doesn't come along very often; that night I was aware of a feeling of joyousness even as I slept, and this feeling stayed with me all the next day. A week later Mr. Dobie said to us when it was time to leave Barton's, "Boys, come home with me and have a cold beer. I've got something I want to show you." We had no idea of what to expect, for he would tell us nothing more. In his back yard he read us our conversation at the restaurant as transcribed from memory. He later published this transcription in the Sunday paper, but it was so bowdlerized that the point of almost every story was spoiled. Whoever read it must have thought that we did not know how to tell a story or that we were foolish enough to laugh at nothing at all.

Later in the same summer, 1957, we planned to have a picnic down Barton Creek after our swim. We went below the bridge not very far from where the creek runs into the Colorado and there we built a fire on the clay bank (later washed away by the same flood that took Mr. Bedichek's tree). Walter Prescott Webb and Mody Boatright joined us. While Mr. Bedichek mixed a huge bowl of salad and I broiled a steak, the other three sat on a tarpaulin and began to talk. After supper Mr. Bedichek told how he had helped one of his daughters, then studying anatomy in the University, find a tomcat for dissection. One afternoon he and his daughter had struck out in the direction of Bastrop for a leisurely ride and had wandered around on the back roads and through the post oaks until they happened on a shack in a clearing. When they caught sight of some cats around the place they decided to stop and see what they could do. A man in faded blue overalls was sitting on the front porch. After passing the time of day with him Mr. Bedichek began to work towards his object. He said something like this, "I see you've got some very fine cats around here. I need a cat and I'd like to get one from you." The farmer at once began to praise his cats for their marvelous rat- and mouse-catching abilities. Mr. Bedichek heard him out and at last indicated that he wanted a particularly large tomcat sleeping under a bush. The farmer said, "Yes, sir, that's a very fine cat. One of the best on the place. He really will keep your place cleaned out of rats and mice." Mr. Bedichek then asked how it would be possible to get the cat back to Austin. The farmer said he could get a tow sack and put the cat in it. He caught the cat, put him in the sack, and tied up the mouth. When he handed Mr. Bedichek the sack, he said, "Now just shut him up in the barn and let him get at those rats and mice. Keep him there three or four days before you let him out, and I'll guarantee you he never will run off from your place." Then Mr. Bedichek asked the farmer how much he wanted for the cat. The farmer said he reckoned four bits would be about right. Not having expected to buy a cat, Mr. Bedichek had come off with only a little change in his pocket. He told the farmer that he would give him all he had, thirty-five cents, and bring the rest the next time he was down that way. The farmer agreed, evidently thinking that he had been bargained out of fifteen cents but glad to get thirty-five. Mr. Bedichek and his daughter took the cat back to Austin, where he yielded up his life to the cause of science.

There was more to the story. Later Mr. Bedichek happened to be down in the same neck of the woods, and he thought he would stop and pay the farmer the fifteen cents that was owing to him. The farmer recognized Mr. Bedichek and immediately began to suspect that something was wrong. He said, "If you're looking for that big tomcat, he ain't come back here. You must not have kept him locked up in the barn like I told you to." Mr. Bedichek said he had no cause at all for complaint but had simply stopped to pay the fifteen cents. The farmer's mouth dropped open and then he said, "I shore thank you. If you need any more cats like that 'un, you know where to come. Yes, sir, I've got one of the finest breeds of rat-catchers in Bastrop County."

Of course I have not done justice to Mr. Bedichek's story. He spent about fifteen minutes in the telling. This is only one of several stories that he told that night, and I have heard him tell many others on Bedichek's rock or at picnics—always where there was no electricity for a tape recorder. Once I tried to get him on tape indoors; I got his voice and his marvelous laugh at someone else's story, but he wouldn't tell a story of his own.

On another afternoon we adjourned from Barton Springs to my house, where we sat in an air-conditioned room and had our beer. We talked and talked; it grew dark but no one thought of turning on the lights. Mr. Dobie said, "Bedi, why in the world don't you write your autobiography? You've known a lot of people, you've done a great many different things, you've thought many thoughts, you know how to tell a good story, and you have copies of all the letters you have written." Mr. Bedichek said he didn't want to sit down and begin with his boyhood and go through the whole history of his life; besides, at the moment he was more interested in the problem of water conservation, and he thought the public at large would receive more benefit if he published a book on this problem rather than on himself. Then he turned the tables on Mr. Dobie, urging him to write the story of his own life. Eventually he put aside the water problem and began to write about another subject that he had often held forth

67

on at Barton Springs, smells and the sense of smell in both human beings and animals. About two months ago he showed me the completed manuscript for a full-length book, which he was tentatively calling *Speaking of Noses*.

Many of the conversations on Bedichek's rock had to do with scientific and philosophic problems. Once when we were talking about the kind of ethics founded on the Darwinian concept of the struggle for existence and the survival of the fittest, I happened to mention Kropotkin's attempt to combat this ethical theory by attacking its biological foundation. I said that Kropotkin has written *Mutual Aid* to establish the thesis that the chief factor in the progressive evolution of both animals and men is mutual aid rather than the struggle for existence and the survival of the fittest. "Do you have a copy of *Mutual Aid*?" asked Mr. Bedichek. "The library does not have a copy of this in book form; I am having to read *Mutual Aid* as it was originally published in a magazine. Would you lend me your copy?" He was working on *Karankaway Country* at the time and he wanted to review *Mutual Aid*, which he had read years before and which he thought a valuable contribution to biological and ethical theory. He kept my book for a year and then returned it. He was always very careful about returning the books that he had borrowed, and he wanted his own books returned too, though he didn't care how long I kept them.

One afternoon while we were sitting on Bedichek's rock I spoke of an essay by Einstein on science and religion. He was impressed by the clarity of Einstein's demarcation between the spheres of science and religion and his statement of what he considered to be the chief present course of conflict between religion and science, the concept of a personal God. In Einstein's view such a conflict need not exist. Mr. Bedichek asked to borrow this book; he liked the essay so well that he read the whole book and kept it by him to look into from time to time. Two years later he came to my office to return it. Not finding me in, he wrote a note and slipped the book in my letter drop: "Dear Wilson—Credit me with returning this book. Sorry you are not in. Am in a jawing mood. Bedi."

In those two years we had of course spoken many times about anthropomorphism. Once I asked him whether, in his own mind, he did not personify nature and think about nature as an all-wise, all-beneficent power that had planned all forms of being, both animate

68

and inanimate, with a purpose. We were with Mr. Dobie at his place in the country, Cherry Springs, this time, not Barton Springs. At first Mr. Bedichek was not willing to grant that the imputation had any element of truth in it, but after a while he said, "But there is purpose!" I tried to argue that after a form of animal life has adapted itself to an existing environment it seems to have been made purposely for that environment, but Mr. Bedichek held that though this was true it did not rule out purpose. Then I cited an explanation given by a French writer in the eighteenth century of why the limbs of fruit trees bend towards the earth when the fruit is ripe; the reason for this, said the Frenchman, Bernardin de Saint-Pierre, is that it was all planned so in the beginning for the convenience of mankind when he comes to pick the fruit. "That is all foolishness!" Mr. Bedichek replied. "That is silly! It doesn't explain why as each apple is picked the limb moves just a little further from the ground until it is out of reach. It ought to stay down until all the fruit is picked!" This was not the end of the discussion; it continued for some time, but Mr. Bedichek remained firm in his conviction that purpose does exist, though Mr. Dobie sided with me.

I did not go to Barton's for a week after Mr. Bedichek's passing. When I did go, I swam over to Bedichek's rock and stood in the water before it. How many hours had he sat there over the years with his friends, talking about birds, quoting poetry, telling anecdotes, recalling passages in his life, analyzing politics, and speculating on the questions of existence! Let Bedichek's rock remain, unaltered in any way, unmarked by a bronze inscription.

FOUR LETTERS

"The days of dizzy raptures . . . gone"

Bedichek wrote his friends J. Frank Dobie and Clara Lewis on old age:

September 27, 1951

Dear Dobie:

Yes, in comparison with the microscopic lapse of time taken up by one's adult years, man's 'progress' or 'retrogression' can only be framed in geologic time.

I have just learned from reading a scholarly and immensely documented history of furniture that from about 400 A.D. to about 1500 A.D. the chair was completely lost. The easy, relaxed postures we see seated on Greek vases of, say, Persephone & Palamedes, with the figure of the Goddess molded into the chair completely reposed, serene and tranquil, is general throughout the Greek and Roman empires for at least a thousand years.

Then man literally forgets how to sit down, and it is a thousand years before he discovers a genuine chair and how to make one. From the Fall of Rome to the Discovery of America man had not where to rest his buttocks, and then it took him nearly three hundred years to fashion a piece in which the relaxed sitting posture of the human body was possible.

So, if it takes a millenium or so—no one knows how long, to make a simple piece of furniture one can sit on—and then after forgetting how [, in] another millenium [we] only re-learn by accidental survival of representations, think how the more complicated things of civilization, not only mechanical but "ways of life" (the genuine essences of civilization)—consider how much is lost in the monstrous

70

churnings about of wars and migrations to which our species is subjected. Truly "we little note nor long remember."

This occurs to me in the context of your "geologic time" remark the other afternoon, and tends to confirm your suggestion. It is also in line with the "no-progress" theory I mentioned. I think it must have been some such staggering discovery as mine of the chair that caused our most robust of optimists, Walt Whitman, to rub his eyes and exclaim, "I know the *amplitude of time*." How much more philosophic is that remark than Tennyson's "I the heir to all the ages in the foremost files of Time." Is he the heir to all the ages? Not by a damnsite. He inherits only a microscopic fraction, and that little will be wiped out and forgotten in the World Hurricane in which we shall shortly be engulfed.

Yours,

Bedi

P.S. An old barber who has cut my hair for forty years confided to my right ear as he was trimming the hairs out of it yesterday afternoon that he can no longer sit down camp-style out in the open—he can no longer naturally answer Nature's call, but must seek a rest of some sort.   R.B.

P.P.S. One of the real tragedies of Old Age lies in its decreasing ability to squat.
ccEugene George, Jr.

This is a young man with whom I sometimes have philosophic discussions.   R.B.

801 E 23
Austin 5, Texas
March 13, 1955

Dear Clara:

Finally, I found your note of March 3 and note that in answering from memory the other day, I forgot all about the quatrain stuck down in the lower lefthand corner.

As a general policy Age should let Youth have its illusions. Maybe you should be permitted to believe that Moore is right, and that, in the darkening years, Memory will serve as their comforter if not their delight. I believed this until I got old. I believed, also, the opening lines of "Rabbi Ben Ezra."

But Moore and Browning were indulging in wishful thinking. The last of life is by no means the best of life. Memory does not half renew our pleasures. On the other hand, Memory makes us more miserable by presenting former joys in contrast with the aches and pains of a worn-out physical machine, and, on the emotional plain, with the mere ghosts or shadows of pleasures once experienced with an overwhelming sense of their reality.

Tennyson comes nearer my experience: "a sorrow's crown of sorrows is remembering happier things . . .

> Drug thy memory lest thou learn it, lest *thy* heart be put to proof
> In the dead, unhappy night when the rain is on the roof.
> (italics supplied)

And, again, he is so mortally right in that immortal unrhymed lyric, finest in the language, "Tears, Idle Tears." Repetition of it renews even now the flow of tears from my dried-up, drouthy eyes.

Once in the beginning of my old age, I drove alone down the beautiful Bosque Valley in the fall of the year. I began repeating that poem looking out upon "the happy autumn fields" and thinking of the days in that very valley when it was the scene, years previously, of one of the great emotional experiences of my life. Tears blinded me and I drove off on the side of the road until I regained my vision.

Fortunately, we have poetry for childhood, and poetry a little more realistic for youth, still nearer the truth for middle age, but finally we must take to prose. Even Browning succumbed to this truth when he admitted into "By the Fireside," "Not verse now, only prose," as evidence that all the days of dizzy raptures were really and finally gone.

All this should not repress the aspiration to be happy in old age. Witness that heroic spirit whose funeral we are attending today.* I gathered great strength from occasional associations with her, of which the last at your home was to me the most inspiring of all. Dobie and I, both doubters, rarely felicitate each other, but we did this very thing right after that memorable dinner. Bless her dear heart, there she sat smiling, dominating completely her terrible physical infirmities. It is hard for me to believe that she ever sur-

---

* Mrs. Morgan Smith.

rendered, even "in the dead, unhappy night," to the sick fancies I have (under a most mysterious compulsion) been sharing with you. Did she ever indulge "tears, idle tears?" I doubt it. But if she did, she was, in her contacts with us, always and indisputably captain of her soul.

Well, I'm afraid it will take another compost-party to dissipate the gloom into which this correspondence has fallen. Until then, I am

Yours as cheerfully as possible,

Bedi

Dear Dobie:

I believe that you and I reached our conclusion concerning help-less old age independently of each other and perhaps independently of our reading, or of our listening to the wise. Anyway, it takes a Greek to put it into words that seem to me to leave nothing unsaid:

Only the base will long for length of life that never turns another way from evil.
What joy is there in day that follows day, now swift, now slow, and death the only goal.
I count as nothing him who feels within the glow of empty hopes.

Yours for a long life as long as it is a merry one, or as you say, as long as one can stay "lit up with life."

R.B.

October 10, 1957

801 East 23rd Street
Austin 5, Texas
August 31, 1956

Dear Clara [Lewis]:

From long habit I never throw away an unfaded rose, but stick it in a little water, not from any sentimental association it may happen to have with an event or personality, but simply because in my religion a trash can is not place for a rose with any life left in it.

Hence, the little rose you pinned on my lapel the other night was thus bestowed as I was disrobing for bed, and it is still there in its

73

berth as fresh as when it was ravished from its bush. Each morning since as I begin my devotional, which consists of merely reading a good book, I see it across the table above the edge of its peanut-butter glass.

So, for my small trouble in extending ever so briefly this little flower's little lease on life, I am rewarded by being reminded of you, your graciousness, of your consideration for others, of your zest in life, your vivacity and ceaseless activity all richly seasoned with what Wordsworth nominates "that best portion of a good man's life, his little nameless unremembered acts of kindness and of love."

And even yet in this dawn nearly a week later, this flower still faces me over the edge of the glass, performing untaught its self-imposed task of reminding.

And thus reminded I am and must remain

Always Sincerely yours

Roy Bedichek

EDGAR E. WITT*

"Today is life—the rest is nothing"

That Roy Bedichek remained my devoted friend for more than sixty years was always a mystery to me—he a scholarly person, I having little contact with literature except in dry law tomes and "political literature"—he a poet in thinking and living, I always engrossed in material things of this practical world. That he found something in my life that gave me his affection and interest has made me think more of myself.

We came to know each other in our late teens in the little town of Eddy. I attended the public schools; Roy went to his parents' private school.

We went from there to Waco in the fall of 1896 to work as stenographers and study law. A year later we decided to go to college before taking up any profession. We both joined Phi Delta Theta Fraternity at The University of Texas on recommendation of our boyhood friend, Tom Connally, who had joined the previous year. We continued for a good portion of our college life as roommates.

During our college days Roy and his and my fraternity pal, the well known Harry Peyton Steger, took an excursion pleasure trip to New Orleans. When they discovered that besides their return tickets they had only fifty cents between them, they invested this in a stalk of bananas and boarded their trains for Austin and lived on these bananas enroute. In those days such trips took much longer than now, but the bananas lasted them. We both earned our way through

* Chief commissioner, Indian Claims Commission, and former lieutenant governor of Texas.

75

The University of Texas, Roy always as a part time secretary for somebody, and I by selling advertising in publications, getting roomers for boarding houses, etc.

After finishing our respective academic courses our lives became separated for around 15 years, during which time Roy was quite a wanderer. I think he tramped over Europe one summer with Steger, and I have a recollection of them reaching Montreal on their return, stranded, and financing trips (Roy to Texas, Harry to New York) by drawing several small drafts on mutual friends in Texas, of whom I was one.

When I became a member of the Texas Senate in 1918, I found Roy with the University Interscholastic League and with a wife and two charming girl children, Sarah and Mary, to whom I became "Uncle Edgar." From 1918 until the day of his passing we remained in constant communication. It was always a "feast of soul" for me to have conversation or correspondence with him. An "illiterate" like myself felt like he was sitting at the feet of a Socrates or a Solomon. He interspersed his talk with profanity not only without giving offense but in a way that made the profane words beautiful. He held demagogues and stuffed shirts in contempt but would not hurt anyone with the stroke of a feather.

Only recently, after receiving from me a letter telling him that neither of us would likely be here much longer, he wrote me:

I note your dismal prognostication concerning the imminence of our demise, and I think the less said about this the better for both of us. George Santayana, the famous philosopher who was given a sad view of life on account of living through two expatriations—one when he came to America at eight years of age and another when he returned to Italy forty years later—tried to live with his old age reducing his comprehension of time to one day. Once you get this psychology, he advises, things are brighter: "The charm I find in old age—for I was never happier than I am now—comes of having learned to live in the moment, and thereby in eternity; and this means recovering a perpetual youth, since nothing can be fresher than each day as it dawns and changes." Of course, Santayana thieves this from the Bible, although he was all his life an uncompromising unbeliever, and infidel. He often said "The material world is a fiction, and any other world is a nightmare." But nevertheless he swipes the thought of Jesus: "Sufficient unto the day is the evil thereof"; and "take no thought of the morrow," etc. I have tried for a long time to do this very thing. It is hope, or looking forwards, and reminiscence, or looking backward, that brings on the gloomy days. Maundering over the "dear dead days gone beyond recall," or Tennyson's cry-baby stuff: "Tears, Idle Tears."

Better turn to Whitman, as I often do, repeating to myself,

This then is life,
Here is what has come to the surface after so many throes and convulsions.
How curious, how real!
Underfoot the divine soil, overhead the sun.

Paul said: "I die daily." And the inference is that he feels that he has a daily resurrection. When one comes out of sleep (temporary death) and experiences a resurrection, he should ask nothing of dead yesterdays or of unborn tomorrows. Today is life—the rest is nothing.

A LETTER TO WEBB

"I . . . hear Time's wingèd chariot"

Dr. Webb drew from his letters from Bedichek the one that follows:

Dear Webb:

The lines you quote are impressive:

> But at my back I always hear
> Time's wingèd chariot hurrying near.

Your comment is deeply philosophic. Instead of being an historian, you should have been a philosopher. You have genuine philosophic insight, but not a professionally cultivated one. But maybe the professional philosophers would have sealed up the outlets of your intuitive wisdom. I have always contended that you are somewhat of a psychic.

A couplet you quote started me digging into my capacious memory for a couplet or two from a poem by some early American rhymster, maybe Bret Harte. Maybe John Hay, maybe someone else—no matter. My digging, as usual, exhumed only the concluding lines which run

> A few swift years and who can show
> Which dust was Bill and which was Joe.

A few more days of digging and the digger brought up another fragment,

> . . . Ah, pensive scholar, what is fame?

This, you see, is a query and must have an answer. So searching

78

the cubby-holes of deposits jumbled and overlaid with dust I un-
covered the title of a poem,

"Lines to a Dying Athlete," but nothing came of it for a day or two,
and then while I was taking a bath and thinking of what a mess of
a winter-garden I have, this couplet popped up uncalled:

> Silence sounds no worse than cheers
> After the earth has stopped his ears.

Do you notice that the rime of this is almost identical with the rime
of your couplet. What strange alchemy goes on in the memory!

Still I knew this was a wrong scent—true it is in the same vein, but
I knew that it didn't answer, except by indirection, the query,

> Ah, pensive scholar, what is fame?

Then I decided to give it up and write to the "memory" column of
the NY Times and get the answer. But I was busy and put off writing.
It kept ding-donging in my memory: "what is the rime for fame?"
Finally "flame" came. It must be flame, but get the line, I could not,
so I decided to build up a line of my own, but with the figure the poet
used clearly before me, that is a comparison of "fame" to "flame." "A
sudden lift of leaping flame" and I repeated it aloud with dissatis-
faction:

> Ah, pensive scholar, what is fame?
> A sudden lift of leaping flame.

Mighty sorry! No poet of any tunefulness would use it, but I knew
the comparison was right. Then since the last couplet of the poem
first dug up mentions "dust" another comparison of fame to dust must
be next, and it came without much trouble:

> A giddy whirlwind's fickle gust
> That lifts a pinch of mortal dust.

So I think I have it, that is the concluding three couplets. There is
leading up to these three couplets a short life history of Bill and one
of Joe. One a "pensive scholar" and the other a hail fellow well-met
who takes life and life's joys and sorrows in his healthy stride.

> Ah, pensive scholar, what is fame?
> A slender tongue of leaping flame,
> A giddy whirlwind's fickle gust

79

> That lifts a pinch of mortal dust—
> A few swift years and who can show
> Which dust was Bill and which was Joe.

You can see what a burden and what superhuman exertion your suggestion put upon me that we are no longer friendly in the mails, or even neighborly, because

> Always at our backs we hear
> "Time's wingèd chariot hurrying near."

I am afraid Toynbee is too much for me. I have read your review in the *Dallas News*. It makes a stimulating introduction to the great man's work, but I hear "Time's wingèd chariot." I must stick to my humble knitting, and try to understand simpler things than the reasons for the fall, rise, endurances and diseases of twenty-five or thirty civilizations since they began recording themselves in enduring and legible form. What does Toynbee say of the Minoan civilization whose record recently discovered has not yet been deciphered?

Don't give yourself any more concern over my arrogance. It is definitely on its way out.

As ever, affectionately

Bedi

December 6, 1954.

EDMUND HEINSOHN

We loved him because of his naturalness

At Bedichek's funeral Dr. Edmund Heinsohn, minister emeritus, Universtiy Methodist Church in Austin, said in part:

Roy Bedichek was an unreconstructed individualist.

He was a renowned naturalist, but we didn't love him because he was a naturalist, we loved him because of his naturalness. There was something earthy about him that made us respect him, appreciate him, and love him.

With all the tramping around in the woods that he did, it was difficult for us to see how he could do any research work for the writing of his books. His books, however, bear the evidences of thorough research. He saw and appreciated nature in the whole, and also in its minutest detail. To read his recent description of the "Silly Bum" thistle is to have an exciting experience.

Whether we think of him as a newspaperman, organizer, and head of the University Interscholastic League, or as the author of important books, we must remember that in all of his activities his work was the natural expression of his personality and of his mind and spirit. Most of us have our persona, our mask, and most of us put on an act. Our persona is frequently the result of a compromise between our real personality and organized society. Roy Bedichek never wore a mask, never put on an act, and was frank and sincere and courageous in what he said and did. There was little difference between his persona and his personality.

81

John Donne, the distinguished British clergyman, had something to say about the death of one man being the death of us all. The death of Roy Bedichek is the death of us all, but the life that was in Roy Bedichek is also the life of us all. The mind and spirit of Roy Bedichek had survival value.

WALTER PRESCOTT WEBB

Dear Bedi:

Ronnie Dugger asked me to send him something to include in his special edition of *The Observer,* which I understand he is making into a sort of Bedichek symposium to commemorate your departure on a long journey. Those of us who knew you would just as soon have had you postpone it, though we all know that such a journey is inevitable.

You will be interested, and perhaps amused, to learn that you took a good deal of the sting out of your going by the manner of it. Those of us who had listened to your vociferous comments on this subject know that you went exactly the way you wanted, as if you had designed it with the skill and determination you used in designing your own life. Few people are able to call their own shots as you did, right up to the end.

After the service by Dr. Heinsohn, which I thought very appropriate for you, three of us went out for lunch where we had a pretty good time retelling the delightful stories which our total association of not less than one hundred years had provided us. (Frank Dobie and I knew you for forty years, and Glen Evans must have known you for twenty or more, and that makes the one hundred years.) I know you would have been pleased to be the subject of such animated conversation, and the center of so many good stories. We were particularly delighted that you had finished your fourth book, all of them written after you were seventy, and that you had got your publisher's signature on the line, and maybe even a nice advance, only a week earlier.

The first time I remember seeing you was during the impeachment trial of a Texas governor when I as a student was in the gallery of the House of Representatives and you as a reporter for the *San Antonio Express* were on the floor. You were supposed to be making impartial reports, but I suspect you may have slanted them just a little in the direction of your sentiment, which is exactly what I would have done had I been in your place. Incidentally that trial is the most dramatic event I have ever witnessed. Later you became an editor on the *Express* and held this position when I decided to quit teaching in the San Antonio schools because I had had a row with the superintendent. I applied to you for a job as a reporter. You not only turned me down, but you gave me a lengthy and not wholly convincing lecture as to why I should not take this step. I didn't take it because nobody would give me a job.

My memory is not very clear as to when or how our friendship developed at The University of Texas. I spent a five-year stretch on your Interscholastic League Council and was struck by the savage intensity with which you enforced the rules made (by you, I suspect) in an effort to preserve some morality in school athletics.

We really got acquainted, I think, when we went to the Big Bend during the Christmas holidays and camped at the mouth of Saint Helena Canyon, camped in a sandbed with a one-armed Real Silk stocking salesman who was trying to get away from civilization and had darn near done it. We cleaned up his camp, fed him good food, and paid him $3.00 for showing us the canyon which was right there for all to see. He was a salesman. It was from him that you learned about a special breed of rabbits, which he called knee rabbits, found only, according to our informant, in the Rio Grande Valley. I'll never forget the expression on your face when, in response to your question, our host told you the origin of knee rabbits. Coming back from the Big Bend we decided that what we had done was foolish and that we liked it; we entered into an agreement to do at least one foolish thing each year. I think I have lived up to that agreement, but I am not sure that you did. Your innate caution seemed to get in the way.

In 1942 I did what turned out to be a wise thing. I bought the Old Johnson Institute in the hills southwest of Austin and changed its name to Friday Mountain Ranch because a hill there is named Friday Mountain and I liked the name. You used the old stone building as a hideout to write your first book, *Adventures with a Texas Naturalist*. You spent a year and a day there, but you came out with the

84

finished manuscript. Your picture hangs in the room upstairs where you did your writing, sleeping and eating. You cooked your own food in the open fireplace or on a hot plate; occasionally you insisted on my eating things you had cooked in the ashes. The potatoes and eggs were all right, but I drew the line on brussel sprouts and spinach, which I don't care for when cooked proper. There was not even running water in the house, but you made out. We still have the big round table you used, one that Captain Ernest Best of the Texas Rangers took out of a gambling house.

Another thing you did was to suggest that Rodney Kidd and I should set up a boys' camp at Friday Mountain. In response to your suggestion we met one rainy day and set up Friday Mountain Boys' Camp, now in its thirteenth year. You had a chapter in your book entitled "The Tree and the Rock." It was the story of how a hackberry tree found root in a giant rock, broke the rock into several pieces and became a big tree. You were explaining how soil is made. The tree died during the drought, only the stump and the broken rocks are left. It is possible that you have conferred immortality on Friday Mountain and that in the future students and curious tourists in search of culture will make pilgrimages there to see where the Texas Naturalist wrote his first book.

Ah well, Bedi, this could go on for a long time if I recounted all the memories of a long association. Perhaps I can sum it up by saying that you made my life richer as I am sure you did the lives of many others. You left Texas a better place than you found it and no Texan should wish for more.

Yours,

Walter Prescott Webb

Mr. Roy Bedichek

WALTER PRESCOTT WEBB

MELISSA GATEWOOD JONES*

His first teacher

I look back with pride and pleasure to the host of children that I have taught in my fifty years' teaching. One who impressed was a five-year-old boy named Walter Webb. He was my neighbor because his family and mine had both bought farms in West Texas. I was teaching the one-room country school of the community. I realized my little neighbor had an unusual mind and asked my school board to let him sit in my school. They consented if it was not too much work for me.

I was a young teacher, nineteen, and loved children. Little Walter was delighted and listened to each class. Geography he loved best. I had large maps on the wall and I taught the pupils the countries, rivers, and cities. I asked a boy in the class, one day, where he lived. He said "Texas." I asked him to point it out. He put the pointer on South America. Walter raised his chubby little hand and said, "He comes a long way to school."

We had a snow storm one night, and we played snowball at recess the next day. Walter fell and skinned his little fat cheek. He was always a chubby little thing. After that I led him over the grounds until they were not so slick.

Friday afternoons quite often we had "speeches." Walter was all ready with something. Once it was:

* Of Corpus Christi, Texas, a school teacher whose recollections, "Teaching in Arizona Territory," were published in the University of Arizona historical quarterly.

> Meet me, sister, meet me,
> And let us run a race.
> Last year you used to beat me
> In every little chase.

One big boy who had no Memory Gem for the day said:

> For a fact,
> I lost my speech
> In a buffalo track.

Walter said, "Miss Lessie, he had better find it." He always called me "Miss Lessie."

When Walter was fifteen years old I was again his teacher. One of the subjects I taught him was Texas history. This school was considered a "tough" school. The year before, two boys carried knives and sometimes guns for a battle at noon, after school, or any convenient place. We had no trouble that year. Walter was such a perfect young gentleman that the "bandits" were ashamed to do wrong. He was the flower on the fig tree.

The next year my husband and I went to Arizona Territory and taught four years. When we returned, Walter had moved and I lost trace of him. When I did hear, he was in Austin attending Texas University. An unknown friend was sending him.

Some years ago I was a delegate to the United Daughters of the Confederacy in Austin. An usher at the meeting came to me and said that someone in the lobby wanted to see me but did not tell his name. There stood a mature man. When I looked at his eyes, I knew he was Walter Webb, my pupil of long ago, now Dr. Walter Prescott Webb. I had a picture of him taken in a school group when he was fifteen, and I gave it to him.

Dr. Webb and his wife, Jane, came to see me in Corpus Christi, and we had a nice time together and enjoyed it.

When he married the second time he brought his bride, Terrell Maverick, to see me. When they left, Walter kissed me goodbye. He always kissed me goodbye and his wives did, too. Bless his heart. He was a sweet little boy and he was sweet till the end.

88

SAVOIE LOTTINVILLE*

"Professor, that was purty"

"Everyone who creates anything needs an audience, even if it's only an audience of one," Walter Prescott Webb was saying. I had asked him when we were together in Lincoln, Nebraska, in 1957 to tell how he had got started in writing. The meeting of the Mississippi Valley Historical Association had closed, and the hundreds of eager and talkative historians who had attended were now on their way home. Walter and I were left in the wake of the meeting. "Come to my room and we'll swap yarns," he said over the telephone.

Fifty years before, Walter said, he had been a teacher in a one-room schoolhouse in East Texas. He taught all grades and did the school chores as well. Among his pupils was a ten-year-old named Henry Woods, who was part Indian. Henry was a helpful and admiring friend to his teacher. He always managed to arrive at school in the morning, as Walter did, much ahead of the other youngsters, to help wash down the blackboards, bring in wood for the stove, and sweep out. He was the very soul of helpfulness.

One spring morning, when the turf under the piney woods was beginning to show early wildflowers, the twenty-year-old teacher hurried along to school a little after sun-up, well ahead of his usual schedule. On his arrival, instead of going about his chores, he sat down at his desk and began writing. Half an hour later, little Henry Woods came through the schoolhouse door, ready to assist Walter Webb.

"Good morning, Henry," said the teacher. "Why don't we change

* Director of the University of Oklahoma Press.

89

our plans a little today? Sit down in your place, if you will. I've written a little word sketch of you that I'd like for you to hear."

Henry Woods took his place and, cupping his chin in his hands, he listened as his teacher read. When the word sketch was finished, little Henry looked up, starry-eyed, and said, "Professor, that was purty."

"He was my first audience," Walter told me. "I've been writing ever since."

Many things could be said about Webb's power as a historian—his skill in arriving at historical meaning, his breadth of concept, his deceptively simple narrative style, his originality, and his courage in taking new paths—but at heart his craft was directed to conveying meaning to people. The lesson the teacher learned from the pupil more than half a century ago had lasted a lifetime.

RUPERT N. RICHARDSON[*]

"Does anyone have a reason to suggest?"

It was in the history class of the late Eugene C. Barker during the spring of 1922 that I first knew Walter Prescott Webb. Both of us had grown up in Stephens County, but our trails had not crossed before. At that time he was an instructor in history, I a part-time instructor in government, and we were both working toward advanced degrees in The University of Texas.

One day Dr. Barker touched upon the subject of western extension of settlements. With his gift for clarity and orderly development of a topic, he made a swift survey, pointed to the Great Plains on the wall map, and said: "Here this advance stopped, or moved very slowly for several decades. I am not certain why. Does anyone have a reason to suggest?" Two or three facts were mentioned; I called attention to the lack of available water; and then Webb spoke up and put the explanation in a form that I had not heard before. "These people came from a timbered country and had developed a timber civilization; when they reached the land where forests ceased they were confused and did not know what to do. Before they could occupy the country they had to develop a new way of life, and it took them decades to do it."

I was impressed with the statement, but I did not then realize that Webb had just set forth the thesis of what was to become one of the great books of our times: *The Great Plains.*

* Senior professor in history at Hardin-Simmons University who has written several books, including *Texas, the Lone Star State.*

Webb was interested in ideas and was a genius at developing them. To him facts were useless unless one was able to discover their meaning. It was with this point of view that he became a great historian. To his friends, however, the man was even greater than the historian.

JOHN HALLER

A most generous offer

During the war years I enrolled in Walter Prescott Webb's graduate course dealing with the history of the American frontier. When I entered the classroom the first time, I saw a short, bulky man with a very large, very round head, no visible neck, owl-like eyes, and paunchy cheeks; with a grave, preoccupied air and slow, deliberate movements. Seated at his desk, he spoke in a measured, resonant, impressive tone, quite lacking in Texas drawl, distinguished rather by a richly cultured quality difficult to define but impossible to mistake.

There will be no daily assignments and no examinations in this class [he said]. Each student is asked to select a project related to the general subject and to write a paper on it. Sometime before the end of the term he will be asked to read the paper before the class. Grades—for whatever they're worth—will be determined entirely by the papers submitted. You are a group of mature men and women, and you will be expected to work under your own initiative. That's all for today.

Altogether it was a very impressive first performance, and I went away delighted.

About this time I formed a small organization composed of myself and several other university students to work on Austin's trees during our unoccupied afternoons. Soon I found that we needed a truck, but trucks were hard to come by. I mentioned this fact to Dr. Webb and he said that he had one he was not using. I asked if he would sell or rent it to me. "I don't want to sell it, and I won't rent it to you," he said, "but I'll let you use it as long as you want to."

93

One unfortunate thing about doing a favor is the fact that the recipient may soon be after you to do him another. Not many days after Dr. Webb loaned me his truck, I decided to buy a mechanical log saw on the theory that the oil that went into the machine was less costly than the sweat that came out of me. The only thing that stood between me and the saw was $266. I wrote to my father, who sent me $100. Then I went to the bank to borrow the rest and learned in a moment the total valuelessness of my signature, of which I had always been rather fond. The next morning found me in Dr. Webb's office, generously inviting him to be the co-signer.

He looked all around the room, up at the ceiling and down at the floor. The silence was more embarrassing for him than for me.

"I've lost on so many notes," he said at last. "I swore I'd never sign another. How much did you want to borrow?"

"One-hundred and fifty dollars," I answered.

"I might go seventy-five," he said meditatively. "I could stand to lose that much."

"Please don't sign it if you don't want to," I said. "I won't blame you a bit for not signing it. *I* know I'll repay the note, but you don't know it. How could you? But if we make it at all, it'll have to be for $150; otherwise I won't be able to buy the saw."

The next morning he took me to the bank personally, introduced me to the president, and signed the note.

Six months went by. I had expanded my little tree company and was depending on it entirely for my living. But work was slack, and I was desperate.

"Are you keeping busy?" he asked me one day, with the same unfailing interest he always took in his students.

"I'm starving to death," I answered modestly.

The next morning he had me and my crew out on the Friday Mountain ranch, going over the trees.

"Work here until business in town picks up," he said. "Don't hurry to get through."

Still once more I worried Dr. Webb with my personal problems. I had had a difficulty with my landlady and was being asked to move. Apartments were harder to get than trucks. Who should I think of in this situation but the man who had thrice befriended me?

He took me in his car to a place on the outskirts of the city, where a small frame house stood vacant.

"It needs a little fixing up," he said. "But if you want, you can live there until you find something better."

"How much is the rent?" I asked.

"Nothing," he answered. "How do you think I can charge you? You are just beginning. I've already lived my life."

As it happened, I found another place closer in and thus was saved from this ultimate imposition.

Sometime during these days I enrolled in another course with Dr. Webb, a seminar devoted to research on the influence of the American frontier on European institutions. There were eight of us in the class, seven men and one woman. Each was allowed to select his topic. I chose the effect of the American frontier on European literature. We met twice a week at night; as we sat around that ovaloid, polished table, our faces reflected on its smooth surface, we felt, and probably looked, very important.

Europe during the Middle Ages was a body paralyzed [Dr. Webb began, developing his great idea in his careful, deliberate manner]. Trade was stagnant; institutions changed little if at all; property was largely inherited; travel was slight; learning was the exclusive occupation of the priests, who had little interest in secular affairs.

The discovery of the New World altered everything. It opened up new horizons, spiritual as well as geographical. It wrought a revolution in the human spirit. It initiated a great expansionist movement that is just now coming to an end. It was the greatest event in the history of the world. It will not be duplicated until another planet is opened for colonization.

The interesting thing about the frontier [he continued] is not how the Old World civilization transformed it, but how *it* transformed the Old World civilization. The frontier was the catalyst that stimulated the Old World into new activity. Every European institution that came into contact with the American frontier underwent a process of erosion. Like European clothes that were found unfit for the American wilderness, so European institutions were found unfit for it and were torn off or discarded, piece by piece.

The project we are going to study is so broad and so far-reaching that we will never exhaust it. I hope each one of you will give it his best efforts. As for myself, I expect to do more work on the subject than any one of you, if my health holds out.

Such was the beginning of the seminar, probably the most interesting course I ever took. Each one of us went about his task with enthusiasm. I was lucky enough to stumble on some material that had not yet come to Dr. Webb's attention and incorporated it as best I could into my paper. When my turn came and I read my paper, Dr. Webb asked me to stay after class. We then got in his car and drove about Austin for three hours or so, stopping at restaurants here and there for coffee.

"I want that paper enlarged into a book," he said, making me giddy with praise. "If it isn't published, how can I quote from it?" And throwing back his head he laughed that hearty laugh for which he was famous—not just a vibration of the vocal chords but a participation of the whole man.

"You have the nucleus of a great book, and you have the ability to finish it," he continued. "You write it, and I'll see that it gets published."

Then to encourage me he told me the story of his life: how he had written *The Great Plains* originally as a Ph.D. dissertation and how he had decided that it was too good to be merely a dissertation and had turned it into the book. He told me how he had dug up material on the Texas Rangers and made that into a book. Growing more intimate, he went on to tell me about his ventures in writing for the pulps and all the interesting anecdotes connected with the struggles of a beginning writer.

"What I did, you can do," he said. "You do it. I'll subsidize you."

Circumstances prevented my taking advantage of this, the most generous offer I ever received. Can it be believed? To such an invitation from such a man I turned a deaf ear! Six months before, and I would have given my right arm for the opportunity. Now, however, I had just married, I was completely engrossed by the tree business, which was beginning to grow formidably under my hands, and I was intoxicated by the sudden and unexpected feel of money in my pocket.

The book he wanted me to write never got written. Nevertheless, he used much of my material in *The Great Frontier,* particularly my translations from Gilbert Chenard, and he was kind enough to acknowledge the use. There is an unfortunate tendency on the part of teachers to pilfer outright the result of their pupils' researches. Nothing of this was to be found in Dr. Webb. Utterly devoid of vanity, he was fairness itself: fair to his students, his colleagues, and his predecessors.

At the completion of the seminar, Dr. Webb invited us to Friday

Mountain ranch for a barbecue. We sat around a campfire eating two-inch steaks by the light of a full moon and talking. In common with many other great men, Dr. Webb has a strong strain of Rabelaisianism in him. I remember particularly one of the stories he told us. It concerned a cowboy who got the habit of visiting a Mexican woman when her husband was out looking after the cattle. On one such occasion the husband returned at the wrong time.

"Queeck!" said Dolores. "Under the bed. Tony will keel you!"

The cowboy managed to get under the bed just as Tony came in the door. The ruse promised to be a complete success until a goose, sleeping under the bed, was awakened by a foot under his wing and suddenly began to hiss.

"To hell with that Aztec!" shouted the cowboy, bursting out of hiding and running out of the door in his underwear. "I'm snake bit!"

Later on, having left the university, I saw Dr. Webb less frequently, although I managed to find a pretext for going by once every six months or so to visit with him. He always found time to talk to me and always manifested the same thoughtful interest in my affairs, as if they were really important. I was working on a book on trees and asked him what he thought about its chances for success.

"Don't plan on getting rich off the book," he said, giving me the same melancholy advice J. Frank Dobie had given me earlier. "It's easy to exaggerate the money to be made from a book. You can make more money cutting down trees than by writing about them."

Several years later when I actually had an offer from a publisher, I again went to see him to discuss the terms, with which, by now considering myself quite a businessman, I was not at all satisfied.

"I told you not to expect much money," he began. "The ideal is to break even. Lots of books lose money; some have to be subsidized. You write the book because you have it in you. If you make any money, that's incidental and so much to the good."

"But what about the seven years I've spent working on this thing?" I protested. "I would have been better off in a barroom."

"That's not the way to look at it," he answered quietly. "You are now an authority on the subject. You will be asked to speak here and there, and the book will bring you new friends and new contacts. The royalty checks don't tell the whole story. There are by-products in books as well as in beef."

Dr. Webb was the most profound and original thinker I have ever encountered in person. I have known other men wittier, cleverer, with more superficial brilliance, but none comparable to him in depth, range, and balance.

More than for his intellect, however, Dr. Webb was admired and loved for his humanity. Here was a man always sensitive to the plight of the unfortunate, always ready with help and guidance, always disposed to extend a hand to beginners, to the dispossessed, the misunderstood, the unrecognized. In some men intellect exists as a cold and independent faculty, unaccompanied by personal warmth. Not so with Dr. Webb: in him the reach of his intellect was matched by the breadth of his humanity.

J. FRANK DOBIE

"For years we three sat together"

Walter Prescott Webb and I were born in the same year, 1888. He belonged to one drouth-scarred part of Texas, I to another. His father was a country school teacher who homesteaded a quarter-section of poor land; mine was a rancher who rather expected that education would lead his sons to a better occupation. Webb came to The University of Texas as instructor in history in 1918, while I was a soldier in France, four years after I had come as instructor in English. We advanced concurrently, along divergent ways, as underlings at the University.

Our friendship developed more after about 1930, it seems to me, but I was never close to him as I was with Roy Bedichek, the dearest comrade of my life. Webb had sides never revealed directly to me.

On the evening of March 8, 1963, two other men and I sat down as guests with Frank Wardlaw in his home. He said, "Walter Webb thought he would join us, but he will be late." After conversation and "the better adjuncts of water," we went to a Mexican restaurant. Nobody knew where we were. Before we got back to our homes a number of people had tried to telephone Wardlaw and me. About six-thirty Webb and his wife had been found on the ground near their over-turned car, he dead and she so severely injured that she had to remain in a hospital for thee months.

Bedichek was a kind of peg on which my happiest associations with Webb hung. For years we three sat together, with other men, at the same table during fortnightly dinners, "papers," and discussions of the Town and Gown club of Austin, but talk at our table was seldom

99

so free and personal as it always was at prolonged picnic suppers in the country. Bedichek was the habitual planner of these supper parties, also cooker of the steaks. A vegetarian by philosophy in the later years of his life, he never threw off on his own steaks. The earliest of these picnic suppers that I remember were not far beyond the Rob Roy ranch, some distance off the Bee Caves road in the hills west of Austin. Bedi liked to camp high up. At one hilltop camp we looked down on bullbats (nighthawks) booming as they dived for insects. After Webb, in 1942, acquired Friday Mountain ranch, a location there on Bear Creek became our supping and conversation grounds, though in the '50's we went several times to a place I then owned in Burnet county named Cherry Springs—on account of wild cherry trees growing by Fall Creek.

I got so that I took along potato salad prepared by Bertha Dobie as nobody else could prepare it. Someone might take something else, but Bedichek brought steaks, bread, tomatoes, lettuce, beer, and so on, and then saw that each man paid his share. Nobody was host and the drinking was moderate—one can of beer for Bedi. Webb did not really care for any. When he took whiskey, on other occasions, a jigger without water would do him all evening. He had not drunk at all until he was about fifty. Sitting with the dons after dinner at his college in Oxford, he had developed a mild taste for wine. He craved coffee, which Bedichek was particular in boiling and which he furnished, along with pot, tin plates, knives and forks.

Mody Boatright and Wilson Hudson, both of The University of Texas English department, were regulars at these campfire suppers. After Frank Wardlaw came as director of the University Press, he added to talk and geniality. Any time that John Henry Faulk or Glen Evans was in town, he was there. One time, during World War II, Faulk brought an Englishman along, and in capping limericks with each other both proved themselves bottomless artesian wells. I remember Coke Stevenson, then governor, saying at one supper— the only one he attended—that the American frontiersman carried a rifle, an axe, and a Bible. This was at Friday Mountain. We were by the same water when Homer Price Rainey, president of the university, told us that the regents were out to get him. Ours was no club in any organized way, and we never had regular gatherings, but all of us were liberal enough to be for Rainey and against the reactionary regents who for several years dominated the university.

While dismissing Rainey, the regents, in October, 1944, elected Dr. T. S. Painter as acting president. Immediately thereafter he said in a letter addressed to the faculty: "I want it definitely understood that I am not a candidate for the position of permanent president, and I would not accept it if it were offered to me." The regents wanted an agent. Before long it was clear that they had what they wanted. When, in May, 1946, they elected him president and he accepted the offer, a caucus of faculty men asked Webb to formulate their opinions. At a special meeting of the faculty a few days later Webb countered a resolution "assuring President Painter of our support and cooperation" with one expressing "deep regret that Dr. Painter has not reciprocated the trust the faculty reposed in him, but has, on the contrary, broken faith and violated his pledge." The Webb motion of disconfidence failed to carry by a vote of 160 to 186.

His *Divided We Stand* (1937) was a stand for fairness. Based on figures in *The World Almanac* and the United States census, it made out a case against the prospering North for keeping the South in poverty as a colonial dependent until Franklin D. Roosevelt and the New Deal reversed the trend. Later Webb made clear that vast oil fields and rising industrialism in the South resulting from World War II advanced the region's prosperity.

Few other men of his stature and intellectual power had experienced so intimately the choke of poverty. The extremity of it is set forth in his essay, "The Search for William E. Hinds." As prosperity made him aware of the independence that it gives to an individual, he became, it seems to me, more actively considerate of that basis of freedom for other individuals and for Texas and the South.

In his later years Webb drew a good salary as distinguished professor. Beyond salaries (and motion picture rights amounting to $10,000 on his book *The Texas Rangers*), he prospered through investing earnings from teaching and writing—especially from two textbooks—in real estate. A few years ago he drew up a plan to enable faculty members of The University of Texas who so wished and who had the money to invest in real estate. This plan, as far as I know, never got into operation.

Several times I heard him speak of the influence of L. M. Keasbey on his life. Before World War I, Keasbey, a professor in the university, gave a course on economics—though it was entitled "institutional history"—in which he emphasized one way to get rich: invest in land

101

that the activities of an increasing population will make more valuable, very valuable if the land be chosen judiciously. At the time Webb was absorbing directions to the "unearned increment," an Austin peddler and then wholesale shipper of vegetables named M. H. Crockett took the Keasbey course. He, as I observed and as I heard him tell with pride, became expert in anticipating traffic routes of the city; he died one of the richest property owners in it.

Webb wrote little on civil rights. A few years after the decision of the Supreme Court of the United States on the desegregation of public schools, he could write and speak on the South's advancing economic prosperity without touching on the Negro economically or otherwise. Yet he did not ignore the subject. In a paper to have been delivered at Rice University shortly after he died, he said:

The Southerner is so concerned with the racial issue that he has no time for anything else. This is the [same] issue that has plagued the South since 1820. . . . The racial issue is too heavy to move; it is too green to burn; the best we can do for the present is to plow around it and cultivate the rest of the field.

Friday Mountain Ranch, in the hills seventeen miles southwest of Austin, consists of approximately a section of land that was, when Webb acquired it, eroded, devoid of humus, bare of vegetation beyond trees, cedars on the hills, and broomweeds in the valley. He had wastage accumulated at cotton gins east of Austin hauled out to spread on the ground. He applied commercial fertilizer to plots no longer tillable. While he was Harmsworth professor of American history at Oxford University, 1942–43, he gave his address to the English *Who's Who* as Friday Mountain Ranch, Austin, Texas. He belonged to it. During the terrible drouth that began late in the '40's and did not end until 1957 he made slow progress in restoring the soil and growing a turf of grass—a turf that reach its climax the spring he died.

He figured that the land should some day pay for the expenses he had been out on it. It did, by increase of real estate prices. Beyond all, he valued and enjoyed grass for itself, beautiful on any land, the mark of bounty on ground once impoverished. Several times when I was with him where grass flourished I saw him gather seeds of sideoats grama, little bluestem, Indian grass, and switch grass to take to Friday Mountain and scatter around. I suppose he bought seeds by

102

the bushel also. In planning near the end of his life to transfer title to the land, he chose as purchaser a friend, Rodney Kidd, who would maintain the turf.

He was not a naturalist in the way that Bedichek was, but he observed. Twice at least he told me that we had missed much out of life by not learning botany while growing up in the country. One time as four or five of us were riding in a car along Fall Creek in Burnet county he called out to halt. He had spotted a hackberry, about twenty feet high, growing up through the hollow trunk of a big dead live oak. He did not swim, but the pools of water impounded by dams he had constructed across Bear Creek gave him as much pleasure as any swimming hole ever gave any swimmer.

His brief book *Flat Top: A Story of Modern Ranching*, printed and published by Carl Hertzog of El Paso in 1960, is on grass and a man of grass named Charles Pettit. In 1938 Mr. Pettit bought 7,000 acres, to which he added 10,000 of wornout, eroded farms. Year after year he combatted weeds, prickly pear, and other competitors of grass. Year after year he applied fertilizer, planted clover, put out seeds of native grasses. He impounded over 3,400 acre feet of water, brought back a turf of grasses waist-high. After living with the land for a quarter of a century, he made the ranch pay. "The man really loves grass," Webb wrote. If Webb also had not loved grass, he would never have written this account of a ranch that was a model in conservation practices.

About the time I was leaving for England late in 1945 to teach in a G.I. university, a civilized man of wealth who demanded anonymity granted a sum of money to relieve Roy Bedichek for a year from his duties as director of the Interscholastic League of Texas. He had a book to write. Webb invited him to take over a big upstairs room with a fireplace in the old Friday Mountain rock house, originally built for a boys' academy. Here, eager in his liberation, Bedichek made shelves of apple boxes to hold his books, carried water by bucket from a dug well, brought up wood, cooked over the open fire. Through the year 1946 he worked at a table in front of the fireplace.

Chickens mechanically grown in rooms downstairs did not bother him. In fact, he based one of his richest chapters on "Denatured Chickens." Associating with himself, letting his richly-stored mind play, adding meanings to long-accumulating observations on people, birds, wild flowers, trees, and other forms of life, he achieved

103

Adventures with a Texas Naturalist. Published in 1947, it was four-teen years later taken over by the University of Texas Press, an insti-tution that Webb, more than any other man in the faculty, had fur-thered. "The Bedichek Room" remains, through Webb and Rodney Kidd, a feature at Friday Mountain.

Webb's *The Great Frontier*, officially published December 8, 1952, won the Carr P. Collins Award of a thousand dollars given annually by the Texas Institute of Letters. His response to the presentation was the after-dinner address to the institute—and mighty fidgety he was before dinner. He asked me, also others, to notice how people received what he had to say, something so intimate to *him* that he shrank from making it public. He read his say. It was the most moving I have heard any man utter: it moved deeply all who heard it. He waited a long time to publish it, with some added details, under title of "The Search for William E. Hinds," in *Harper's Maga-zine*, July, 1961. *Reader's Digest* published a condensation of it the following month.

The subject of autobiography came up several times among us while Bedichek was still on hand, iterating that he lacked the genius of Jean Jacques Rousseau for confession. As Webb was leaving my room one day in 1960, I again spoke about autobiography. He volun-teered that he had written one while at Oxford University, 1942–43. He did not go into detail. The whole cannot, I believe, have anything else so intensely, so poignantly personal as the chapter in which he tells of a response received in 1904 to a letter he had written to the letter column of the Sunny South. It was from William E. Hinds of New York, an utter stranger, not only commending his ambition to be a writer but offering to send him books and magazines. Later this William E. Hinds urged him to get a college education and loaned him money while he was attending The University of Texas. Hinds died forty-five years before Webb's obligation to him became a chapter in published literature.

It resulted in many letters from unknowns, some sending money to help students as Hinds had helped Webb. For years he had been concerned over some way to requite Hinds and had given financial aid to able but needy students. He now set up the William E. Hinds scholarship fund at The University of Texas. After his death a check donating money to it was found in his pocketbook; it is an ultimate beneficiary in his will. The Hinds-Webb scholarship fund is now the official name.

I have no recollection of having heard Webb speak at any time of his soul, his religion, or God. He belonged to no church, ignored churches, liked some free-thinkers, some churchmen, especially Dr. Edmund Heinsohn, long pastor of the University Methodist church in Austin. After Heinsohn became a member of Town and Gown years ago, he often sat with Bedichek, Webb, and Dobie. He conducted Bedichek's funeral services, reading into them an interpretation of the man's character. At Webb's funeral he read an interpretative sketch of Webb's life. "I remain an agnostic," Somerset Maugham wrote in *The Summing Up*, "and the practical outcome of agnosticism is that you act as though God did not exist." As far as I can see, Walter Webb's positive goodness bore no relation to what is called God. His conduct was not determined by Biblical injunctions or by expectation of reward in some sort of post mortem existence. His mother is said to have been a fundamentalist, his father a skeptic who read the Bible in order to refute more specifically some of her credulities.

I cannot imagine Webb's "praying for guidance," but at one time he believed in something beyond. After he married in 1916 he was teaching in San Antonio and became so low-spirited over the future that he, as I recall his story, was about to take a job in a jewelry store. He consulted a noted fortuneteller known as Madam Sckerles. She said: "The child will be a girl. I see nothing but books." With books he continued.

If the radical right appeared unjust and undemocratic to him, the radical left increasingly annoyed him. He was not a crusader and was not contentious. He sometimes wished, he once told me, that he did not have to think. He hungered after brightness and cheerful talk. His sense of humor tended to progress from anecdotes of rusticity to sharp wit. He loved stories, especially of people, and told them well. He held—at one time, at least—that a certain strengthening of the mind comes through playing poker. He liked to play poker and played with skill.

One time while we were walking along the railroad about Third Street in Austin, we stopped beside an old-time locomotive, stationary, throbbing with power. Webb said, "That is the greatest manifestation of power in the world." I told him that out of respect for its symbolism of power, Doctor Sanders, professor of Latin and Greek at Southwestern University about the beginning of the century, would remove his hat in salute to a steam engine pulling a train past him.

Whether Webb actually ever hated anybody I cannot say. I never heard him express hatred of any kind. He could be caustic, as when he wished that birth control had been in practice before a certain individual was born. He was more inclined to set forth the facts about a man than to praise or condemn. He inclined to the policy of Governor Jim Ferguson, who said, "I never use up energy hating." He was tolerant of human vagaries. He had developed as professor and historian under the late Dr. Eugene C. Barker, for years head of the history department of The University of Texas. Barker's directness and his integrity were admirable. I myself owe considerable to him. The older he grew, the more conservative, even reactionary, he grew. He seemed in his later years to think that the masses of mankind need a kind of dictatorial direction in religion, politics, and other regions of life. While Dr. Barker became hostile, in his acrid way, to the New Deal and a strong bolster to the by-no-means-intellectual regents who deposed Rainey, mainly for being a New Dealer, Webb was strong for Franklin D. Roosevelt, as he was later for Truman. But he was never against Barker. "I did not understand him," I heard him say, "but he was my friend and supporter. He was open, generous, fearless. I remember him with respect."

Webb maintained a dim view of certain English teachers under whom he had studied in The University of Texas. He acknowledged no debt to them in mastering the craft of writing. Some time in the 1920's he was avidly reading O. Henry and trying out his own hand on short stories. I remember one based on an electric sign above Joske's store in San Antonio that every night flashed on the picture of a cowboy roping a steer.

I wish he had written more on the craft of writing. I quote from his essay "On the Writing of Books," published in *The Alcalde*, June, 1952, (and repeated with changes and additions in his presidential address to the American Historical Association, reproduced in the *Texas Observer*, January 24, 1959):

It takes a good deal of ego to write a book. All authors have ego; most of them try to conceal it under a cloak of assumed modesty which they put on

106

with unbecoming immodesty. This ego makes itself manifest in the following ways: (1) The author believes he has something to say. (2) He believes it is worth saying. (3) He believes he can say it better than anyone else. If he ever stops to doubt any one of these three beliefs, he immediately loses that confidence and self-deception—that ego, if you please—so essential to authorship. In effect, the author, to write a book, spins out of his own mind a cocoon, goes mentally into it, seals it up, and never comes out until the job is done. That explains why authors hide out, hole up in hotel rooms, neglect their friends, their family, and their creditors . . . they may even neglect their students. They neglect everything that may tend to destroy their grand illusion.

The longer Webb jousted with words and thoughts, the finer-tempered his blade became. His use of the specific to bring home an idea suggests in style Jesus' application of the parable. His "The American West, Perpetual Mirage" (*Harper's Magazine*, May 1957) is as brilliant as any historical essay I have read. With what economy does he set forth the core!: "The overriding influence that shapes the West is the desert. That is its one unifying force. It permeates the plains, climbs to all but the highest mountain peaks, dwells continuously in the valleys, and plunges down the Pacific slope to argue with the sea."

Webb's generalizations are conclusions drawn from and supported by the concrete:

Western history is bizarre because of the nature of what it has got. The historians and other writers do what men have always done in the desert. They make the best of what little they do have. Westerners have developed a talent for taking something small and blowing it up to giant size, as a photographer blows up a photograph.

They write of cowboys as if they were noble knights, and the cowmen kings. They do biographies of bad men, Billy the Kid, the Plummer gang, and Sam Bass, of bad women like Calamity Jane, of gunmen like Wyatt Earp and Wild Bill Hickok. . . . They blow the abandoned saloon up into an art museum, and Boot Hill into a shrine for pilgrims. In Montana Charlie Russell is better than Titian, and in the Black Hills Frederick Remington is greater than Michelangelo. Custer, who blundered to his death, taking better men with him, found a place in every saloon not already pre-empted to that travesty on decency and justice, Judge Roy Bean.

Some commentators have characterized Webb as "a great Texan." "We Texans," he wrote me in 1957, "have been as insular as Kansans

—God save the mark." I remember well, with a certain personal shrinking, a period when his boundaries and my boundaries were to an extent circumscribed by the boundaries of Texas. Each of us in his way passed to a perspective beyond geographical lines, though each remained deeply marked by the land he lived in and by the inhabitants of that land. The greatness of Webb was as a man. "Man thinking"—Emerson's definition of a scholar—does not have around his head a band welded there by the confines of a province, by clerical ukases, or by any other mundane restrictions. Webb was not "finely suited" to life at Oxford University. He belonged to and marked The University of Texas. Only a few months before the end he published an opinion that it now had "within its grasp" the long sought-for status of "a university of the first class." All the while he maintained the critical judgment of "man thinking":

Men at Oxford are free to follow their compass of truth wherever the needle points without looking over their shoulders to see what hounds are pursuing them. Professors are not even under suspicion. An Oxford man can attend a mass meeting in London and participate without jeopardizing his job. England is not afraid to have views expressed. England, with all its apparent stupidities, seems to know what a university really is.

In "For Whom the Historian Tolls," in *An Honest Preface and Other Essays,* with an introduction by Joe B. Frantz (1959), Webb provided this economical illumination:

[Articles by historians in historical journals] are correct, the sentences usually—after the editors get though with them—are grammatical, and the footnotes are properly right at the bottom of the page. But one finds in them little charm, few vivid figures of speech, and practically none of that soft luminosity—an undefinable quality—which suffuses good writing. The reader may be informed, but he is rarely lured, enthralled, or captivated by the art of the performance.

Webb's chief research was for facts to lead to understanding. His superiority as an historian lies in his perception, his power of thought, his mastery of language, his interpretations of the land and the ever-evolving currents of human affairs. Not long after his first major book, *The Great Plains,* came out in 1931, Clem Yore of Colorado reported on a gathering of Western fiction writers who had been unaware of the meaning of barbed wire, windmills over wells drilled into the ground, and treeless plains themselves until Webb enlightened them.

In his last big book, *The Great Frontier,* he interprets the western hemisphere as a frontier for the expansion of Europe. He says plainly and emphatically that America has been consuming irreplaceable natural resources and that prosperity based on such procedure cannot continue. He even questions the continuance of democracy. This book came out during the outrage of McCarthyism and the House Un-American Activities Committee's blackguard betrayals of human rights. Some fanatics, without reading the book, slammed it as an "un-American" rebuke to "free enterprise." Webb never considered boosters as exemplars of patriotism.

The first Mrs. Webb, Jane Oliphant, after having been married to Walter for more than forty-three years, died in the summer of 1960, survived by a daughter, Mildred, of whom father as well as mother was very fond. In December of 1961 he married Terrell Maverick, widow of the late Maury Maverick of San Antonio, vivacious in mind and body, delightful and sensible too.

Considering his love for her and considering her marrying him, he said, "This is an unexpected dividend from life." He was openly naive in expressing joy in her being. He had, as it were, been born again. His happy ardency made his friends rejoice. During the summer of 1962 while he was lecturing at the University of Alaska, she unable to accompany him as both had planned, he airmailed a letter to her every day. He had never seemed so eagerly active over the publication of one of his own books as he was over publishing *Washington Wife,* by Ellen Maury Slayden, the manuscript of which Terrell Webb had inherited and which both of them foreworded. They autographed the book in a San Antonio bookstore the last afternoon of Webb's life.

Any man who has seen and been a part of life wants to leave it before decomposing into a juiceless vegetable. Webb died standing up, as Caesar considered it meet for a man to die. In a flash he passed from wisdom and happiness to the finality of death. No person who has added as much to the heritage of human life as Walter Webb added ceases to be. His thinking, his writing, and his standing up will surely continue as elements of his projected shadow.

JOHN FISCHER*

An unfashionable kind of historian

To the joy of his editors, Walter Prescott Webb was an unfashionable kind of historian. Some of his colleagues, indeed, regarded him as a scandal to the profession, because he shamelessly practiced three heresies:

1. He believed that history was a branch of literature. Consequently he tried to write as well as he could; and he was still laboring to perfect his craftsmanship in prose almost till the day of his death. He had no patience with the view, so widespread among his contemporaries, that any scholar who writes with grace, clarity, and style must be a "popularizer," and therefore unsound. Quite the contrary: Dr. Webb cherished the old-fashioned notion that anything worth writing ought to be worth reading too, and that a wide audience in no way cheapened a conscientious author. The result was that he earned himself a place among that handful of contemporary American historians—including such people as Garrett Mattingly, Bernard DeVoto, and Barbara Tuchman—whose work is read by laymen with genuine pleasure. (In England of course this sort of historian is less rare; but the tradition there has seldom confused scholarship with pedantry.)

2. He believed that a historian's objectivity need not bar him from holding, and expressing, strong convictions. His studies—and his deep involvement in the life around him—led him to certain conclusions about American politics, economics, and leadership. He

* Editor of *Harper's Magazine.*

110

urged these views right out in public, even when they were considered unseemly—or downright dangerous—for a man in academic life. Dr. Webb expected retaliation, and he got it. For example, he always believed that his appointment to a distinguished professorship was delayed for years by members of the board of regents who felt that teachers should keep their mouths shut on public issues—especially when they disagreed with the Texas Establishment. But I never heard him complain about such treatment. "Anybody who walks into a fight," he once remarked, "has got to expect to get some lumps." I got the impression he enjoyed the fight, and felt he had dealt out more lumps than he got.

3. He wasn't afraid to tackle big subjects. Now and then he would talk—with a mixture of sorrow, amusement, and contempt—about fledgeling historians who would devote years of labor to some safe, respectable little theme. Such as "Some Aspects of Southwestern Agrarian Policy Between 1868 and 1875," for example, or "Sources of Economic Data on Early Settlements Below the Brazos"—two mythical Ph.D. dissertations he used to cite when bemoaning the caliber of latter day graduate students. For himself, Dr. Webb preferred subjects that offered plenty of elbow room. How the South and Southwest had been treated like exploited colonies of the predatory Easterners . . . what the closing of the last frontier would do to society, not just in America but throughout the world . . . what price we would have to pay for our folly in building cities where God meant to have a desert: these were ideas of a size he thought worth tackling.

Some critics objected that his subjects were so sweeping as to be unmanageable, and that his intuition and eloquence occasionally outran his documentation. (They also were horrified when he expounded them, not in professional journals, but in *Harper's Magazine* and other lay publications.) This didn't bother him. Dr. Webb thought of himself—if I understood him correctly—as a kind of scout on the frontiers of history. His job was to explore the terrain, to spot the big ideas, to discover new watersheds of the mind. More pedestrian characters could follow later, to document his findings and stake out the section lines with surveyors' accuracy. After all, Kit Carson never had time to carry a theodolite and plane table, either.

Immodesty? Maybe so. Most big men (and good writers) are not

111

noted for their modesty. In demeanor and personal behavior, I never knew a man more modest than Walter; but about his work he did have an out-sized self-confidence. Indeed, I am convinced that this is an essential characteristic of any writer who amounts to much. The vocation is so lonely, demanding, and beset with discouragements that men with shrunken egos are likely to give it up pretty quickly for some less demanding work, such as plumbing or the oil business.

So I was not surprised when Walter told me one night, over a glass of bourbon, that his main ambition was to found a school of historians. He wanted to gather a band of disciples, who could grasp his main ideas and develop them in a series of books to be written over a period of maybe twenty years. He would like to serve as general editor for the series, and if he could get a foundation grant perhaps he could gather the main contributors together under one roof somewhere in Texas . . .

Well, it didn't work out quite that way; and perhaps he never really expected it to—after all, he was nearly seventy at the time of the conversation. But I could never be sure how serious Walter was about his future plans, because it never seemed to occur to him that he was growing older. He was always as eager to take on new projects—a major television series, a marriage, the editing of the Slayden diaries—as if he were a youngster just starting out.

It was significant, I think, that the magazine article which gave him most pleasure was "The Search for William E. Hinds," published in *Harper's* in July, 1961. This was really the story of his own beginnings, and of the unknown benefactor who helped Walter to climb up from the cotton patch. In his later years he had become obsessed with the notion that he ought to find out all he could about this obscure and long-dead New York businessman, and to create a literary memorial to Hinds' goodness. The result, in first draft, was over-written and sentimental. A suggestion that a little editorial pruning might help made Walter indignant; but after snorting and stomping for a few days, he came around. The final version was still charged with emotion—with a deep feeling that the Webb debt to Hinds still had not been fully repaid—and it evoked a remarkable response from hundreds of readers. When the article was reprinted in the *Reader's Digest*, the flood of letters redoubled; many of them contained checks for the Hinds Fund, which Walter had established to help students as needy as he once was.

In our last conversation, Walter told me he was as proud of that article as anything he had ever written "because it moved so many people to do something worthwhile." This, I suspect, was the yardstick he applied subconsciously to all his writing. Unconventional as it may be for a historian, I don't know where any writer can find a better measure.

RONNIE DUGGER

The Great Plains

"For what do we *know*—and what *do* we know—what do we *really* and *truly* know about what a friend of mine will insist on calling our 'insides'? Meaning not our lights, livers, and other organs, but that part of us where the mysteries are." Thus wrote W. H. Hudson, the field naturalist, who loved to seek truth, which so often eluded him and so often eludes us all, in the recesses of the unknown.

—Webb in *The Great Plains*

Walter Webb's article in *Harper's* late in his life on the great American desert is one of the best essays written by a man from this part of the country. Its themes were not new in his work. In 1931, there appeared under his name a clear, witty, and original book of history, *The Great Plains*. One cannot read it now without knowing from the occasional loveliness of language and the occasional flights of fancy that Webb never gave up wanting to write novels; from his contempt for hidebound laws, his yawps of exhiliration, and his sardonic jests that he was himself a westerner; from his splendid powers of generalization that he was one of the most intelligent men we have had to think about our ways; and from certain other passages that, though his experiences went back to ancient scenes of travail on the farm and his attitudes on race were narrow then, he had no fear of radicalism, whenever it is called for.

Not many historians, accustomed to withering scrutiny of the form of their footnotes by septuagenarian Ph.D.'s, would have dared leave in their manuscripts this passage on the cattle kingdom, in *The Great Plains:*

A thousand farms in the East will each have six or seven cows, with as many more calves and yearlings—ten thousand head. But they attract no attention. They are incidents of agriculture. In the West a ranch will cover the same area as the thousand farms, and will have perhaps ten thousand head, round-ups, rodeos, men on horseback, and all that goes with ranching. Hot days in the branding pen with bawling calves and the smell of burned hair and flesh on the wind! Men in boots and big hats, with the accompaniment of jangling spurs and frisky horses. Camp cook and horse wrangler! Profanity and huge appetites! . . . The East did a large business on a small scale; the West did a small business magnificently.

To get at the truth of the past, Webb wrote, ". . . we must make use of the imagination," and in a single sentence he could send a reader into a wonderland of future possibilities: "If the Mississippi, draining the humid eastern country, could be induced to flow into the arid West, it would be almost impossible to imagine the possibilities of irrigation." While portions of his work in 1931 thudded along the way most scholars' do, he tended, even then, toward rhythms—"If the rain falls on the windward side of the mountains, the leeward side must suffer all the more"; a buffalo's sense of smell was useless to it "when it was approached from down the wind"—and toward romantic musing: "Cowboys at work, eighteen hours a day, for the herd left the bed ground by daybreak and kept it until dark; cowboys at work, riding, singing, nursing the cattle; yet it is difficult for those who now read of their hardships to realize that they worked at all." As far as Webb was concerned, ballads, songs, and novels were part of the historical evidence, for the literature of the Great Plains had to deal "with the aspects of nature—the somber, far-spread, ocean-like plain; the arid mountains; the quicksanded rivers; the drought, the hail, and the wind." In the last chapter of the book, "Mysteries of the Great Plains," he wrote that the evidence indicated that "the plain gives man new and novel sensations of elation, of vastness, of romance, of awe, and often of nauseating loneliness." He knew that a book of history is only a man writing about the past.

He was not a nit-picker; he wanted to have some fun as he went along with his work. Plains Indians were willing to eat their horses if they had to—"The Indian rode his commissary into battle." When the settlers from the East first crossed the ninety-eighth meridian onto the plains, there was little thought of general irrigation. "The people

115

were settling there under the illusion that rainfall would follow agriculture." It did not. "In the shadow of the drought men turn to prayer (at least some of them do), led by the more religious-minded, and the skeptical acquiesce, with the stoic philosophy that it may do no good; but they guess it won't do any harm. Sometimes the rains come, proving the efficacy of faith."

As his whimsey did not get in the way of his intelligence, neither, he said, did facts that fall contrary to a general truth. Again and again, discussing geology, rainfall, "the horse culture of the woodland" and "that of the plains," the great configurations of environment and civilization, he attained generalizations no man could have without first storing up the facts and then extending the powers of a lithe intelligence. Consider these scattered passages:

The position of the grassland in the United States and in North America may be most accurately pictured when taken in connection with the timber regions or the rainfall map. The eastern forest and the western forest come together in Canada, where they form a continuous subarctic forest extending from ocean to ocean. In the south the two forest belts unite in Mexico. Between these belts is a great oval whose characteristic natural vegetation is grass and desert shrub. This grassland "acts as a barrier between the species of the two regions even more effectively than a body of water of the same extent."

.   .   .   .

The history of the Plains is the history of the grasslands. Civilization develops on level ground. The fundamental problems that man faced when he crossed the line are not problems of the mountains but of the Plains.

.   .   .   .

The Great Plains presented a barrier which arrested for a time the whole westward movement, but the barrier was greater for the South than for the North. The Northern system, founded in individual ownership of land and free labor, was *modified* when it entered the Great Plains region, but its essential character was not changed. The Southern system, founded on slavery and cotton, was *barred* by an infrangible law—bounded on the west by aridity just as effectually as it was on the north by cold. Thus did the Great Plains break the balance between the North and the South and turn the advantage to the Northern section, making its ideals, rather than those of the South, national.

Webb's approach to history sometimes seemed racial. The blood of pueblo or sedentary Indian stock, compared with that of the Plains

116

Indians, "was as ditch water"; on Southern plantations, worked by Negroes before mechanization, "one man was doing only the work of a man, if that"; "For ingenuity of design no one can beat a Mexican"; the Spanish failed at conquering the Plains Indians, and "The problem of subduing them had to be solved by another race." Yet it would not be fair to hold these ways of thinking to the standards of current times. His life began a long time ago, and when he wrote *The Great Plains* he could say, as none of us who have been city-raised could say now:

> We are still a farm people. . . . There is for us nothing new on the farm. We know it all intimately—the long hours, the sweaty, stinking underwear, the debt and the mortgage, the way it feels to drag in at twilight after a day in the field and to sit on the doorstep and pull from our aching feet our brogan shoes before we eat the coarse evening meal. That is the common heritage of the majority of American people.

Webb's freedom of spirit was a freedom of his own times and place—a frontier honesty. He had, for instance, nothing but contempt for Spain's church-shielded forays in America.

> Spain's fourfold purpose [he wrote] was to conquer, convert, exploit, and incorporate the natives. . . . For conquest, there was the *conquistador* . . . for conversion, there was the friar, the emissary of the church, the religious campaigner; for exploitation after the conquest was over, there was the *encomendero*, whose function it was to make a profit from the native and share it with the king. . . . Finally, in 1772 the whole policy of peace was abandoned in desperation, and the Spaniard undertook the destruction of the Plains Indian even before his soul had been saved.

He did not blink the fact that after the Texas Revolution, Texans stole the cattle defeated Mexicans left behind, or the probability that during the Civil War some Texans got rich staying behind while their neighbors were off fighting. He persistently sided with the plainsmen who practiced "a little judicious fraud" to evade unreasonable laws, passed by uninformed Eastern lawmakers, limiting arid-land ranching.

Political radicalism on the plains began, he wrote, with the farmers—the Grange, the Farmers' Alliance, the Farmers' Union. "They were far from markets, burned by drought, beaten by hail, withered by hot winds, frozen by blizzards, eaten out by the grasshoppers, exploited by capitalists, and cozened by politicians. Why should they

117

not turn to radicalism? When men suffer, they become politically radical; when they cease to suffer, they favor the existing order." Women got the vote first on the plains. Why was that? "There is hidden somewhere in the cause the spirit of the Great Plains which made men democratic in deed and in truth," Webb said. He hoped that out of the high adventure and intense suffering of the plains "may come in time a mystical and spiritual quality contributing much to a civilization that thus far is notorious for its devotion to material things."

I did not know Webb. We exchanged remarks on a few occasions; once or so I was able to see through his storied gruffness to a warm, heartily-laughing man. Just one memorable thing happened between us. We were having lunch over a manuscript of a speech he had made that I was going to print in the *Observer*. We found ourselves in a congenial rapport over political matters (though we must have differed some on what a man should do as to politics). As we parted, he quoted something out of John Dewey, a passage that was, as I vaguely recall, intelligent and idealistic in Dewey's matter of fact way. It has been in my memory that it was from *Human Nature and Conduct*, at the end of a chapter, but I have looked and cannot find it there. Anyway, I remembered the passage at the time, and also, as I said to Dr. Webb, that Dewey had gone on in it to conclude that human affairs are necessarily tending toward more and more socialism.[1] I didn't ask Webb why he had not recited this conclusion, but that question was an import of my mentioning it. He replied, I remember very clearly (for I thought about it a good deal afterward, and my mind has come back to it occasionally since then), that the role of some men is to work within existing institutions, cultivating the ground for the changes that are to come.

[1] Subsequently an *Observer* reader suggested in a letter that perhaps the passage was one from the chapter entitled "Socialism" in Dewey's *Individualism—Old and New*, a passage that concludes, "We are in for some kind of socialism, call it by whatever name we please, and no matter what it will be called when it's realized." The reader said Webb once quoted this passage in his course on the Great Frontier.—Ed.

H. MEWHINNEY

The Great Frontier

Walter Webb's great quality was a sort of massive and inexorable common sense.

In this respect he was something like Charles Darwin. And it was this quality that finally led him, when he was almost an old man, to write what I think is likely to prove the most important book written anywhere in the world during this century. This was *The Great Frontier.*

I knew Mr. Walter for almost forty years. But he had other friends who knew him better and longer. If nobody minds, I should prefer to use this space to write about that one book and the effect it had on my own thinking rather than about Mr. Walter himself.

It is worth remarking that the three friends so often called the triumvirate—Webb, Bedichek, and Dobie—were all clearer thinkers and sounder artists as they grew older. That is unusual in our country and in our century. Most American artists, and the novelists in particular, commit themselves to certain views and attitudes before they reach thirty. Then they never outgrow those views. They are much like the Mexican axolotl, who matures enough to reproduce his kind but never enough to grow out of the tadpole stage.

In *The Great Frontier* Webb addressed himself to the grand and terrible theme of our times, to the theme that under varied aspects so fascinated Oswald Spengler and Arnold Toynbee and even, for that matter, H. G. Wells. What really made the Western world what it is?

How was it that the petty and insignificant kingdoms of Western

119

Europe—almost beneath the contempt of the Ottoman Turk—
peopled by men so poor, dirty, and ignorant that they took Marco
Polo for a liar when he came home to tell about the magnificent court
of Kublai Khan—how did these fellows ever manage to set forth and
plunder the world?

And all the more especially, how did it happen, after technology
had been nearly at a standstill for something like three thousand
years, that the Western Europeans began that astonishing career in
the physical sciences that brought us steamships, electric lights, air-
planes, spacecraft, and nuclear bombs, so that now we wallow in our
own riches and tremble at the deadliness of our own weapons?

So that now we are astonished and outraged when those peoples
of a different complexion, whom our plundering forefathers somehow
forgot to annihilate, suddenly come forth demanding a share both in
the riches and in the knowledge of the techniques.

The Tasmanians and the Karankawas are gone. But the Chinamen
are very much with us.

We are taught in high school, although none too clearly or ex-
plicitly, that Western Europe did not amount to much until Henry
the Navigator came along in the middle fourteen hundreds and
started sending out expeditions to reconnoiter the coast of Africa
and look for a way to the East.

Webb set out to clarify the matter. He had been influenced by
Frederick Jackson Turner's famous paper about the influence of the
frontier on American history. He had been prepared by years of
studying the frontier, especially of studying the effects of inventions
so simple as that of barbed wire. That is to say, like Darwin, he was
not offering a theory that nobody had ever thought of before; he was
systematically arranging the arguments for the theory or perhaps
even the proofs.

He contended that it was the white man's looting and plundering
of the frontiers—of the Americas, Africa, Australia, and the ancient
kingdoms of the East—that really created the modern world; that
brought on the sudden acceleration in technology, in the study of the
physical sciences, and even in literature; that but for Columbus and
Vasco da Gama there might never have been a Shakespeare or even
an Einstein. That is, it was simply the loot—gold, silver, fish, furs,
ship timber, sugar, chocolate, tobacco—that furnished the capital for
the fantastic development of Western Europe in learning, science,

120

and inventions; that for a few centuries made those petty peoples the lords of the earth; that led Kipling to write such nonsensical and pharisaical admonitions as *Take up the white man's burden.*

One may reflect sardonically that if there had been no plundering of the frontiers there would have been no Industrial Revolution, no Marx, and no Stalin.

All this from Webb, basically simple as it is, is far more convincing than Spengler's hypothesis that the major cultures grow, flourish, and decay as inevitably as the individual organism, like so many rose-bushes or cockleburrs; more convincing than Toynbee's ideas of challenge and response.

For the sudden technological flowering of Western Europe was quite unlike anything that ever happened in Egypt, or Mesopotamia, or Greece.

When Henry the Navigator came along, the techniques and the sciences had been at a standstill, or worse, for many centuries. Remember that Phoenician seamen in the service of Pharaoh Necho had actually circumnavigated Africa two thousand years earlier, about 600 B.C. Eratosthenes had measured the circumference of the earth quite accurately about 200 B.C. There had been palaces in Egypt, in Babylon, in Crete, and in Nero's Rome larger and more magnificent than anything standing in Europe in the times of Prince Henry. The very Aztecs had botanical and zoological gardens long before any such thing was thought of in Madrid.

Prince Henry's men had only one item of technology that really worked. That was the sailing ship. And it worked none too well. Remember that Pharaoh Necho's men circumnavigated Africa on their first and only attempt. It took Prince Henry's captains years of trying.

Prince Henry's men knew the use of gunpowder but the arquebus was a less efficient weapon than the crossbow. Not even the flintlock had been invented yet.

There was not a telescope anywhere in Europe. There was not a watch that would keep time. The peasants tilled their fields with much the same sort of wooden plow that had been used in Neolithic Egypt. There was not an electric light, a kerosene lantern, or even a whale oil lamp. The rich had torches. The poor had the light of the hearth. The roads were far worse than in Roman times. The rich went on horseback. The poor walked through the mud.

121

There actually must be some kind of determinism or inevitability in mankind's affairs, whether it is the kind suggested by Webb, or by Spengler, or by Toynbee, or even by those Nineteenth Century socialists whose doctrines are now most familiar in the version offered by Karl Marx.

For it is at last becoming plain—and more so from what the pre-historians rather than the historians have learned in the past century —that certain advances or at least certain changes occur in techniques, sciences, arts, modes of thought, and modes of behavior whenever particular conditions occur.

The British anthropologist Gordon Childe argued brilliantly that the two most important things that ever happened in mankind's career on earth both happened before written history, as such, even existed.

The first was what Childe called the Neolithic Revolution, when bands of men settled down in particular places and began to make their living by growing crops rather than by hunting, or fishing, or gathering nuts and berries.

The other was what Childe called the Urban Revolution, when men began to live in true cities, when trades became specialized, when the social structure, too, became more elaborate, when there were kings, priests, and nobles rather than chieftains, shamans, and warriors, and when writing was invented.

The prehistorians are still far from sure about the details. But it is fairly certain now that both revolutions, in all their complexities, occurred quite independently in Eurasia and in the Americas. Likely enough, there were independent developments in several centers.

There seems to have been little interchange of views between Webb and Childe or between Childe and Spengler. I am not even sure that Webb ever read a line that Childe had written.

The changes in the Western world that Webb, Spengler, and Toynbee discussed in their several ways have no name in common use as yet. But in essence this is a third revolution and likely to prove even more fateful than the other two.

Nowadays for the first time since the gorilla-brained Australopithecinae were hunting pigs and antelopes on the thornbrush-studded plains of South Africa—and that was a million and three-quarters of years ago, if Leakey's dates turn out to be right—men have learned in a few happy countries of the West to grow more food than they

122

can eat and to manufacture more devices than they can use or can even sell to one another. Not Sesostris, nor Sardanapalus, nor Nero could have imagined such luxuries as an automobile mechanic or a television repairman now enjoys every day.

Both we and the Russians are preparing to send explorers to the moon—certainly the most expensive luxury ever imagined.

But a great part of the world enjoys none of the luxuries, is restless, and is envious of them. And the Russians, to the deadly danger of us all, have made a sort of lunatic religion out of the doctrines of a fellow who was merely one more misinformed Nineteenth Century economic theorist, with little knowledge of prehistory, of ancient history, of anthropology, or of human or of animal behavior. Why, Marx wrote that book before Schliemann excavated Troy, before Evans excavated Knossos, before Sautuola found the paintings in the Altamira cavern, before the Wrights flew the first airplane, before Ford simplified factory production.

If only the Russians could read Webb instead of Marx.

WILSON M. HUDSON

Webb my teacher

On March 2, 1963, Walter Prescott Webb wrote this on one of the
end leaves of *Washington Wife*: "To my friend from away back."
Our friendship began in 1925 and lasted until the fatal automobile
accident on March 8. Through all the phases of his career he was the
same—straightforward, cheerful, and companionable. He was always
ready for a chat or a cup of coffee, no matter how busy he was.

It was my good fortune to take History 9 as a freshman under
Webb and Duncalf, who has also left us. They took turns in lecturing
to about one hundred and fifty students in the big auditorium of the
old Law Building. On Fridays we were divided into quiz sections,
and Webb happened to be my quizmaster.

He lectured from notes, with the corners of his mouth turned down
as if he were not particularly enjoying what he was doing. It has
been my impression that he did not care to speak before large groups
of people, nor did he like to get very far from written copy. He had
the information and he knew how to impart the maximum in fifty
minutes; he did not consider himself an entertainer and he made no
use of attention-catching tricks or gadgets. In the Friday quiz sessions
he would give us a short discussion question and then make us talk
about the week's work. He dealt in ideas and drew us out. In taking
notes on the Monday and Wednesday lectures and making summaries
of collateral reading, I wrote much more than in freshman English
and learned a great deal more about writing.

One of the books on the collateral list was Ellen Semple's *Influences
of Geographic Environment*, which Webb later told me he had placed
there himself. In the first week of school I dipped into this book and

experienced a strong intellectual thrill. The first sentence was loaded with implications: "Man is a product of the earth's surface." In a wide-ranging discussion Semple showed that men's way of life, laws, myths, mental attitudes, and even their bodies vary according to their geographical situation. To someone who had not gone very far beyond the dogma that man is a special creation of the deity formed in his image to do his will, this was illuminating and liberative. In Semple's book I was being introduced to a basic element in Webb's approach to history: environment comes first and strongly influences human institutions. This, I learned years afterwards, was the orientation of Lindley Miller Keasbey, Webb's teacher at the university. As the shadow of the library crept up the side of the old Main Building, I sat reading. I was late for supper that night.

I took no more courses in history but continued to see Webb from time to time. I became a page in the library, and he was a frequent visitor to the stacks. When he began to work on *The Great Plains* he went at such a pace that he could not come for the books he needed but would leave a list to be gathered together and brought to his office. He paid another page, who came at seven in the morning, to bring the books to him. He was so immersed in study and writing that he seemed to be in a daze; the unifying idea for *The Great Plains* had come to him so forcefully that he had set aside *The Texas Rangers* and was working at a white heat. He practically lived in his office.

A graduate student who had seen some of Webb's manuscript made this comment on his style: "He's no Macaulay, but he gets there in his homely way." Today we give thanks that he didn't take Macaulay for a model. No small part of the merit of *The Great Plains* is its directness, simplicity, and clarity of expression. In freshman English, which he took at the university, Webb had not fared well under the instruction of a man who wanted his students to write like Charles Lamb. As a writer Webb totally eclipsed this instructor, who in a long life of composing little articles never faced a task of any magnitude or produced a single book. When *The Great Plains* appeared in an inexpensive edition, at my suggestion it was made one of several optional texts in freshman English. I have taught it repeatedly as a model of historical writing, first at the University of Chicago. It has a clear-cut pair of basic terms, *land* and *people*, and it is beautifully organized.

It is well known that Webb befriended many students and lent money to them. Once he gave me some much-needed help. On the eve of graduation day in May of 1930, when I was to receive an M.A. in English, I was walking along Congress Avenue. As I approached Sixth Street I heard someone call to me from a car stopped in the middle of the street. I went out and found Dr. Webb (as we always addressed him even before he had the degree) seated beside the driver.

"You're getting your master's degree tomorrow, aren't you?" he asked.

"Yes, sir."

"You want a job this summer?"

"Yes, sir."

"This is Mr. Ferguson, dean of Stephen F. Austin State Teachers College in Nacogdoches. He's taking his doctor's tomorrow. Meet him after the ceremony and he'll tell you how to get to Nacogdoches and when to be there."

This was all. The next afternoon I was on board a train for Jacksonville, where I had to change to a bus in order to reach Nacogdoches. Of course I was very grateful to Webb at the time. When I reminded him of this incident years later and expressed my gratitude again, he said, "Wilson, you shouldn't be grateful to me." I was puzzled, but after the appearance of the story of how William E. Hinds had helped him obtain an education I understood.

In the fall of 1930 I began teaching at Rice and continued there until 1937. During these years I saw Webb on occasional visits to Austin, and I bought and read *The Great Plains* and *Divided We Stand* when they appeared, in 1931 and 1937. Through his books he has continued to be my teacher down to the present day.

The publication of *Divided We Stand* came just at the time when I had become a traveler for a publisher whose home office was in Massachusetts. In this book Webb stated that if everyone in the South and West who was working for a Northern firm were in uniform the South and West would look like any army camp. The book made me acutely conscious that the more successful I was in obtaining orders in my territory the more I was contributing to the economic dominance of the North. Not long after the appearance of *Divided We Stand* Webb made a talk at the Cokesbury Book Store in Dallas which I was able to hear by accident of being in Dallas at the

126

same time. He told a story to illustrate how he felt when he sold Hollywood the movie rights to *The Texas Rangers*. A Texas cowman was riding a Pullman to Kansas City for the first time—he had always ridden up with his cattle on a freight and back on the chair car. He knew he was to tip the porter but he didn't know how much.

"George, how much am I supposed to tip you when I get off at Kansas City?" he asked.

"Just whatever you think right, suh."

"How much do they usually tip you?"

"It ranges. Some tips one way and others another."

"Well, George, what would you say your average tip is?"

"A dolluh, suh."

When the porter brushed him off as they were pulling in, the cowman gave him a silver dollar.

With a big smile George said, "Thank you, suh! That's the first time I ever made my average."

The fee for the movie rights gave Webb a start toward a fortune. With it he bought an old church bordering the Capitol grounds, rented the building to the state for years, and eventually sold it to the state for a good profit. He made other investments in Austin. Webb was a fine businessman as well as a fine scholar.

He loved a good story, though he was not given to joking in the classrooms. Once I heard him tell a story which he later used, in a revised form, for the conclusion of "How the Republican Party Lost Its Future," which appeared in 1949. A certain man kept telling himself about the great things that he would do in the future, but he never got down to work. One morning while shaving he was struck by the lines in his face and the thinness and greyness of his hair. After a long look he exclaimed, "My God, my future is now my past!" This story is capable of producing a bad case of the midnight shakes— even of extracting work from ex-fairhaired boys.

Webb liked folk sayings, though he did not use many himself. One day while he, Mody Boatright, and I were having coffee together, he suddenly asked, "Mody, what was that about the cat?" Mody's reply, " 'I'll do it if it hairlips all the cats in Grimes County'," brought a burst of hearty laughter. The laughter of Webb and his good friends Dobie and Bedichek was marvelous to hear. It rang out on the picnics we used to have. It might not keep a man from committing suicide, but it

127

would make him laugh before pulling the trigger. Webb, Dobie, and Bedi were accustomed to thinking about and discussing the world's most serious problems, but they had a playfulness of mind on appropriate occasions that indicated freedom and flexibility. In this respect they were like Erasmus and Sir Thomas More. To be deeply concerned for the welfare of mankind in perilous times and yet to be able to laugh at the right moment, not to lose the joyousness of life—this is a great gift that perhaps can be cultivated.

After World War II and four years in the Air Force I had returned to Texas to teach in the university. I just missed the time of troubles set off by the Rainey affair, in which Webb played a courageous part representing the faculty. One day at coffee Webb told me about his experience at the University of Chicago, where I had taken my last degree. At his oral examination he "froze" when the first question was asked, nor could he say anything in response to the second question. He turned on his heel and walked out. "My mind was racing. I went straight to the apartment and told my wife to pack. We got out of Chicago before sundown." Webb was always kind to nervous doctoral candidates at their orals; he found the right questions to get them started and give them a chance to show their knowledge. Eugene Barker, recognizing that Webb was an original and independent thinker who had to make his own way, had asked for two copies of *The Great Plains,* which he accepted as Webb's dissertation, and granted him a degree.

Webb was a learned man with a capacity for hard thinking and sustained effort, but he was not academic. He did not immure himself in the university or cut himself off from the outside world. He wanted to communicate with the general reader and he succeeded admirably in doing so. Once at a meeting of the university faculty he alluded to "professors who write little articles for their colleagues to read." His unemphatic tone gave no clue to the scorn he felt.

In an essay solicited but rejected by the editor of *American Heritage* because it was too strong, he charged that academic training produces timid and self-repressed historians who write in a colorless way on the assumption that they are being objective.

In graduate schools the student is taught to select a subject of such small dimensions that it offers no challenge to the intellect, does not develop the mind, and has little or no significance when developed. He is encouraged to write without benefit of imagination, to avoid any statement based on

128

perception and insight unless he can prove by the documents that his idea is not original.

"An Honest Preface" is a brilliant satire on the academic game of writing a little book to get a little promotion; the central idea of the professor's book is "an entirely new theory as to the relationship existing between the physical law governing the refraction of light and the incidence of the high cost of living on tenant farms among the Esquimaux."

Webb had intellectual daring. Without this quality he would not have attempted the grand synthesis of modern history represented in *The Great Frontier*. Once while he was on leave to work on this book I met him on the campus as he was walking along with his slow, swinging stride, looking at the ground and putting a cigarette to his mouth. I had to call his name twice before he noticed me. Over coffee I asked him what he was working on. After telling me he said, "This is the biggest thing I've tackled yet, but I think I can handle it." And handle it he did. About a year later I happened into his office at the moment when he was putting the manuscript into a box to send to his publisher. "I wonder how they'll take this," he said when the package was wrapped and addressed. He did not mean the publishers but the historians and critics who would read the book. At such a time a writer almost always experiences a moment of self-doubt. "Well," he said, lighting a cigarette, "if all you write is what everybody agrees with, you haven't said much. Let's mail this and get a cup of coffee." Some months after the book was published I asked him what the reviewers were saying. "They say it isn't Toynbee." And he laughed with amusement.

In his choice of subjects Webb showed courage and a high regard for the public good. He was not afraid to deal with "controversial" subjects—a word now beloved by radical rightists and moral cowards. In the manuscript of *Divided We Stand*, in which he attacked the economic dominance of the North, there was a chapter on the ruination of a small independent bottle factory at Santa Anna, Texas, by the monopolistic Hartford Empire Glass Company. The publishers removed the chapter, but Webb restored it in augmented form when he republished the book at his own risk in 1947. "The Parabola of Individualism," a chapter in *The Great Frontier*, is the best existing explanation of what has happened to individualism in America.

129

Webb wished to see an increase in the well-being and prosperity of the West, the state of Texas, and his city. Aware of the basic importance of water, he studied and wrote about this problem in the West and in Texas as a part of the West. He rewrote a government report in an effort to reach the general public and show what could be done to utilize the water of Texas streams for manufacturing and urbanization as well as agriculture. In *More Water for Texas* he explained, with his usual lucidity, a breath-taking plan which one day may be put into effect. To the Austin paper he contributed articles on the future development of the city and of the South. Webb was no cloistered man shrinking from the world and its problems.

As honest as he was courageous, Webb was committed to the truth. He was not like some Westerners of the booster type who are unwilling to admit that there is a shortage of water in the West. When in 1957 he published "The American West: Perpetual Mirage" in *Harper's*, he offended many Westerners with his thesis that the key to the understanding of the West is the existence of a vast desert in its heart. Several senators, led by Goldwater of Arizona, vilified him and even accused him of historical ignorance. Protesting editorials, some later inserted in the Congressional Record, appeared, and letters came through the mail, one Denverite saying he would like to use Webb for target practice.

Webb had pointed out that the West has certain negatives or deficiencies (water, timber, cities, industry, labor, Negroes) and certain positives (land, grass, minerals, natural wonders, Indians, and Orientals) and that historians have not written about the negatives but have made the most of the positives. The Westerner, he said, is like a musician performing on a stringed instrument with many of its strings missing; he has to make up in agility and virtuosity what the instrument lacks. Webb grew up in West Texas on the edge of the desert and he loved the West, but he possessed clarity of insight and powers of self-criticism beyond the capacity of most Westerners.

He had a capacious and penetrating mind. Recently I have been turning over many books written about the West, and again and again I have found them illuminated by what he said in the essay in *Harper's* or in *The Great Plains*. He also has a very fine article "On the Cultural Resources of Texas" buried in a book that became a casualty of the Rainey troubles, an article that I might never have known about if it hadn't been mentioned to me by Mody Boatright when I began to teach Life and Literature of the Southwest, a course which J. Frank Dobie originated and made the most popular elective in the university as long as he taught there. "My theory holds that the true distinctive culture of a region, in this case of Texas, springs from the soil just as do the plants." First there was the land and then came the people, whose lives were shaped by the land. An indigenous culture should and does make use of locally available materials; this is true of literature and art as well as of architecture. As an example of a man who made use of locally available materials for cultural purposes, Webb referred to his friend Bedichek (without giving his name), who in the course of traveling over the state incidentally observed birds and built up a remarkable knowledge of them. Webb was not boasting about the cultural attainments of Texas; rather he was pointing out that the materials were plentiful but as yet had been little used.

Webb used the materials that were available to him, including his own mind and energy. He was not erratic, but moved steadily in one direction. His was a fine contribution to the university and the state of Texas and to the nation. He was an intellectual and moral force in our lives.

In the last year I frequently saw him as he walked past the window of my office on his way across the campus. Sometimes we would meet and he would tell me about the video series of lectures on American life that he was supervising. He was happy to be at work. No more can the tall man be seen striding along, wrapped in thought and carrying his head low.

JOE B. FRANTZ*

His politics

By nature and upbringing Webb was a devoted liberal in the best
sense of that often-bromidic word. He believed that the world could
be improved, that truth was sufficient excuse for objective investigation, that a weak link anywhere in the complex of civilization represented challenge and opportunity. He saw no contradiction in
being for Ralph Yarborough *and* for Lyndon Johnson, and indeed
counted both among his close friends. Whenever he thought either
was right, he gave that one his unqualified support; if he thought
either was wrong, he was equally unhesitant to upbraid, or perhaps
"chide" would be a more precise word.

As far as party affiliation was concerned, he lost his objectivity
somewhat. He welcomed "that other party" into prominence in Texas,
but he was almost yellow-dog in his devotion to the Democratic ban-
ner. With characteristic quick humor, he was wont to say, "I believe
in a strong Republican Party, but not strong enough ever to win—
only to keep the Democrats honest." Or in another vein, "What did
the Republican Party ever do for Texas?"

In another sense he reflected his boyhood background in barren
West Texas with a true agrarian brand of old-time populism. Deep
down, one suspects, he distrusted urbanism, bloc voting, and bankers.
Certainly he showed strong nativist tendencies and his views on racial
matters were not exactly progressive, were even a bit barbaric.

* Professor of history at The University of Texas at Austin, past president of
the Southwestern Social Science Association, and author.

132

On the other hand, he went into the state of Mississippi and told the local citizenry at Oxford that the state was plain stupid if it permitted its historic adherence to racial segregation to bar its material progress. The talk was straightforward enough that the professor who invited him, a head of a department, was promptly removed from that position for having imported such a radical.

Again, he told an audience of several thousand at Texas A. & M. that conditions that had spawned the capitalistic, democratic world of the United States up to 1920 had passed, and that his listeners could be wistful and sentimental if they chose, but they might as well accept the fact that a new social, economic, and political order was at hand and figure out their place in this new world. Before he could drive the 110 miles back to Austin, telephone calls and telegrams were being sent in numbers to the board of regents demanding his resignation.

"I must not have given them enough hope," he said half-ruefully, half-impishly.

In 1959 Houghton-Mifflin brought out a collection of his essays, "some . . . written in blood, some in lye, some in honey." The collection included two of his presidential addresses before major historical associations, essays in which he purposely set out to be significant and profound. But the essay which he often said was the best in the book was neither of these, but the one entitled "How the Republican Party Lost Its Future," which he dashed off for the *Southwest Review* in 1949.

When General Eisenhower spread his arms V-fashion and grinned his then irresistible smile in 1952, many people twitted Webb for his article, suggesting that few essays purporting to be historical and objective had ever been refuted so quickly. Webb didn't think these gibes were especially funny, nor did he lose his confidence that he was essentially right. As the congressional races of the later 1950's showed a rising Democratic tide and much of the leadership of the Republican administration seemed to be in the hands of Democrats, especially Sam Rayburn and Senator Johnson, Webb felt confirmed. Never did he retreat from his position that the Republican Party had "successively turned its back on one great segment of society after another, on the farmer, on small business, on labor." The party, in his words, "quit the people long before the people quit it."

His political value lay in the fact that people could examine issues in his presence, aware that he did not operate in spiritless objectivity but also aware that somewhere in the conversations and examinations would come a moment of revelation, of crystallization, of insight, of simplification. The man who sat with him over coffee might go away with views diametrically opposite to Webb's, but he would know why. To my way of thinking, this is teaching at its best.

DUNCAN ROBINSON

J was regarded as a bumpkin indeed

For a few days each spring from 1939 through 1944, I was closely associated with Dr. Webb. He selected me to assist him in getting the newspapers of Texas to devote some space to the annual meetings of the Texas State Historical Association, held then, usually, in the Driskill Hotel. At the time I was a teacher of English and, in an extra-curricular capacity, publicity director of North Texas Agricultural College.

He sometimes invited me to eat with him at a place called Toonerville, where he was fond of the hamburgers, and once he took me to play poker with him and some of his cronies—former Texas Rangers and professors. Not one cent of money was involved, but never did I encounter such intense competition. I was regarded as a bumpkin indeed when I declared jacks, queens, kings, aces, and jokers wild. After this crude pronouncement, Dr. Webb appeared glum.

In the evenings after the meetings there was usually good talk in our hotel rooms. In those far-off, trying times, Dr. Webb, tired from a long day of acting as host, would usually sit quietly as Frank Dobie and Evetts Haley talked of Charles Goodnight or tending cows in a blizzard. Sometimes Roy Bedichek, as well as Maury Maverick, Herbert Gambrell, Herbert Fletcher, and other well-known and gifted Texans called in.

I did not realize then that I should have aped Boswell and put on paper that marvelous talk—that urbane, trenchant, witty talk, the like of which is probably not to be heard again in these dull urban times when it is regarded as provincial to care about rivers and wind-mills and coyotes.

HART STILWELL*

Webb as a sinner

I spent quite a bit of time around Walter Webb between 1947 and 1955, much of it "shading" under those big trees in Pancho Dobie's back yard—drinking Dobie's fine red whiskey.

At least Pancho and I were drinking it. Webb usually drank nothing, a failing I set out later to remedy.

I didn't get one-tenth the pleasure I should have from Webb's conversation. The reason: I talk too damn much myself. It's a fault I haven't been able to cure any more than Webb could cure his withdrawal from the wonderful world of sin.

And here I give the word "sin" its Puritan meaning—anything calculated to give somebody else a kind of pleasure denied you. Included in, as Mr. Goldwyn might put it, are, of course, drinking, poker playing, cussing, dancing, and that old bugaboo, sex.

From all that I could put together, I judged that Webb denied himself the joys of all sins. I don't recall his ever saying "damn."

On one occasion Joe Small and Fred Gipson and I were sitting in a hotel room with Webb, and the talk turned to the Puritan ethic, which is, of course, the determining moral force in our attitudes, even though it may not control our actions.

All four of us sort of took turns at a frontal assault on the Puritan concept, berating it for the abnormal frustrations it has caused, and I derived my customary satisfaction from explaining with what exhiliration I busted the bind all to pieces, way back there.

Webb more or less went along with us in the opinion that the bind

* A writer, who lives in San Antonio, Texas.

136

was pretty doggone tight, considering the basic drives of the human animal. But he said, a bit wistfully, I thought, that he had accepted the bind.

Well, we may have failed miserably in our later efforts to teach Walter Webb how to drink booze, but we did take him by the hand and lead him into one form of sin—poker.

I can rightfully claim credit for a major part of the leading, since the poker games were played at my apartment in Austin at a time when I was living alone. I mean by that, I wasn't married.

Of course Joe Small was the catalyst, which you would expect, since he and Webb were real close friends for many years, and I saw Webb seldom except during the time we were trying to teach him how to sin.

He had never played poker for money before that first session at my apartment. Long before, when he was gathering material for his book on the Texas Rangers, he and Frank Hamer and some others, including rich bankers, played poker quite often, Webb said.

They'd make huge wagers, ten thousand bucks. And they felt perfectly at ease wagering that amount for the privilege of drawing to an inside straight. For they used play money.

We used *real* money, even though most poker players would be amused at the thought, the stakes were so small. We played nickel ante.

I figured up later, after I moved from Austin to Houston, and discovered that teaching Walter Webb to play poker cost me $347.50. It seems incredible, since there was seldom a swing of more than twenty bucks at one of those sessions. At least few of us ever lost more than that, although one lucky person might accumulate forty bucks or more from the gathering.

Webb became a real tough poker player later, Joe tells me. "Any time you could beat him, you had to be doggone lucky or pull some smart ones—and most of the time the smart ones backfired."

Well, I wonder, in view of that, how Webb might have fared in the other areas of sin. I conclude he would have done real fine.

We did manage to talk him into drinking a highball now and then, but he never would take more than two in an entire evening. And usually he would stick to wine, drinking only two or three small glasses during a long poker session.

Anyway, he sure didn't make much headway toward what I call first rate, enjoyable sin. But is there anyone among us who can say that Walter Webb didn't lead a *full* life? I think not.

RODNEY J. KIDD

Going to places in the pasture

Dr. Webb and I met at the Night Hawk on South Congress on a wet, rainy November day in 1946 and decided to open a boys' camp at his Friday Mountain ranch in the summer of 1947. He gave his word and I gave mine and the agreement was in effect. He liked to operate on a simple, man to man basis, your word and his word. We did business that way for seventeen years and never a cross word passed between us.

Mr Bedichek told me:

Kidd, Dr. Webb is a very sensitive person. His feelings are very tender and they can be hurt easily. He is a man of few words. He will not impose on you and neither will he let you impose on him. You will always know how he stands on matters. You will find him intensely honest, and he knows how to make money.

After we had been in business for about a year, I found out that Dr. Webb had borrowed $10,000 to repair the old Johnston Institute building on the ranch and to get things ready for the camp. I was a country boy from Georgetown and Kingsville, just out of a long depression and Southwestern University, and this move by Dr. Webb scared me. When I mentioned it to him, he said he did not tell me because he was afraid I would "back out."

The ranch seemed to provide him the kind of relaxation, rest, and diversion he wanted and needed. He enjoyed going to the auction barns on Mondays with Mr. Garrett, either to sell or buy a few head of stock. Many times in the summer he would go without a coat, and

139

one could see his wallet in his back pocket, with several hundred-dollar bills exposed.

The year the camp opened, a five-year drouth began. Bear Creek and Onion Creek dried up, except for potholes of water. Windy Cove, a favorite swimming hole, and the Archer pool were not fit for swimming. While I was primarily interested in working with the boys and developing their capacities, Dr. Webb was interested in restoring the soil, in resodding the native grasses, and in having fun with Mr. Garrett in his ranching program. Dr. Webb refused to have anything to do with running the boys' camp. However, he liked to see the crowds from a distance, enjoying the beauty and tranquility of the ranch. When the last parent had pulled out, he would come up to find out how things had gone. "Rodney," he would say, "you talk to the parents and run the camp. I will communicate with the grass and with nature. There is no back talk from my project."

Mr. and Mrs. Garrett were devoted to him. Mrs. Garrett always prepared the kind of meals he liked. Dr. Webb furnished the money and materials and Mr. Garrett the labor for a cottage that was the site of many happy story-tellings, domino games, and plans to get rich in the livestock business. Dr. Webb told me he never expected to make any money from his farming, ranching, or hog-raising. He explained that some men spent their money for country clubs, travel, wine, or other things, but he liked to spend his at the ranch, experimenting with Mr. Garrett's get-rich plans. Together they built barns, bought cattle, sold cattle, bought hogs, sold hogs, planted grass, cut cedar, and cleared land. They told a lot of stories but they never made money on a single project.

Mr. Garrett had a great deal of native ability but very meager education. He was a carpenter, mechanic, electrician, plumber, and stockman; he could do all kinds of chores around the ranch. Besides, he was a marvelous story teller, and I think this is what Dr. Webb loved most. Gathered around the Garrett table, we would listen to the host tell about the time he was electrocuted doing some repair work at Robstown. The people called a doctor, and the doctor pronounced him dead; they called for the undertaker to come and pick him up. He could hear all of this, but he could not move an arm or a muscle, or raise his voice. He said he realized that unless something was done he would wind up in the funeral home and in a hearse on

140

the way to the graveyard. Finally, he was able to move an eyebrow, and someone happened to see it. An hour later he was back on the job.

When Dr. Webb and Mr. Garrett were in the cattle business, Mr. Garrett would get out his pencil and paper, and they would sit around the dinner table, figuring how they could make $10,000 next year by planting a certain field in oats, another in maize, and by marketing their stock at certain seasons. Dr. Webb knew very well that these figures would not work out, but he said that this was a better life than belonging to a country club.

In June of 1962, while Dr. Webb was in Alaska, Mr. Garrett went down to the field to check on some sheep. While there, he had a heart attack and passed away. When I drove my car into the field to pick up the body, I watched his eyebrow for some time, hoping to see it twitch again. But the man Dr. Webb described as "the bull of the woods" was gone. I called Dr. Webb in Alaska. With the death of one of his best friends, Dr. Webb found that the ranch had lost some of its appeal, and his interest in farming and ranching began to wane.

Frequently I would look out across the pastures at Friday Mountain and see someone moving about, bending over, examining the flowers, the weeds, the blades of grass. It would be Dr. Webb, going to places in the pasture where he had planted native grasses. He liked to bring to the ranch people who were interested in the soil, the water, and the grasses. Annually he purchased commercial fertilizer for the pastures where the land had been barren for many years. Bulldozers were brought in to remove the cedar from the hills so the grass and the oaks could grow. For many years no hunting was allowed.

Dr. Webb loved the simple, quiet things of life. He did not indulge in strong drink; he did not relate dirty and smutty stories; he was a great lover of the out-of-doors. I have been with him at the camp, in the woods, around campfires, at banquets, in hotels, with his family and with my family. At all times he was the same: humble, quiet, and considerate of the wishes and desires of others. He never pressed or pushed for the things that he personally might choose to do.

JACK CARGILL, JR.*

His last project

Old, frail. Using a cane, and wearing a pinstriped suit slightly too large for him, along with a big Stetson hat. This is how I first saw Dr. Webb as he entered room 101 of Texas' business and economics building for the first meeting of his history course based on and named for *The Great Frontier*. I was trying hard to be impressed, to see the greatness which I had always heard ascribed to the man, which I had felt while reading *Divided We Stand*, and which had prompted me to enroll in the course. But there was no aura about him, and my disappointment increased when his first lecture was almost directly quoted from his first chapter. Dr. Webb was not a man who impressed people at the first meeting; he put on no show. He was the most thoroughly honest person imaginable.

He said that the members of the class had undoubtedly signed up for one of two reasons: either to catch the old man before he kicked off, or to take a crip course. Webb's philosophy of teaching became evident as the course progressed: he was not interested in lecturing; the material was available; those who wanted to could learn a good deal; those who did not could have their easy grade.

At the age of seventy-four, when most educators, if not retired, are only repeating the knowledge they have learned over a lifetime, Dr. Webb was pioneering. There was much talk of the value of educational television, but one lecturer taping a course, and the TV set then just acting as a stand-in for him, was of small benefit. A TV

* Of Marshall, Texas, an honors graduate student in history at The University of Texas at Austin.

course, under this system, was inferior to an ordinary lecture course: questioning and spontaneous give-and-take were sacrificed, and no added feature counteracted the loss.Webb envisioned a type of course that was feasible only through the medium of videotape. Through his prestige and the wealth of the Ford Foundation, the groundwork was laid for *Topics in American Civilization,* a course wherein top American historians from all over the country were to record a lecture or set of lectures on their specialties. The result was to be a course too broad in scope for one teacher ever to have covered, yet with a measure of depth, because each field was to be discussed by a specialist.

As one of the twelve students given permission to view the first semester's tapings, I came to see at first hand the greatness of Webb. He demanded personal thought and personal responsibility when we answered his questions; he was unsparingly truthful in discussing his eminent colleagues with us; he described some of the speakers' books as frankly boring; and he generally showed us the humanity of great men, himself included.

When, on the night of Friday, March 8, 1963, Webb was killed, he had not yet taped the lectures on his specialty. But his enthusiasm had inspired others, and the leadership of his project was assumed by his colleague and protégé, Dr. Joe B. Frantz. The TV series, renamed *American Civilization: By the Interpreters,* continues, offering students far away from his beloved University a glimpse of his ever-youthful creativity.

LON TINKLE*

Meetings in Dallas

When *The New York Times* celebrated its one-hundredth anniversary in 1951, its Sunday Book Review assessed American writing during the first fifty years of this century. Henry Steele Commager, writing on history, concluded that Walter Prescott Webb's *The Great Plains* was entitled to be called "the best single-volume contribution to American history" published between 1900 and 1950. As Walter Webb commented so often to friends, honors and recognition seemed to have been reserved for him for his last years. He was not ungrateful about the sudden avalanche of acclaim—but he noted the irony of it with a wryness that had become habit. Unorthodox and ferociously independent, he must have thought of himself as an ugly duckling of the academic world.

At any rate, he had a great fondness for the Hans Christian Andersen tale, and gave it a personal twist. Once, in a fit of weariness and self-pity, I raged for an hour over the penalties and miseries of a Texas rearing for a man who wanted to be an expert on European literature. I related to Walter the backgrounds (privileged, as I thought) of some of my classmates at Columbia and the Sorbonne, specialists of whom people have heard. He listened with sympathy. A few days later I got from an Austin book store a very handsomely illustrated copy of Andersen. "Read this," his note urged, "it will do you good." He told me later it was one of his favorite gestures to cure depression in his friends. I rarely think of the Andersen fable,

* Book editor of the *Dallas Morning News*, teacher of French literature at Southern Methodist University, and author of *13 Days to Glory*.

144

but, in these days when nearly anybody over thirty thinks himself an anachronism, I do often think of Webb.

Two years after Commager's tribute, the president of Oxford University Press told me in New York that Arnold Toynbee was coming to this country and wanted to come to Texas to see Walter Prescott Webb. Toynbee did come; his plane had a lay-over in Dallas, and the Oxford Press man advised me to run out and talk to him at the airport about a plan for him also to speak in Dallas, a plan he had steadily rejected. Bolstered by a promise from the late E. DeGolyer of Dallas to post any necessary fee, I met the plane. Toynbee, his white mane of hair afloat in the airport blows, was polite but unshakable. "I have only limited time, as I stated by letter," he explained, "and I want to spend what time I have in Texas with Professor Webb."

I told Walter this later, when *he* was killing a lay-over at the Dallas airport. It became a sort of ritual after that for me to visit with him during stop-overs in Dallas, and his many engagements brought him through with regularity. When I recall memories of talks with him, the scene is usually the airport. He was, of course, brimming with ideas and projects every time I saw him. He had a plan for the Texas Institute of Letters, or a program for the *Southwest Review*, or some advice for the *Texas Almanac*, or a way to revolutionize book selling in the nation (it was a wonderful idea, too), or more mundane things about how to improve the duck situation on a little pond our house overlooks or how to arrange the education of the Tinkle boys, or where to buy up land in North Texas. I do not recall ever encountering a more fertile mind.

One night in the summer of 1961, Walter called me from Austin to say he had an hour's wait next morning in Dallas. He had something he wanted to tell me. There was a crush at Gate Twelve, where his plane was to leave, so we turned a corner and sat down at vacant Gate Thirteen.

What he had to tell me was engrossing indeed. So much so, it was I who had to remind him it was about time for his plane. "Oh, they'll announce it, don't worry," he said, and told me some more. But presently, he asked, "Why don't they call that plane?" and we got up to check.

Outside Gate Twelve, both signs were astounding—the gangplank had been removed and all propellers were whirling.

"Why, that fool plane's trying to take off," he exclaimed as he dashed out and, as though heading off a West Texas mule, ran in front of the ship and signalled the pilot to be sensible.

Airport flunkies, recovering, began to run around in circles. A jeep scouting the field made a bee-line for Webb. The pilot sadly shook his head, "no." On Webb's heels I too was making frantic and righteous signs when the man in the jeep grabbed me. Luckily, he was Braniff's station master and had sized up the situation at once.

"Jump in!" he yelled above the engine roar, "another plane leaving over here." The jeep made a broken field run through taxiing and arriving planes and its driver said, "I know who you are, Professor Webb."

Not much mollified, Webb spoke scathingly of planes that leave unannounced, especially when he had to be in Minneapolis on time for a speaking engagement. The second plane was also already locked tight. Our jeep-host was undaunted. "Maybe I can get you on an American Airlines jet leaving for Chicago." We whipped across the field again. "I'm sympathetic to an absent-minded professor," the station manager said, "but you know, Professor Webb, that plane was announced several times."

Walter ignored the latter comment. Cutting his eyes at me, he muttered, "two absent-minded professors." But after a bit more maneuvering, we made the jet. Walter had to wait in Chicago for his baggage, on the first plane, to catch up with him.

It made an amusing story for the paper and Paul Crume, former Webb student and longtime friend, wrote it up with style. We didn't hear the plane called because Walter was telling me he thought he had been lucky enough to persuade Terrell Maverick to marry him in the autumn. He was a happy man that morning at Love Field.

Joe Frantz characterized him as a man whose sophistication was generally unsuspected. I remember, though this is only marginally what Joe meant, a dinner Herbert Gambrell and I once had with him at Dallas' Old Warsaw restaurant. After a meal that would have satisfied even Alfred A. Knopf, Walter asked the waiter to bring an orange, a sharp knife, and a bottle of cognac. With precise skill, he cut the peeling around the middle of the orange, gently worked the top and bottom parts of the rind loose from the pulp, and turned the top half into a cup and the bottom half into a base for the cleanly skinned fruit in the middle. Into the cup at the top, Webb poured

146

cognac and then set it aflame. A round of applause came from neighboring tables, where guests had watched the maneuver with fascinated attention. Webb set the orange cup on a plate and asked our waiter to offer ceremonial sips to our neighbors. They spooned it out. A memorable literary occasion at Old Warsaw which several have tried to duplicate, always without success.

The last time I saw him, two weeks before his death, he gave a talk at Southern Methodist University on Feb. 17, 1963, then came over to our house for a little meal. "I have no more books in me that I want to write," he said. "At my age you live from day to day. Terrell and I aren't waiting to celebrate our anniversaries in terms of years. We celebrate each month. Just last week we observed our fifteenth anniversary. I am a happy man, a very happy man."

GLEN L. EVANS[*]

Free of both hate and fear

I first saw Walter Prescott Webb in the middle 1930's when I was a student at The University of Texas. We exchanged a perfunctory greeting; I was struck by the solemn expression on his face, and I guessed him to be a severe and unapproachable man. Several years passed before I realized how mistaken this was. I did not have him as a professor, although, in an informal sense, I was always his student. From the time we first became well acquainted, around 1940, until I moved away from Austin in 1954, we met for long or short talks perhaps once or twice a month. Thereafter I saw him only once or twice a year. Most of our meetings were over a cup of coffee or at lunch, but occasionally they were in his office. Sometimes I made notes on what he had said.

During periods when he was not actively engaged in writing, he was engrossed with his Friday Mountain ranch, and it was one of his favorite topics of discussion. The ranch, as J. Frank Dobie has said, "entered into his bones—into the very fibers of his being." He was primarily concerned with restoring its depleted grassland and water, but nothing about the place was too insignificant to escape his interest. He once told me that no horned toads were ever seen there and wondered whether I could suggest why. We talked about releasing a few of the small lizards around the ranch house to see whether they would survive, but we never got around to doing it. There is a well preserved dinosaur track in one of the limestone ledges near the house. After examining it one day, I suggested that a little excavation

* A geologist living in Midland.

148

might expose more of the trail, which, it seemed to me, would interest the members of the boys' camp that Rodney Kidd held on the ranch during summer months. After a little reflection, Dr. Webb said that he had been trying hard to get the soil to heal over the natural erosion, and he guessed we wouldn't do any more excavating.

Occasionally in our conversations I would get carried away with some opinion, and he would bring me firmly back to my senses. One day we were talking about governmental programs on water conservation. I spoke bitterly against a senator whom I accused of being interested in the issue principally because he wanted to wring every drop of favorable publicity out of it. After reflecting for a few moments, Webb replied:

You work for a company that is in the business of finding and producing oil. You know that you have to make a profit if you are going to stay in business, and that no one should blame you for trying to make a profit. A politician has to make a profit, too, in the form of voter approval, if he wants to stay in office. If he serves effectively in his office he should not be blamed for trying to make a favorable impression on the only people who can keep him there.

It was typical of Dr. Webb that he offered this as a friendly observation and not as a reprimand.

Most memorable of my associations with him were those occasions when I was included in the periodic steak-supper outing which he, J. Frank Dobie, the late Roy Bedichek, and other friends held for the primary purpose of enjoying each other's company. Those I attended were held variously on Webb's Friday Mountain ranch or on Dobie's old Cherry Springs ranch, or sometimes on a site selected by Roy Bedichek on some secluded creek bank in the hills west of Austin. The peaceful, open-air setting had an enlivening effect on every member of the supper party. The talk was brisk and witty, and it seemed to improve steadily as the evening wore on. Certainly the three exceptional men who composed the nucleus of the group and their friends who were present on these outings produced the most delightful and enlightening conversation that I have heard in my life.

In a stimulating group Dr. Webb was not an aggressive talker. More often than not he would sit quietly, listening intently. Now and then he would break in with a pertinent remark or a short, illustrative story. He knew, as others who regularly attended those camp suppers knew, and as most people do not, how to contribute to a conversation without dominating it. At times when something was said that amused him he would burst out in a roar of laughter that was utterly contagious.

Despite the mournful expression he wore, Dr. Webb was a skilled dispeller of gloom. In 1959, after we had attended the funeral for Roy Bedichek, Webb, Mr. Dobie and I went out together for lunch— a meal for which we had no appetite, Mr. Dobie was suffering in his depths. I, too, felt the loss acutely and was becoming terribly depressed and lonely. Dr. Webb had known Roy Bedichek much longer and more intimately than I, and was certainly not less conscious of his loss. Yet he talked more freely than usual, recalling cheerful and witty things that Bedi had said. He reflected that the only way that life might be thought to have a happy ending was when death came, as it had come to Bedichek, suddenly and painlessly after a long, happy, and useful career. His statements were logical and soothing, and as free of inanities and sentimentalities as always. I feel sure that he intended to help lift our spirits, and he succeeded.

He was a deep and complex man. I suspect that he had the quality of greatness within him. About a year before Bedi died, he remarked to me, in substance if not exactly, "Webb shows no sign of mental aging. Instead, he gets stronger every year. He has a source of inner power that the rest of us don't have—or if we have it we don't know how to reach it." Thinking for him seemed as natural as breathing. It gave him dignity and serenity, and freed him from emotional strains. In the time I knew him I don't believe he feared anything in or after life. He seemed free of both hate and fear, but I don't believe that he had ever made a conscious effort to divest himself of either. It seemed that acts or events that normally incite hate or fear got digested in his thinking processes and never entered the emotional part of his being.

The last time I saw him was around the middle of February shortly before his death. I was in Austin for the day, and he invited me to join him and his wife, Terrell, whom I had not met previously, for lunch at the Night Hawk cafe near The University of Texas campus. During the hour or so we spent together he was brimming over with enthusiasm. He talked mainly of *Washington Wife,* the book which he and Mrs. Webb had helped bring out, and of which he was in-

150

ordinately proud. His unconcealed devotion for Mrs. Webb and the joy he derived from her companionship was as pleasing for me to observe as it has been for his many other friends. When I left him I knew that he was happier than I had ever seen him before. His death was a shocking loss to all of us who knew him, but according to his own standards, his life had a happy ending.

TOM SUTHERLAND*

The power of land and the power of mind

I agree with you that there is a natural aristocracy among men. The grounds of this are virtue and talents. . . . There is also an artificial aristocracy, founded on wealth and birth without either virtue or talents. . . . The natural aristocracy I consider as the most precious gift of nature, for the instruction, the trusts, and government of society.

Jefferson to John Adams

Walter Prescott Webb, the historian, was killed by a machine, an automobile, in 1963 while riding happily with his sixty-year–old new wife. He left us the largest legacy of any man, an idea. No one, as far as I know, has made a straighter statement of what machines have done to us in removing our land frontier. At seventy-four Webb was weighing in the bumper harvest of his own frontier, human thought.

What Webb said, mainly, in his last historical analysis, *The Great Frontier,* was that the world, by the use of designs of finance and new machines, had consumed the chief historical source of our prosperity and that, believe it or not, we face some kind of radical change. Land, new land, the sudden use of the great frontier of unoccupied land that became accessible four hundred years ago, had moved money and all it buys up and down the arteries and capillaries of the Western world. Webb set forth with lucidity how man's invention

* A member of the English faculty of The University of Texas at Arlington.

When he was a young man, his wife said, Roy Bedichek had "lots of yella hair, and green eyes with lots of spots in them."

Walter Prescott Webb as a young man (left) had grown up with a love for geography. After early indecision his major interests settled on teaching and writing. Photograph at right was made during a 1937 Big Bend trip with the Texas Rangers, whose definitive history he wrote.

Two early photographs of J. Frank Dobie show him at the age of ten, and as a first lieutenant in the Field Artillery in 1917. "When I was young," he once said, "I preferred to be around old people, because I felt I could learn most from them."

For Bedichek, "back to nature was not back to the primitive," said Dobie, "there to be saved from 'poring over miserable books'." Bedichek is shown (left) in Deming, New Mexico, in 1911. His bride is shown in the photograph at right, accompanied by Bedichek's dog Hobo.

Bedichek "loved children." At Barton Springs he posed with his daughters Sarah (left) and Mary Virginia. Bedichek continued to be a summer swimmer at Barton's even to the day before he died.

Bertha and Frank Dobie were photographed
about 1933 during a visit to a hacienda near Mexico City. Mrs. Dobie was important to Frank's
work, particularly as a critical reader of manuscripts.

In April, 1936, Frank Dobie visited the last survivor of Old Tas-
cosa. "He values the past," Editor Angus Cameron said of him,
"but he has no use for those who worship it."

Dobie's lectures were lively; his course in the Life and Literature of the Southwest, begun in 1930, became the most popular elective at The University of Texas. He spoke in an "earthy growl which no amount of culture could rob of its cow-country qualities." These photographs were taken during a 1939 talk at Texas Christian University.

To get a book done, Frank Dobie said, a man has to "associate with himself." This photograph (by F. Wilbur Seiders) was made in 1941 beside Waller Creek.

Webb was a quiet man who nevertheless spoke and wrote on controversial subjects. The "reach of his intellect was matched by the breadth of his humanity," but his sophistication, said Joe Frantz, was generally unsuspected. At Oxford in 1943 (bottom picture) Webb stood in the top row, second from the left.

Dobie enjoyed talking with people, whether at Cambridge (top, 1944), where he became "not just a successful teacher but an ambassador at large," or at home (bottom, photograph by Russell Lee), where he always had time to hear a story.

"Webb was a learned man with a capacity for hard thinking and sustained effort," said his friend Wilson Hudson, "but he was not academic. He did not immure himself in the university or cut himself off from the outside world." This photograph was made about 1945.

It was said of Dobie that "with a minimum of reverence for age and baldness, he indicated that he was capable of running his own life."

Bedichek "liked to cook outdoors, eat outdoors, sleep outdoors, look and listen ou[t]doors, be at one with the unexplaining wind from the south." The top photogra[ph] shows him with his grandsons Alan Pipkin, Jr., and Roy Bedichek Pipkin.

Dobie's face always reflected joy of life. "Somehow around Frank," observed book critic Lon Tinkle, "everybody feels intelligent and life seems good."

Dobie was as close to his beloved land as is possible to be, yet he was anything but provincial. "A good regional writer deals with the culture of a region," his friend Mody Boatright said. "Dobie has done this." Picture at left was made during a 1931 panther hunt.

Left: Walter Prescott Webb's first wife, Jane Oliphant Webb, and daughter Mildred posed for this picture about 1919. Right: "Despite the mournful expression he wore," Glen Evans remarked, "Dr. Webb was a skilled dispeller of gloom." He is shown here about 1935, with his dog Gigolo.

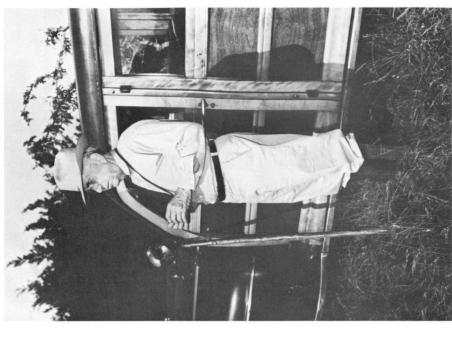

Two strong feelings, among others, characterized Bedichek: "Only Nature is normal," he once wrote. And on trips into the country (right) "Mr. Bedi" carried binoculars, not a gun.

Dobie said of Bedichek: "He was as unenvying and as free from greed and jealousy as any man could be." (Photograph by Walter Barnes Studio.)

This photograph of Dobie was snapped by a *Houston Post* photographer December 27, 1949.

The Golden Wedding Anniversary picture of Walter Prescott Webb's parents—made on October 19, 1931—pictured (seated, center) Mr. and Mrs. C. P. Webb and, standing to Mr. Webb's right, Betty Jean Kennedy. Behind them are (left to right) Mrs. George Kennedy, Mrs. Jane Oliphant Webb, Walter Webb, George Kennedy, Oleta Hewlett, and Mildred Alice Webb.

Hold before the young, Bedichek said and did, "the great theme of superior performance and the vision of greatness it inspires."

"By nature and upbringing Webb was a devoted liberal in the best sense of that often bromidic word," said Joe Frantz. "He believed that the world could be improved." In the foreground is the late Bill Kittrell.

One of Mrs. Dobie's favorite photographs of her husband shows
Dobie with Caroline Wardlaw.

"He is as good a listener as he is a talker," Dobie's friend Frank Wardlaw said of him. His face often reflected his reactions as in these two photographs (by Russell Lee). With Dobie is Hart Stilwell.

Bedichek was a man at peace. "To live is to be sufficiently stimulated," he once said; his drinking was limited to an occasional can of cold beer.

"Dr. Webb was not a man who impressed people at the first meeting; he put on no show," said a former student. "He was the most thoroughly honest person imaginable." (Photograph by Neal Douglass.)

Dobie's friends will remember forever the pleasure of sitting with him in the back yard by Waller Creek, "surrounded by Bertha's wonderful flowers." (Photograph by Russell Lee.)

"Plato helped start the day for [Bedichek] on a noble plane and put him into a creative mood." He died suddenly on a late summer day in 1959 while waiting for his wife to finish cooking corn bread. "There was little difference," said the Reverend Edmund Heinsohn, "between his persona and his personality." (Photograph by Neal Douglass.)

Terrell and Walter Webb. A few months after this photograph was made in 1963 (by Charles Smith) Webb died in an automobile accident, in which his wife was seriously injured.

Bertha and Frank Dobie. Frank Dobie died in his sleep Friday, September 18, 1964. "His was the kind of freedom," Edmund Heinsohn said, "that made it possible for him to stand in the presence of royalty and not feel inferior, and stand in the presence of the lowly and not feel superior." (Photograph by Evans Studio.)

The men are gone but the memories remain. Top, Bedichek (left) and Dobie were photographed on "Bedi's Rock" at Barton Springs; when their discussions became heated one of them would take a dip in the chilling waters and help in a mutual cooling off before conversation was resumed. Bottom, the stone house at Friday Mountain, owned by Webb, was where Bedichek was "held in benignant captivity" while he wrote *Adventures with a Texas Naturalist*.

and passion for life had made the Western world blossom and freedom thrive. He could show the most childlike of students the way the Constitution made the individual into a citizen. On a blackboard he wrote an *I*; around it he drew a circle which he let stand for the Constitution. For a long time no individual had such a circle to hold out kings, but in necessity men had at last invented this defense against the state. Webb could also show readers the way the American West was won, when, and only when, new defenses were devised against the reluctant aborigine and drouth. Guns fired without need of reloading, barbed wire to hold cattle in vacant land where men were scarce, and life-giving water pumped by wind where no rivers ran—such things now quaintly simple in a rocket age—are clearly explained as instruments of profound change.

Our present predicament, proceeding from the point when repeater gunfire ran off the hostiles and the range was put under barbed wire, is, Webb said, a dilemma: either to invent a substitute boom-maker for land or to decline from the exceptionally happy estate of our four-hundred–year boom.

The world still contains an abundance of wealth [Webb granted] and we are becoming more skilled in its conservation. Even though we are faced with change, much of which we heartily dislike, we shall be better prepared to make the necessary adjustments if we recognize the reasons for making them. . . . Here are some changes which are at hand and must be accepted.

Society as it thickens will become more closely integrated and its members more interdependent. Governments will tend to become stronger, using more compulsion in order to meet their obligations. There will be a tendency toward socialization as now exhibited in the United States and Great Britain or toward absolutism as exhibited by the fascist states and by Russia. The loose democracy belonged to a frontier stage of society. The individual will become relatively less important and will tend to lose his identity in growing corporate life. . . . Capitalism of the Nineteenth-Century type will decline with the passing of the boom on which it was based.

Webb stated these prophecies with lucidity—and with tears in his eyes, for he had seen and tasted that sense of maximum freedom and greatness that for a time the Western world produced for new large groups of common men; he now stared with his special insight and honesty into the fact of unavoidable change.

By others Webb's views of history and the future were not ac-

153

cepted, for our very success has made us so optimistic that we will not believe that it is over—or even modified. But whatever the answer to our dilemma, it is difficult to think of an argument against its existence. Administrations have thought of slogans, "The New Deal," "The New Frontier," "The Great Society." Senator Ralph Yarborough thought up a dynamic speech, saying that we are not a people whose dream has somewhere died—as Faulkner once said— but that we will move on to new horizons as our habits prompt us to do. Jolly good show! One applauds. It is good to know that the pilots of the ship of state have not lost their pluck. But assertion, even in stirring slogans and speeches, is not proof. Webb was a logician and teacher, not an orator or maker of slogans, and he has brought us to a central question of our time: What do we do with our growing family now that the land is sold off?

He said that he hoped for an answer, knowing that whatever we do, it will be different; but no one has answered. Neither America nor Russia nor China nor the old states of Europe nor the new ones in Africa seem to be able to contrive another Eden in our time. America, where hope is highest and for the best reasons, finds its saving grace of basic democracy obscured by rampant commercial activity that snows a lovely continent and a good people under one loud big sell. The common man, whom the American frontier elevated, is in all parts of the world as neglected as ever, if not more so; his present condition is brain-washing and a progressive regimentation—his only certainty is crowding. Our government makes gallant gestures toward common men, as in its civil rights legislation. One of them was kept at the University of Mississippi at a cost of two million dollars. But such action will not fundamentally modify the mediocrity of mind the society now cultivates and rewards.

The answer to Webb's question, "What next, after the land is used?" is another question, "What next, if the power of the human mind is kept in jail?" Permit me, in memory of an honest inquirer and for the sake of useful discussion of his question, to suggest a line of thought: that to advance thinking, we must release the freely-ranging brain power that has been taken up like land.

Webb's own story symbolizes the process by which brains may fructify. At the age of ten he was leaning on a primitive plough in an arid part of the world when a letter, instrumental to his fate, was handed him by his mother. The plough was the one that broke the

154

plains—a Georgia stock. If you know West Texas, you can see in your mind the weathered land, the immense blue and cloudless sky, the sun so fierce that the shade under the boy's hat or the woman's sunbonnet is at first glance like the darkness of night. The letter was from a Brooklyn bachelor, William Ellery Hinds, who had read, in a Southern magazine, a letter the child Webb had sent saying he wished to become a writer. Hinds helped Webb for many years, by the blind trust of the mails. The two never saw each other face to face.[1] This accident made Webb's honest thinking accessible to the human race.

The mystery haunted Webb. In his progressively rewarded life, he made efforts to know more about Hinds, while assisting students needy as the boy on the plough had been. The man who could master historical details, from the population-to-land ratio of 1492 to barbed wire, died without knowing the man who had fostered his career, or why he had done it.

A letter that Webb wrote in 1961 shows him in natural friendship, passing on encouragement to those who stand where he had stood.

In short [he says of certain written matter to a younger man who showed the letter to me], I detect here a real and special talent which I think you should cultivate and develop. An example is your description of how your father sat on the porch and leaned back against the 2 x 4 or 4 x 4 gallery post.

. . . if you decide, as some other of my talented young friends have, to sit on your tail and do nothing I want these pieces back. I want them back anyway because I do not trust people who have talent and have cultivated . . . laziness.

Is honest independent thinking then so difficult? Extremely difficult in an even more interdependent world! Whether the thinker is in the pay of government, business, or the colleges, the forces that confine his mind make it most difficult and dangerous to his career for him to lift his eyes above the grindstone of his specialized assignment. Anyone who doubts this fact is invited to present some of Webb's questions to any banker, executive, or employee in our 500,000 corporations, any bureaucrat in our far-flung bureaucracy on which the sun never sets, any teacher in our 50,000 school districts

---

[1] I believe that this story, which appeared in *Harper's* under the title "The Search for William E. Hinds," is the most stirring ever written by Webb.—T.S.

where understaffed schools do baby-sitting for mothers who resign from motherhood in order to work and pay the price of prosperity in Go-Go Land. Ask the next hireling you meet in our Great Society Beehive:

"Do you think that we are destined to make drastic economic reforms away from Nineteenth-Century capitalism and toward socialization?"

"Will you say so for the public record?"

Webb himself has been given grudging acclaim and little serious audience where it counts in the affairs of men. Scholars trained to the esoteric have disregarded him because he is simple and easy to understand; he writes too well. Yankees have not liked his analysis of how they milk the South and West; Republicans abhor his argument explaining how they lost their future by not understanding the necessity of change; Democratic politicians have taken him more as an ornament of their program than as an adviser on the fundamentals that escape them. But honest, broad, and creative thinking is necessary to show us the way out of our Twentieth-Century wilderness. How can we cure the conditions that make inoperative the good minds found throughout government, business, and the colleges? Where are the new Webbs, where are the environments to produce them? When it is proposed that we invade a Bay of Pigs, who shall advise us? On these occasions of great decision we seem more ignorant than children.

In another letter Webb writes, about an election: "If I have dignified 'the people' I have done it because I really believe in their judgment and wisdom, and also in their power, once they can see the fundamental issue." There is no better example of his power to explain clearly than an allegory by which he shows the way the frontier in America wiped out the old institutional classes of Europe. He takes five men into the western wild country exploring for land. A bemedalled general leads; a sleek banker follows; then a learned professor with his notes and indigestion; then a clergyman robustly thinking of a report to his church; and finally a plain man named Jim Brown who has had some direct experience with the American wilderness.

The general loses the party by insisting they follow his leadership. Jim Brown dissents, saying something about the lay of the land. He has to show them the way out. He shoots the game by which they survive and shows the others the best way to hunt. When their clothes are ripped to pieces and worn off, Jim Brown shows them the way to make clothing by tanning deer hide with ashes and brains. After a while, they are all alike in looks and good health, surviving by acting as a unit with the single goal of survival and with Jim Brown as their natural and acknowledged leader. This, in a few words, explains how Americans acquired new and more workable social traits as a result of the frontier.

If I were told that by a mystery too vast for understanding the individual will endure in some Valhalla where the soul selects its own society, I would imagine Walter Prescott Webb in conversation with a former soldier, a banker, a professor, a preacher, and a plain man named Jim Brown. They are camped by clear water in a pleasant grove deep in the virgin continent. They have come a long way from where they started. Exposure to this life has erased their differences. Their clothes are buckskin tanned with campfire ashes. They carry rifles, knives, and an axe. There is no distinction in their keen glance and appetite. They are discussing how next morning they will push on west. They see themselves moving through the boundless buffalo grass that springs up quickly where their unshod ponies' hooves have pressed it down. Jim Brown, the common fellow whose readiness and sense have been honed and set free upon that great frontier, will show the way.

What we can do—and must do to survive the end of one frontier— is to harness the philanthropy of a William Ellery Hinds to the liberation of superior, undiscovered minds: the final frontier. One of them, whether he is Jim Brown or another Walter Prescott Webb or Thomas Jefferson, may show us the way.

EDMUND HEINSOHN

To the basic loyalties of life he was true

In the course of his eulogy at Dr. Webb's funeral, Dr. Heinsohn said:

He loved all kinds of people. He loved the sinners, but not their sins. Shine boys and members of all classes and races were his friends. He and an associate made a trip to Kingsville where he was to deliver a commencement address. It took him five days to go and return. In every community he wanted to stop and get some friends for a coffee-drinking conversation. Many of these friends were not academicians. But to him they were important persons. . . .

To the basic loyalties of life he was true. The elemental human relationships he would not violate. He was also true to himself, and to be so he kept himself in proper perspective. He said that when he thought himself "a big shot," all he needed to do to get himself in right perspective was to go to San Antonio and stand on the street corner at the Gunter Hotel and ask himself how many of the passing crowd had ever heard of Walter Webb, and how many knew of The University of Texas and had any interest in it. Seeing himself in proper perspective made it possible for him to be courageous and un-afraid. A short time before his controversial article in *Harper's Magazine* appeared, he and two friends were together in El Paso. Both of these friends warned him that if that article was published he would lose every friend he ever had. He was silent for a few moments, and then answered: "I can't help it. I'll have to publish it."

He had a conscience about helping students who were in need of

158

help. Applicants for help were never asked about their grades. This was his way of trying to pay the debt he owed to William E. Hinds, the man who had made possible his early college education. A man came into Dr. Webb's office one day for financial assistance. Another faculty member came in a short time after the visitor for help had left. The faculty member inquired if Dr. Webb had had a caller and if he gave him anything. Dr. Webb replied that he had let the man have $100. The faculty member retorted: "That fellow is a professional bum; he has gotten money from a number of men, is leaving the city and is down at the railway station now." Dr. Webb jumped up and said: "I'll get that guy." He rushed down to the station and boarded the train and found his man. Later in the day the faculty member saw Dr. Webb and asked him what had happened when he confronted the man. Dr. Webb answered: "You know, that fellow was so open and above board about the whole matter, I let him have another $100." Dr. Webb always liked a consummate artist, even though he be a crook and a scoundrel.

Beneath his occasional bluntness and gruffness there was a fine sensitivity. He could even become deeply sentimental. The Friday Mountain camp had meant much to him: he could cry while giving expression to his great concern for the preservation of the grass there. He was asked one time if he had ever done anything that he looked back to with regret. The answer came in the affirmative. He had been visiting Houghton Mifflin in Boston, and he was given a copy of Walter Millis' *The Road to War* to look over. The jacket on the book was vivid red. He went out into a park to sit down and laid the book on the bench beside him. Two little Italian children, a girl about nine years old and her little brother about five, came by. They were poor and dirty. The little boy was attracted by the book, and as he edged up to the bench and was reaching his hand out to it, Dr. Webb reached out and pulled it away. As he did so, the little girl very calmly said to her brother, "Don't touch the book, it's too nice for you." There was no resentment and no complaining by the little sister, just a statement of fact. "It's too nice for you." Dr. Webb said: "I would give anything to be able to live that over, and not to move the book away. It has bothered me for years."

PHOTOGRAPH BY GUY GILLETTE

J. FRANK DOBIE

ROCKY REAGAN*

We came from the same range

Frank Dobie and I came from the same range. I have known him for many years. In fact, since our school days. His parents were the salt of the earth. They were the early settlers in Live Oak County and staunch Methodists.

I can but think of the spring I met a lone rider leading a horse packed with bedding and a coffee pot strapped on the side. It was Frank, on his way West to join the Jim Dobie outfit. They were to ship six thousand aged steers to Oklahoma for summer grazing.

Then the afternoons we spent on my front porch or beside the evening fire, reliving those old range days, of a stampede, a fall, or some unusual camp cook.

Frank had it in his blood but was too smart to fight the game and chose the wiser course of recording, in his own rare style, for the future generations, those unusual legends.

J. Frank Dobie or "Pancho" is bone and sinew a frontiersman, a rare character, and I'm proud to say a friend of mine.

* Of George West, Texas. He calls himself "just a cow man."

AL MELINGER*

Poetry in an earthy growl

Back in the late Twenties J. Frank Dobie would light up each winter with the most picturesque case of hayfever in Travis County. Probably he still does. Some of the finest polemics ever printed in Austin were his diatribes against the male cedars whose pollinating he blamed for his agonies. Once he offered publicly to axe every offending tree in the area, but property owners ignored the proposition. Only one other subject inspired him to such rancor—the patriotic doggerel penned by one W. Lee O'Daniel during his gubernatorial career.

I shall not forget my original experience with the Dobie catarrhal affliction when, as a sophomore, I watched him snorting and blinking red-eyed and runny of nose through the introductory moments of a lecture. He had forgotten his handkerchief. Finally, his sturdy figure bolted from the room, rounded the corner to the men's room in Garrison Hall, and returned a moment later trailing several yards of toilet paper. He wadded it into a basketball-sized mass and snorted lustily into it.

"A damn fool would have swallered that," he commented, sniffing contentedly as he thrust the remaining yardage into his pocket.

Years later I discovered that the remark was a derivative of a statement attributed to Sam Houston after he had expelled a mouthful of hot sweet potato during a state dinner. It was only then that I began resenting Mr. Dobie's criticism that my own ideas in English themes were all "derived." Now, in relative maturity, I recognize ruefully

* A businessman in Baytown, Texas.

that had I understood what he meant, I might have saved myself several bales of rejection slips.

By some curious maladjustment of University programming I had found myself, an English and journalism major, in an engineering English class. Because my sole academic strength was in the field of literature, I promptly presumed that I was slated for a leading role in that roomful of slide rule dummies. I had not figured on Dobie's standards.

Up to that point in an otherwise undistinguished academic career, I was a solid *A* student in English, a source of massive satisfaction to me in rationalizing the occasional *F*'s which decorated my papers in such inhuman disciplines as mathematics and chemistry. My genius was lost on Professor Dobie. Under him I learned to cherish even a *B*-minus. His hasty scrawl pulled no punches as to why he thought my efforts were mediocre, so I probably learned more from him than from any of the other several remarkable educators who sowed their seeds so hopefully into the fallow soil of my teen-age intellect.

He was a rumpled, solid man with sunbaked skin, and in those days that shaggy mop, now white as Carl Sandburg's, was iron-grey. He would stride vigorously into Garrison Hall, bearing an armload of papers and exuding a truculent disdain for whatever popular vanity was in current ascendancy.

On a particularly hayfevered morning he drew attention to a football team which preceded each game with a full-squad prayer for victory. "Who believes," he snorted, "that God cares whether one bunch of young apes or another has the most success with an inflated pig bladder?"

Then, his scalding mood tempered by appreciative laughter, Dobie's blunt, brown fingers would open the Snyder and Martin textbook and he would plunge with catholic enthusiasm into Romanticism, Classicism, or the Age of Victoria. He liked to read poetic passages aloud, and when he did in that earthy growl which no amount of culture could rob of its cow country qualities, something vital happened to Wordsworth, Coleridge, Shelley, and Keats. No one who heard him snarl through Browning's hate-filled Soliloquy of the Spanish Cloister could ever again think that poetry is sissy stuff.

He left at midterm to engage in one of those sabbaticals—either to lecture at Cambridge or exploit *Coronado's Children* which was then filling bookstore windows or maybe just to help round up stock on the home place. Anyway, Mrs. Dobie took over and finished the year, and I didn't get many A papers back from her either.

Mr. Dobie was back on the Forty Acres in the late Spring and had been made chairman of a Dad's Day barbecue during the annual Roundup. As undergraduate publicity chairman for the event, I was in officious evidence, glamorous in big black Stetson, genuine leather chaps, and flowing orange neckerchief which bespoke my membership in the Texas Cowboys. I bore a platter of barbecue to my former mentor. He nodded acknowledgment and then, narrowly eyeing my cowpoke trappings, grunted:

"My God, MeLINGer [he always pronounced it that way], I didn't know you was one of THEM."

Four decades later my soul still shrivels at the way he rasped the word "them." I never did enjoy wearing my cowboy uniform much after that.

ELOISE ROACH*

A quatrain forty years ago

Of course everyone knows J. Frank Dobie as the peerless spinner of
yarns, the master teller of tales, the welder of folklore and reminiscence into unforgettable stories. But perhaps it is not so widely
known that he has versified on occasion. For forty years I have treas-
ured a quatrain of his in heroic couplets, his comment on a paper I
handed in for one of his courses at The University of Texas.

It must have been the spring of 1924. At any rate, it was the time
of flappers and jelly beans. We were all very modern—in dress, in
hair styles, in make-up; we had "new" ways of being and of acting,
"new" approaches to all circumstances and to all personal matters.

In Mr. Dobie's course we had read Milton and Alexander Pope, in
particular *Paradise Lost* and *The Rape of the Lock*. Then we had to
write a "theme," a paper of some one thousand words. We must have
been given a good deal of liberty in the choice of subjects, though
evidently it had to have some relation to what we had read. I do not
remember the title of my essay, but my subject was my sad discovery
that there is nothing new under the sun. There had been flappers
and jelly beans in the eighteenth century, though they were called
belles or Nymphs and beaux or fops or witlings. And all our "new"
approaches had been practiced two hundred years ago!

Imitating Pope, I wrote my paper in heroic couplets and freely

* Of Austin, Texas. Her recent work includes her translation of Juan Ramón
Jiménez' *Platero y Yo* and her selection of his poetry.

paraphrased both Milton and Pope. I have forgotten how my essay began, but the ending said something like

> Weep, earthly Muse, with sorrow we are smitten:
> Even our themes are old before they're written.

To which Mr. Dobie affixed the comment "This one is not!" and added:

> If I so well could write heroic rhyme,
> I'd lecture in the pentametric line.
> But positively, all that I can say
> Is, with my thanks, Here, take your A.

ANGUS CAMERON*

Fellow countryman

When my sixteen-year-old daughter was a little girl she saw a picture of Frank Dobie on the back of the jacket of one of his books. It was a shot of him hunkered down by the fire of a hunting camp. That picture caught her imagination. Soon she had an inscribed glossy print of another favorite picture—"the one with the friendly, twinkly eyes" was the way she always referred to it. Frank Dobie had found another admirer. As she grew older she once asked me, "Why do you love him so much?" In a way this piece is an explanation for her.

I served as Frank Dobie's editor for five years when I was on the staff of Little, Brown & Company, his Boston publisher. While I had this privilege we published *The Longhorns, The Mustangs, A Texan in England, The Voice of the Coyote,* and *Ben Lilly.* Anyone who knows Frank Dobie and his works knows at once how much of an education that was for me, an ex-Hoosier sojourning in Boston. It has always seemed the truth of it was that Frank Dobie was my editor, for I know that I got more out of his unintentional revisions of me than he ever got out of my advices to him.

I have always looked back on a weekend spent high above the Devil's River as a time when the full rewards of friendship and professional relationship with Frank Dobie were most evident. Mister Frank was then writing *The Mustangs* and he had come to one of those periods, as writers and long distance runners always do, when the second wind was expected but had not quite arrived. He didn't really need advice; he needed someone interested in the same work to be

* Senior editor at Alfred A. Knopf, Inc., in New York City.

around for a couple of days. He needed someone to talk to, to read what he had written, to have the same high expectations for the remainder that he had. He wrote me that he had taken a cottage at the invitation of a friend of his in the power business, one of those used in later months as weekend and vacation spots for the employees of the company. He drove me out there from Eagle Pass. When we arrived, I found a comfortable cottage in which he had arranged on tables and boards laid on sawhorses the chapters of that fine, free book. He had said we'd bach it, but I didn't realize at first that we'd live off the land as well. The cottage was right at the brink of the high bluff; the dam was in sight; far below the Devil's River curled away from the foam at the bottom of the falls like a silver ribbon. It was February, winter in Boston, but the first edges of spring were showing in Rio Grande country. Later I came to understand fully what that spot meant to Frank Dobie—to any Texan for that matter. I came to realize how much that much water meant to a man who lived in a country that was dry. Back of the cottage lay the high dry country of South Texas. And Frank Dobie and his work were firmly imbedded in that piece of Texas nature.

For two and a half days we talked about mustangs, Cunninghame Graham and Bedichek, Texas lore, world literature, politics, people of both cultures, animals and birds, cacti, and, later, fishing. There, surrounded with the colors, sounds, and life of Texas nature, I experienced all of those qualities that make this unique man. Whether we were frying white bass we caught in the river below (with the rods and invitation and even bait of the brothers Erwin who were supplying a fish fry out of those abundant waters), or collecting a delicious white, gardenia-like bloom of a cactus which Mister Frank prepared as one would prepare green peas, or enjoying a pot of frijoles prepared by a Mexican friend, or finishing up a meal with juajillo honey, we seemed imbedded in local nature.

As a man close to nature, Frank Dobie is a sensualist. He likes good food and remembers vividly notable gustatory experiences such as those memorialized in his article *The American Gun.* He doesn't like substitutes and claims "there's nothing feebler than a milk-fed chicken" or "as tasteless as baby beef." "They've got no strength to them," he says. His fine relish of eating and drinking makes everything taste better in his presence. I know only one other man who

168

can, by the mere act itself, endow the pouring of a drink of whiskey with so much promise of forthcoming pleasure and good fellowship.

To me this sense of being a part of nature is one of the first qualities of Frank Dobie. He knows he is a creature of nature; he feels its immanence at all times; he is not alienated from it. This seems to me one of his first and basic qualities as a man. From it stem, I think, his peculiar art and character. He showed me a painted bunting and a canyon wren; he talked about the pack rat; he named the cacti for me. All of this was a natural by-product of his universal interest in life.

His "editing" of me continued when we talked about the book. His conversation on that occasion was a good example of how literature has "civilized" him, as he is wont to put it. As we went about our chores or sat down with a glass of Jack Daniel's and talked, he vented his frustration that he could not write about horses the way Cunninghame Graham had written about them on the pampas of the Argentine. He quoted phrases and paragraphs from *his* mentor as I listened raptly to mine. I couldn't imagine that anyone could catch the spirit of the horse as he had in his own manuscript, but *he* could imagine it.

On that same occasion this editor-of-life added another revision to me. In speaking of a book he had tried to read as a young man, but had never finished, he said:

Hell, I learned one thing not too long ago that I should have learned when I was twenty. Never try to force a book. If it can't talk back to you, or better make you talk back to it, don't feel guilty about it—put it aside. If it's a great book you'll just have to grow up to it, and you will if you keep yourself in motion. A man has to have a dialogue with a good book and with a lot of such books you just don't become man enough to read them with profit until you've grown up to them.

He once told me that the only way a man could "get civilized" was to realize as early as he could that his chief purpose in life must be "to become a contemporary of himself." He explained that for a number of years he had not been such a contemporary, that he had been too much a folklorist, not enough a modern man. "Yes, and I wasn't *free*," he said. "I was too much caught up with the olden times and not enough a man living in the present." He then explained to me how he had grown up, how he'd been foreman of his uncle's ranch, how he'd got a powerful interest in Texas folklore as a natural by-product of his life. "But I had got too narrow, too regional," he said. He explained how a man has to welcome change in life about him, change that may sometimes harshly conflict with his background, with his predilections. Of course, I was avid for more of that past and I got it as the years went by and in the process I learned something too about the relationship between regionalism and universality.

Like any good radical, Frank Dobie is a reluctant one. He values the past, but he has no use for those who worship it. He welcomes the future, however, and tries to influence it. As all know who have heard him make the air crackle with diatribe, both scornful and profane, or who have revelled in the cactus-thorny prose in the syndicated columns, he is a partisan, a tough in-fighter, and a great hater with a long memory. And his scorn can be heroic when it is directed against such good targets as a handful of ignoramuses trying to run a university as they would an oil drilling crew or a loud-mouthed demagogue like McCarthy trying to run the whole country. He smites hip and thigh against purveyors of lies, vulgarity, ignorance, venality, bigotry, and injustice. He is a staunch champion of beleaguered nonconformists and delights in a man under fire who takes a "go-to-hell" attitude towards those who are trying to intimidate him.

As an integral part of his struggle to become contemporary with himself, there is the parallel struggle to develop universality out of regionalism, a subject he later developed in full in a notable essay. His editing of me continued as he revealed how his trip to London during the war, when he served as exchange professor from The University of Texas to Cambridge University, had advanced the struggle toward contemporaneity. He spoke of "civilized man" in a way that few people understand it. He combines for my taste the best of a man who has become universal to the marrow by being regional to the bone.

Frank Dobie admires scholarship as much as any man I know. At the same time he abhors narrow academic outlooks with as much contempt as any man I know. His own ideals were to be found in his friends Bedichek and Webb because they were both men first and scholars second. The three of them make a formidable trio of Amer-

170

icans who have reflected a universal wisdom by knowing more about their home region than anyone else knows.

My own friendship with Frank Dobie began while I was the New York editor of his publisher. Through the late Raymond Everitt, the editor in chief of Little, Brown & Co., I had met him when assigned to do some editorial chore for him. The next time he came to New York he called me. "Angus," he said with that tone of half query he can get into his voice, "Charlie Everitt and I are having lunch to-morrow and we'd like you to join us." There began a number of these meetings. Charlie Everitt was friend, crony, and adviser of Mister Frank. "Hell, Charlie Everitt knows more about the sources of Western history than any professor I know." From his little bookshop on 57th Street, Charlie Everitt dispensed bourbon and information to a host of grateful and admiring scholars of Americana. These meals together were a delight to me. The last one we had with Mr. Everitt was during the war. Mister Frank was on his way out of the country, his destination unknown to all but a few people. I had got them together at the old Murray Hill Hotel, where we had dinner and spent the evening until Mister Frank took a plane to England. We knew about his exchange fellowship, and over drinks Mr. Everitt and I discovered that we had to convince Mister Frank that he could teach American history to British undergraduates. Mister Frank was doubtful, impressed as he was and as he should have been by the great scholarly tradition of the university whose faculty he was about to join. But Mister Frank's humility was a powerful thing. Finally, in a burst of impatience at our encouragement he said, "But, hell" ("hail" is the way it always sounds to me from Mr. D.), "what if one of those boys asks me about the Webster-Ashburton *Treaty?*"

Now I tell you what you do, Frank [Charlie Everitt said]. If you find yourself momentarily stumped by such a question, just remember that treaty had a clause in it about cod-fishing rights on the Grand Banks. This will remind you of water, which will remind you of liquids. Once you're there you can switch to anything liquid—bourbon, branch water . . . Hell, just tell them the story about the railroad engineer who was spitting champion of the state of Arkansas.

As we all know, Frank Dobie's sojourn at Cambridge was a triumph. There he and his tall tales and his tall hat and his interpretation of the history of England's ally became a legend. The first real-for-sure Westerner these boys, who had themselves grown up on stories of "cowboys and Red Indians," had ever seen, Frank Dobie became not just a successful teacher but an ambassador at large. He says the trip helped to civilize *him*, but the editorials in the London papers when he left England proved that the Texan in England had added more to them than he'd got even from their hallowed halls.

When sensitive critics begin to write about Frank Dobie's work, someone himself not too far removed from the great tradition may discover that the artistry of the work lies in its sensitive blend of the overtones of the teller of tales with the phrasing of the stylist who admires the formal beauties of the English language. Somehow the urban life does not develop tale tellers and yarn spinners. You have to have solitude, quiet, and a small audience of friends who share your life and work to develop the storyteller's art.

A friend once said to me that poetry in our times suffered because the rural idiom, the idiom of nature, was disappearing from the language. The further we get from nature, the poorer the language becomes. I'll let experts argue that one, but I do know that alienation from nature is something we can't afford and still remain whole, and neither can the language afford it. Rural men, men who have handled stock, who have been close to the land or to the frontier or to the wilderness, develop a way of talking which you don't hear very often these days. (Frost retained it and maybe that is one reason Frank Dobie admired him so much.) Frank Dobie has retained it. The verbal echo runs through his writing. The formal phrase is made rich by it.

As a lover of literature he always took a bibliophile's interest in his own books long after they had left the author's hand. As reader and collector himself he had a sound feeling for how a book should be made. When it came time to find an illustrator for *The Voice of the Coyote* and he was asked for advice, he put his finger on precisely the right man. "Olaus Murie knows more about how coyotes really look than any formal animal artist I know of." As all Texans know, *The Longhorns* was illustrated (one might say illuminated almost) at Mr. Dobie's request by the art of Tom Lea, who could draw a longhorn bull or a picture of Bigfoot Wallace sitting on a rail fence with equal evocation of the real thing. Once we were horrified way off there in Boston to discover that we had almost bought sheepskin

172

instead of cowhide for the cover of the de luxe edition of that same book. When we finally told Mr. Dobie how we had saved ourselves and him from such humiliation, he answered, "Romantics always *have* made too much of the rivalry between sheepmen and cow people, and besides I'll bet only an old bootmaker I know in Austin would have recognized the difference." I know he was glad we had discovered the mistake, but I realized how characteristic it was of him to poke fun at hackneyed notions about the West, perhaps in this case as much the result of Eastern fiction as Western faction.

Indeed, his love of the real West makes him impatient with the Wild West of romantics who have sopped up the "Western" notion from books and movies. Once while Mrs. Cameron and I were visiting Mrs. Dobie and him in Austin, he received a phone call. I gathered from his end of the conversation that he was talking with a newspaperman or journalist who wished to interview him. When I realized that he was about to turn them away because of our presence, I urged him to let them come on out. A research and photographic team from *Life* was doing a feature on The Real Cowboy. They wanted to get Frank Dobie's notions on this subject. He gently led them to more workaday ideas about the life of a modern cowhand. He joshed them a little when he discovered that they thought the cowboy worked more for the love of it than for the wages, and gave them a real steer when one of them queried, "Mr. Dobie, I understand that when you were a cowhand you stuffed your pants down into your boots. . . . Do you think the modern cowhand wears his pants on the outside of his boots because he's learned that he can better keep the dust and grit out in that way?" Mr. Dobie grinned, rumpled his white hair with a gnarled hand, and answered, "Well, no. I reckon these boys have noticed just like everybody else from all the Western moving pictures they see these days that their silhouette just naturally *looks* better with the pants outside the boot."

Always the teacher, the interpreter of the West and its lore, Mr. Frank gave a kindly interview to these two men. In their story they lost nothing of the flavor of the old west from having talked to J. Frank Dobie; they gained much of the reality of the present from his gentle humor and advice. He took them on a tour of his Charlie Russell prints and water colors. While he talked I noticed one of the visitors pick up a wood carving of a strange bird. He thought to ask about it but changed his mind. He should have followed his hunch,

173

for the carving was that of a roadrunner. Because I knew that Mr. Frank loved the roadrunner so much (and has named his place on Barton Creek *Paisano*), I had made it a point long before to learn more about this fine, free spirit of the brush country. I liked the fact that the Mexicans call this bird "paisano," fellow countrymen, and I felt that Frank Dobie's love of the roadrunner epitomizes his fellow feeling of kinship with nature. I discovered that this bird has a four-toed foot and two of its toes point forward, two point backward—equally divided then in passage between the past and the future. Wherever Frank Dobie sets his foot down now he is a contemporary of himself but his life points in two directions. Master of the finest traditions of our country's past, his spirit runs swiftly toward the future.

WILSON M. HUDSON

Love of life and freedom

In September of 1957 J. Frank Dobie was taken to Saint David's hospital in a serious condition. Just what was wrong we weren't told. Not much news cames to us. Knowing that Roy Bedichek, if anybody, would have some information, I paid him a visit. He was working in his garden.

"Yes, he is doing as well as can be expected, but is not out of danger. I've seen him. He's had to use an oxygen tent. He gave me that big smile of his and said, 'Hello, Bedi. I'm all lit up with life.' It's remarkable, just remarkable!"

Dobie had had a close call. For more than two weeks only Mrs. Dobie had been allowed to see him. Bedi was the first after her to go into his room. Dobie had been brought in from Cherry Springs, his place in the country, where he had spent two or three nights alone. Pneumonia had run up his pulse and put a strain on his heart. His strength had been low but his vital spark was strong. A month later he told the story himself in an essay called "Camping Beneath an Oxygen Tent." He spent many hours on the border of consciousness. "Down there in the deep well I saw hardly anything, heard hardly anything, remembered hardly anything that was not beautiful." One sound that he did hear was that of roosters greeting the day; it took him back to "a simple and kindly world of a long time ago."

Dobie has always loved life; never has he doubted or mistrusted it. He has loved freedom, which encourages life to develop and reach its fullest possibilities. And he has hated whatever thwarts or strangles the life of man, a creature compounded of body and mind.

175

He has loved literature as "the essence of life." He has waged war on academicians who are afraid of life and would treat literature as a thing apart, a lifeless world on paper. He cares not for the puny or precious in literature. The kind of writing that he likes best has vitality and gusto.

In 1931 he said, in an essay written for the Literary Guild to send out in connection with *Coronado's Children,* that "the qualities most lacking in American literature are flavor and gusto" and that these qualities existed in the pioneer stock of the Southwest, which was relatively free of Puritanical restraint. His most general statement about the necessity of putting life into art was made in 1960: "The one thing needful to all scholarship, as to all literature and art, is vitality." One of his latest statements came after Walter Prescott Webb's death in 1963: "The one thing needful for a writer is vitality of mind. Webb had it."

And Dobie has it too. He has sought subjects crammed with life and has presented them with gusto. Dobie has made frequent use of the word "gusto," a favorite of Hazlitt's in his critical essays. Dobie can forgive deficiency of form if vitality is present. In quoting N. A. Taylor's narrative of travels in Texas he said, "Taylor was young and in love with life. His writing is weedy, but it is full of gusto and honest sympathy for what he met."

Dobie became an English teacher because he fell in love with English poetry while a student at Southwestern University and wanted to communicate that love to others. After a boyhood on his father's ranch in Live Oak County he went to Alice to attend high school for two years so that he could go on to college. In his freshman year at Southwestern, Professor Albert Shipp Pegues's survey course in English poetry "transmuted the world" for the young Dobie. There were other courses with Pegues later and other good intellectual influences at Georgetown.

Immediately after graduation in 1910 Dobie got a job as a reporter for the *San Antonio Express* at $12 or $14 a week. He had such a good time writing that he was reluctant to go to Alpine in the fall, where he was to be principal of a school and to teach also. He was back at Southwestern from 1911 to 1913 as a teacher of English and secretary to the president. Then he spent a year at Columbia and earned an M.A. degree. He came to The University of Texas as an instructor in 1914, and left in 1917 for two years in the field artillery.

Back from France, he resumed teaching at the university; but he was dissatisfied and resigned in the spring of 1920.

While acting as Uncle Jim Dobie's majordomo on Los Olmos Ranch in La Salle County, Dobie would sometimes be visited at night by Santos Cortez, a vaquero who tired of his companions' unvarying talk about the work of the day. Santos told tales about deer, men, and ghosts. One night after Santos had gone it occurred to Dobie that he should collect "the tales of my folk and my land" as Lomax had collected cowboy songs. He now had a definite direction to take, and he has continued in this direction ever since, widening his horizon and gaining perspective as he went along.

During the year I spent on Los Olmos Ranch while Santos talked, while Uncle Jim Dobie and other cowmen talked or stayed silent, while the coyotes sang their songs, and the sandhill cranes honked their lonely music, I seemed to be seeing a great painting of something I'd known all my life. I seemed to be listening to a great epic of something that had been commonplace in my youth but now took on meanings.

In the fall of 1921 Dobie was again instructing at The University of Texas. He took over the editorship of the Texas Folklore Society, founded in 1909, and began to write down and to urge others to write down legends and tales about Texas.

The Legends of Texas was published in 1924; of the Society's books, as Dobie says, it has been "the most influential in opening the eyes of people to the richness of their own traditions." Bertha McKee Dobie, whom he had known at Southwestern and whom he married in 1916, assisted with the editing and contributed some legends also. She helped on all the other folklore publications that he edited. In later years she would sometimes teach for him while he was seeking material and writing. She has always been the first and most helpful reader of his books in manuscript.

Dobie's salary and rank were low, and since he did not intend to take a Ph.D. his prospects of advancement were not good. In the fall of 1923 he accepted the headship of the department of English at Oklahoma A. & M. in Stillwater. From Austin, Webb wrote in 1925, "We are both in a hole on this Ph.D. degree proposition." While at Oklahoma A. & M. Dobie had a stroke of luck, which he defines as being ready for the chance when it comes. E. H. Taylor of the *Country Gentleman* paid a visit to Stillwater and was introduced to

Dobie by Ed Hadley, a teacher of journalism. Over a bottle of smuggled tequila they talked, with the result that Dobie began to contribute to the *Country Gentleman*. First there was an article on cowboy songs and then two articles on the Old Time Trail Drivers' meeting held at San Antonio in 1924. Many more followed.

Leonidas W. Payne and H. T. Parlin of the English department, along with Professor Eugene C. Barker in history, persuaded President Splawn to bring Dobie back to Austin in the fall of 1925 with the rank of adjunct professor. This was the year when I entered the university and came to know by sight the man with the Western hat and the perpetual pipe. The senior professors in the English department weren't pleased to have Dobie back. Dr. Callaway was chairman; it was he who had advised Lomax years earlier to give up his interest in cowboy songs. Dobie had backing outside the department now, and he had a feeling of independence because he could earn money by writing what he wanted to. He began to stand up to Callaway, who had written treatises on the infinitive and participle in Old English and had a distaste for Dobie's articles. Dobie was not humble and meek, as he should have been. I have heard Dobie say this of Callaway: "Dr. Callaway thought everybody ought to have somebody to look up to and he was that somebody."

Dobie argued in 1927 that The University of Texas should have a real relationship to the history and traditions of the state, that like all great universities it should blend the universal and the local. He complained, justly, that some departments had "no more sympathy for the life of the Southwest than they have for life in Patagonia."

In 1929 Dobie published *A Vaquero of the Brush Country*, which was about his part of Texas and had as its starting point the life of John Young, whom Dobie talked with in Alpine. With another book on the way, *Coronado's Children* (1930), Dobie proposed and obtained, against opposition in his department, an advanced course of his own, Life and Literature of the Southwest. When the senior professors objected that the Southwest had no literature, Dobie replied, "It has plenty of life. I'll teach that." He was "on fire with the idea that genuine literature in this part of the world could come about only from an understanding of its life, lore and history."

Dobie's new course became the most popular elective ever given in the university. He presented the subject matter with vitality and gusto, but did not maintain that the Southwest had produced great literature. He wanted Texans to become aware of the traditions and materials which were theirs and which they might put to literary use. There should be a connection between a literature and its land of origin, he maintained, but this alone does not assure greatness. Regionalism is not enough in itself; there must be something wider. "Great literature transcends its native land," he said in 1936, "but none that I know of ignores its own soil." In recent years he has spoken out emphatically against a narrow regionalism: "Good writing about any region is good only to the extent that it has universal appeal." This statement was made in 1950. Ten years later he said, "Unless the regional has elements of the universal it is county-minded and is, therefore, damned."

The treasure legends that Dobie had written down for *The Legends of Texas* put him on a track that led to *Coronado's Children*. The selection of this book by the Literary Guild in 1931 and the attendant publicity made Dobie a nationally known figure. The press presented him as a cowboy and treasure hunter who had become a college professor and writer. Since *Coronado's Children* he has published fourteen books, and another, *Cow People*, is due to appear this fall. His magazine articles are numerous and he has written many prefaces to the books of others. For years he has provided weekly articles for certain Texas newspapers. In all of his books except *A Texan in England* (1945) he has dealt with the Southwest and the West, and also parts of northern Mexico. Even *A Texan in England* keeps coming back to the Southwest as W. H. Hudson's *A Hind in Richmond Park* returns again and again to the Argentine. Dobie has made the nation and the world conscious of the Southwest in tradition and story.

Dobie is not a folklorist or a historian but a storyteller. He has told hundreds of stories about pioneers, cowboys, cowmen, treasure seekers, longhorns, coyotes, mustangs, hunters, rattlesnakes, paisanos, and other indigenes of the land. A good story is a good story for him, whether it is reminiscence, anecdote, or folktale. He admits to having a "constructive memory"; that is, in recalling a tale he might improve it, make it better than it was originally. He loves to hear or tell a story. I have heard him say that he doesn't care how many times he hears the same story provided that it is good. On picnics he would say, "Bedi, tell us the story about the sow and the stalk of bananas" or something else, and listen in great enjoyment to what he already knew by heart.

As a young writer Dobie was wrapped up in "the pageantry of the past," to use his phrase. Once his mother said to him, "Son, why are you always looking backwards? You are acting like an old man." At that time he was not interested in contemporary problems and referred to the present only occasionally for the sake of contrast with the past. World War II brought him face to face with the modern world. In 1943 he was quoted as saying, "After living in a kind of storybook way, allied to the past, for many years, I have been forced by this war at last to become a contemporary with myself." After a year of teaching American history at Cambridge University, 1943–44, and a year of lecturing to American soldiers at Shrivenham and in Germany and Austria at the close of the war, he said, "I have come to think that perspective on any segment of life is as important as knowledge of and sympathy for that life, that wise evaluation of any where depends on knowledge of other wheres."

A *Texan in England* tells the story of Dobie's year at Cambridge. Before the Japanese surrendered I happened to see a copy in the officer's club at an air base where I was stationed near Memphis. I had not even known of the book's existence. I sat down and read through it without stopping. In England Dobie experienced a greater feeling of harmony with his total environment than he ever had known with American "civilization." He said he had thought that "the greatest happiness possible to a man . . . is to become civilized, to know the pageant of the past, to love the beautiful, to have just ideas of values and proportions, and then, retaining his animal spirits and appetites, to live in a wilderness where nature is congenial, with a few barbarians to afford picturesqueness and human relations." But such an ideal, he realized, was impractical in this shrinking world. He was in the midst of a real civilization and he liked it. The manners of the English, their attitude to life, their intellectual tolerance, all gave him serenity and a sense of freedom. And England gave him more—"a more critical attitude toward life."

The contrast was great when he returned to America with its noise, selling, self-trumpeting, and intolerance. The dark days of McCarthyism were upon us, and he found his own university in the hands of "a gang of fascist-minded regents." At a time when intellectuals and liberals were intimidated all through the land, Dobie was one of the few to speak out in this part of the world.

In an article entitled "Texans Need Brains," contributed to the *Texas Ranger,* a student magazine, Dobie made a notable statement. "I do not see," he said, "how anybody who cherishes liberty for others as well as for himself can be intolerant of ideas. I do not see how a vast country the life of which is bound up in vast complexities can be governed wisely except by intellectual ability. Liberty means liberty of mind as much as it means liberty to make a profit." The governor is reported to have said that Dobie should be "summarily dismissed" as a "disturbing influence." Dobie had been appointed a member of the United Nations Educational, Scientific and Cultural Organization; in the minds of some, this was enough to make him guilty of treason by association.

Dobie asked for a leave of absence in the fall of 1947, but was notified that he must return to the classroom or be severed from the university. When September 15 arrived he did not sign in, and his official relationship with the university was terminated. Thus the University lost one of the brightest lights ever to shine forth from the Forty Acres. The students marched in protest. They loved Dobie and what he stood for. The *Daily Texan* and the *Texas Ranger* have asked for and received articles from him since his severance. In 1950 the *Texan* reported that a movement led by Walter Webb and Alton Burdine to restore Dobie to the faculty was underway, but it came to nothing. Mody Boatright was also one of the leaders in the effort to bring Dobie back.

"Any strong-willed and strong-minded individual who does not fit the moulds determined upon for its members by a conventional society will sooner or later have his character attacked," said Dobie in 1936. This proved true when he began to speak out in the days of the McCarthy oppression. In April 1951 the House Un-American Activities Committee listed him as a sponsor of the Mid-Century Conference for Peace, said to be communist inspired. He defended himself by saying that he believed in peace and did not have time to investigate the membership of organizations backing causes which he approved of.

In these years Dobie spoke out with force and energy against the enemies of life and freedom. It was perfectly consistent for someone in love with life to hate whatever sought to stifle life. Once at Barton's

181

I quoted Burke on the subject of hate as related to love: "They will never love where they ought to love, who do not hate where they ought to hate." This he thought was good and repeated in later conversations. In 1956 he wrote, "Positive zest for life and positive opposition to the strangling of life go together." He said he wanted "the stranglers of life strangled." It is true that "the best books and the best pictures infuse life, add to life, are life," and it is wrong to demand, for prudish or political reasons, that they be removed from libraries and museums. Because the love of life has always been dominant in him, hatred of the enemies of life has left no scars on Dobie. "I confess to having had feelings of hatred at times, though life has been too bright and good and energy too precious to spend in maintaining hatred."

For the coronation of Queen Elizabeth the BBC asked the Department of State to help prepare a salute from America. Dobie was invited to take part in this salute. He appeared in a short sound film, telling three anecdotes to show similarities between Texans and Englishmen.

After Dobie had returned from abroad I was seeing him every day during the swimming season at Barton Springs. There was a period in the summer of 1951 when he was very tired. He had sent off the manuscript for *The Mustangs* and was feeling spent. He said he doubted that he would ever write another book treating the whole life of its subject. When the proofs began to come in, he cast off his fatigue and read them with satisfaction in the completion of a difficult task. Late one afternoon while we were drinking beer in his back yard after a swim, he said with a chuckle, "Wilson, I could get my Ph.D. with this book." He never did have a high opinion of degrees, because he had "seen so many sawdust brains with nothing else but degrees and so many active, well-informed, observing, witty, interesting brains without any degrees at all." In 1959 he wrote that the "Teutonic Ph.D. system" had "dehumanized the humanities in American colleges and universities."

Dobie is of course an intellectual with a wide range of knowledge and a great deal of wisdom. "First-class education is always intellectual," he has said. His count against Education spelled with a capital E is that it does not improve the mind. He wants no technicalities or pretenses mixed in with the training of the intellect.

The summer of 1957 was a fine one for swimming and talk at Bar-

182

ton Springs. Roy Bedichek would arrive at about three-thirty to take the heat of the sun on Bedichek's rock, and Dobie and I would come out about an hour later. Sometimes we would talk until the sun went down and then go somewhere for a beer and more talk. Any subject at all would draw Bedi and Dobie out, perhaps on different sides but most often in agreement. They would sometimes lock horns and push hard, because each knew his own mind and did not express lightly formed views. When Bedi had the bit of conversation in his teeth and was running away, Dobie would plunge into the cold water for a moment and then return.

We hated the juke box that would now and then blare out—another form of the "murder of silence" Dobie called it. We were incensed when the park department put up a sign reading "Zilker Springs." Why change the name of Barton Springs? Dobie told a story about a trial that he had attended in Georgetown while he was a student. Frank Taulbee was arguing a case against a man accused of moving a boundary marker to steal a strip of his neighbor's land. The lawyer for the defense quoted Plutarch several times in the course of his speech. Taulbee began thus:

Gentlemen of the jury, we have been hearing over and over what Plutarch says about this and what Plutarch says about that. Who is this man Plutarch, anyhow? I don't know. Perhaps some of you don't know. But I can cite you an authority that we all do know—the Good Book itself. Therein you'll find written these words: "Cursed be he that removeth the ancient landmarks, for the buzzards of the air shall pluck out his eyes."

That night Dobie found in his Bible a curse on the remover of ancient landmarks but it didn't correspond to Taulbee's version.

Towards the end of this same summer Walter Webb and Mody Boatright, nonswimmers, joined us in a picnic on Barton Creek below the bridge. There were other picnics for the five of us at other times and places, always with marvelous talk and hearty laughter. The conversation turned on serious matters too—the international situation, national and state politics, and the condition of the university.

After his bout with pneumonia in the fall of 1957 Dobie had to give up swimming at Barton's. There were too many steps to go up and down. Knowing how much he loved the sport, I gave him a color photograph taken from the high bank and showing the bottom through the transparent water.

I remember particularly well one trip to Cherry Springs, Dobie's place near Spicewood Springs. I think it was in early June 1958; the day was beautiful and the mountain pinks were blooming in the clay and limestone along the highway. I was driving. As we approached Bee Creek Dobie said, "It's a beautiful world, isn't it?" Bedi was on the back seat and didn't catch Dobie's remark. "Hunh? What's that?" he asked. "I said it's a beautiful world," Dobie repeated with some emphasis. "Oh, yes. Of course. I never doubted that," Bedi replied as if it were altogether unnecessary to tell him something that he had known well for a long time.

While Bedi fixed a green salad, I broiled a steak outside. Dobie, having to take things easy, stayed in the kitchen. I couldn't catch what they were saying, but I could tell that a good discussion was going on. Now and then I could hear Dobie say, "Now, Bedi, do you mean to tell me that—" And Bedi would say, "Dobie, you know there's not a thing in the world to that." At another time that day they had an energetic argument about the best way to prepare compost, Bedi standing up for his way and Frank for Bertha's, which she had learned from Lady Eve Balfour's *The Living Soil.*

After steak and salad we had a nap and then sat on the front gallery. Dobie's two horses had got into the yard and left their signs. He said, "Wilson, kick those droppings around so they'll do the grass some good." I kicked them around. This amused Bedi. "You don't have to do everything he says. I'd be durned if I'd kick manure around to fertilize his grass."

After a while we got in the car and drove to the springs. I wanted some of the little cherry trees to bring in to town. Dobie remained above while Bedi and I went down in the moist canyon with a shovel and a tow sack. Bedi pointed out the ones he thought easiest to dig up and even dug up one or two himself. He cupped damp earth around the roots and we put them in the wet sack.

Back at the house we sat on the porch again and rested with a can of beer in our hands. I remember very well two stories told by Bedi, both from life, and one by Dobie about the visit of a Yankee to a Rebel after the Civil War.

On May 21, 1959, the three of us were to go out to Paisano, a place nearer Austin that Dobie had bought after selling Cherry Springs. At about noon the phone rang. It was Dobie. "Wilson, do you know that

Bedi died this morning?" I was astounded. Only the day before, at six o'clock, I had seen him hale and hearty at Barton's.

Walter Webb's death came with great suddenness and shock too, on March 8, 1963.

Four of the little cherry trees that I brought home and transplanted have lived and grown to a height of six or eight feet now. One I named Roy, one Walter, and one Frank. The last one I have dared to name Wilson. It gives me great pleasure just to see them there, greening and blooming in the spring and gaily fluttering their leaves all summer.

"The wild flowers of a rainy spring and the grasses of a showery summer are good and beautiful and sufficient even though they vanish." This poetical sentence is Dobie's. It belongs to a man whose prose was first nurtured by the King James Bible. Life is transient but it is good just the same.

Once at Barton's after we had spoken of death as the completion of the biological process I asked Bedi point-blank about his attitude to death. "I know it's coming," he said, and finished humorously, "but I can't say that I am looking forward to it with any pleasurable anticipation." At another time he told me he had received a letter from Webb containing a complaint about "this tag end of life." He had written Webb and taken him to task. For the Bedichek number of the *Observer* Webb addressed a letter to his old friend in which he said that Bedi had taken a good deal of the sting out of his going by its suddenness—the way Bedi had wanted.

Two days after Webb's passing Dobie wrote this for the *Texan*: "Any man who has seen life and been a part of life wants to leave it before decomposing into a senile vegetable. Webb died standing up..."

Time and again Dobie urged Bedi to write his autobiography, and Bedi in return urged Frank to write his. I have taken over this urging now. I have heard Dobie say, and I feel sure he has said it in print somewhere too, that a writer should be greater than all of his books put together. This is true of Dobie, as fine and as extensive as his literary achievement is. No one can tell of his life as he can. His greatest book is yet to come. In fact, since 1950 he has published autobiographical essays sufficient in number to make a large volume, but when I urge him to put them in a book as "Chapters in an Autobiography" he replies that there is more that should go in—"the rest isn't written yet." In 1957 he announced in the *New York Times Book Review* that he was thinking of an autobiography but foresaw a problem. He took pleasure in writing about his boyhood, youth, and early manhood (the far away and long ago, the pageant of life), but was not anxious to deal with the clashes and controversies (the critical side), nor did he want to omit them. "I have come to value liberated minds as the supreme good of life on earth. The subject is very complex and proliferates into many areas of living. I should not be satisfied with an autobiography that did not bear witness to my passionate belief in freedom of thought."

Freedom of thought! The poem that closes *The Mustangs* is the finest poem on freedom in the language, an ever-living testimony to Dobie's devotion to freedom. This I knew when I heard it recited by Angus Springer at Southwestern on Dobie Day in 1952.

> I see them running, running, running
> From the Spanish caballadas to be free,
> From the mustanger's rope and rifle, to keep free,
> Over seas of pristine grass, like firedancers on a mountain,
> Like lightning playing against the unapproachable horizon.
>
> I see them standing, standing, standing,
> Sentinels of alertness in eye and nostril,
> Every toss of maned neck a Grecian grace,
> Every high snort bugling out the pride of the free.
>
> I see them vanishing, vanishing, vanishing,
> The seas of grass shriveled to pens of barbwired property,
> The wind-racers and wind-drinkers bred into property also.
>
> But winds still blow free and grass still greens,
> And the core of that something which men live on believing
> Is always freedom.
>
> So sometimes yet, in the realities of silence and solitude,
> For a few people unhampered a while by things,
> The mustangs walk out with dawn, stand high, then
> Sweep away, wild with sheer life, and free, free, free—
> Free of all confines of time and flesh.

Here's to life! Here's to freedom! And here's to Dobie, who loves them both!

186

JOHN HALLER

I helped Frank Dobie cut down a tree

Although I never attended one of Dobie's classes, I met him for the first time when he was a professor and I was a student at The University of Texas. At that time I wandered about Austin with an axe on my shoulder and knocked on doors wherever there were trees that needed to be cut down. Such a tree stood in Dobie's yard, and I knocked on the door. As good luck would have it, he was at home, answered the summons himself, made a trade with me, and in a few minutes we were busy cutting down the tree together.

A newcomer to Austin, I knew nothing of Dobie, and he knew nothing of me. Although instructor and student in the same department, neither of us realized the fact. Hence without any preconceived notions on either side, we cut away diligently at the tree, and half a day later, by the time we had it cut up into firewood, we were friends. Not until several weeks later did I find out who Dobie was.

This incident throws much light on the man's character. Unpretentious, modest, and unassuming at all times, he consorts with his fellow men on their level. How many other English professors, of much lesser merit but much larger sense of self-importance, would have calloused their hands with an axe-handle? How many would have fraternized with a passing door-knocker? Frank Dobie would, and did, and does, and in this fraternization with the ordinary man lies his strength.

Many literary people fraternize in the same spirit in which rich people go slumming. They condescend, they make a great sacrifice with perhaps the hope of picking up a little local color or stumbling on some material for a story. There is nothing of this in Frank Dobie. If he fraternizes, he does so because of genuine democratic instincts. He enjoys visiting with people of every social rank; ranchers, cow-punchers, cedar-cutters, Mexicans, clerks, taxi-drivers. He likes anything and anybody that is genuine, because he himself is genuine. What a difficult thing it must be to remain one's self as the world persists in puffing one up, and what a charming thing is simple naturalness in those rare men who have been able to keep it!

A year or so after I came to know him, Dobie left the University for a number of reasons, chief of which was his attitude of protest against the firing of President Homer Rainey. At about the same time I left to go into professional tree surgery. In this capacity I was to meet Dobie over and over again, working on the trees at his residence on Park Place and at his ranch south of town.

There are few better ways of seeing a person as he actually is than by having business dealings with him. If anywhere a man shows up his true colors, it is when his pocketbook is involved. As a business-man, Dobie is no fool. He knows values, and wants to know ahead of time what he gets for his money and how much it is going to cost; moreover, he has a way of asking disconcerting questions that would make things uncomfortable for anyone disposed to cheat him. But he never takes unfair advantage or strives to exploit labor in any way. If he feels that he cannot afford to have the work done, he says so. On one occasion when I told him I could do some work for a certain price but that I would just barely make ends meet on it, he said, "Don't do it. I don't want you to lose money. I want you to *make* money. Otherwise, how can you stay in business? Let's wait a few months until I sell a piece of property. Then I'll pay you what the job is really worth." We waited, he got the money, authorized me to do the work, and paid me what he had promised.

Mr. Dobie spent $550 with me for working on a group of live oak trees on some acres he owns along the San Antonio Highway. He does not live on the land, and he draws no revenue from it beyond cheap rent for an old cheap house. He had the work done simply because of regard for the trees, because it hurt him to see them un-attended. Since he was born and reared among mesquites and live oak trees, these trees are for him in a sense a symbol of the Southwest. He loves the live oak, and when he sees its branches outlined against the sky, he feels the same emotions that other men feel at sight of their country's flag rippling in the breeze. Can anyone doubt his feelings for nature? Although many men love nature, how many are willing to spend $550 on a group of trees in the middle of a pasture?

MODY BOATRIGHT*

A mustang in the groves of academe

In Texas Folklore Society Publication II (1923), the first of the series
he edited, J. Frank Dobie identified himself this way in his notes on
the contributors: "J. Frank Dobie, editor of the present volume, was
born and reared on a ranch in the Texas border country, and although he is now an instructor in The University of Texas, he will
always belong to the range." There is no reason to assume that Dobie
was unaware of the implications of this statement: that there was a
conflict, not to say an incompatibility, between the range and the
grove, or at least he had found it so in Texas, and that his primary
loyalty was to the range: its history, its people, its myths and legends,
and its traditions of freedom he was later to symbolize by the mustang. The statement was prophetic of a long career as teacher,
scholar, writer, who, never provincial, never merely picturesque, was
chiefly concerned with the matter of the Southwest.

Dobie had graduated from Southwestern University at Georgetown, had served a year as high school teacher in Alpine, and returned
to Georgetown as secretary to the president. He received the M.A.
from Columbia in the spring of 1914, and in the fall became instructor
in English at The University of Texas. In 1917 he went to war, and
when he came back, he had a hard time deciding whether to be a
teacher or a ranchman. The teacher won out, and he returned to the

* Professor of English at The University of Texas at Austin and author of
many books and studies on folklore.

university. He admired John Lomax's collection of cowboy ballads and had set for himself the immediate goal of collecting the legends of Texas. Stith Thompson in 1916 had brought out the first annual publication of the Texas Folklore Society, which had been organized by Lomax and Professor L. W. Payne in 1909. Dobie had paid his dues and learned, not that he had been speaking prose all his life, but that he had been hearing folklore ever since he could remember. At that time the professors of English, in a laudable but mistakenly rigid attempt to improve the staff, required the Ph.D. as a condition for promotion above the rank of instructor. Dobie refused to take the degree.

It is doubtful whether any university at that time would have accepted a dissertation on such a subject as legends of Texas. Harvard might have. The ballad scholars there had given Lomax the moral and financial encouragement he needed to collect the cowboy songs and had approved a dissertation by Stith Thompson on folktales of the American Indians. But had even the liberalized doctoral programs typical of the best graduate schools of the present been available, my guess is that Dobie would not have been interested. He has said repeatedly that the usual procedure in writing a dissertation is taking bones out of one graveyard and putting them in another, a conclusion Dr. Johnson had come to many years before about the writing of books. Furthermore the doctoral program had been imported from Germany, and in Dobie's book anything imported from Germany was more than likely to be bad. Conversely, anything imported from England was more than likely to be good. His ideal of higher education is exemplified by the British universities, where the reading is more diversified, less emphasis is placed on formal research, and the terminal degree is the M.A. Also, he agreed with Emerson, his favorite American writer, that whoso would be a man must be a non-conformist. He would get along without a badge in which he saw little honor.

Temporarily he paid for his nonconformity. Still an instructor in 1923, he went to Oklahoma A. and M. College at Stillwater as head of the department. In 1925 he was called back to The University of Texas as adjunct professor under conditions that indicated tenure and advancement, contingent, of course, upon his continued productivity. In approving Dobie's appointment the president of the University acted upon a minority report of the professors. I have only an outline of the debates and procedures as they were related to me many years later by some of the men who had participated.

The spokesman for the majority was senior Professor Morgan Callaway, who raised no personal objection to Dobie, but held that unless he took the degree he should not be promoted, and that unless promotion was open to him, he should not be recalled to the staff.

The opposition of R. H. Griffith was of a different sort. He once told me, I think for my own benefit, that Dobie was trying to perpetuate the very thing a university should educate its students away from. He seemed to think that an interest in Texas longhorns was somehow incompatible with an interest in *Paradise Lost*; or that before one could properly appreciate *The Rape of the Lock*, he must be refined beyond any serious interest in vernacular culture. At one time he must have had a plan for Dobie's redemption. He stopped him on the campus one day and said, "Dobie, I'll tell you what you ought to do." But Dobie never learned what he ought to do. With a minimum of reverence for age and baldness, he indicated that he was capable of running his own life.

The academic honors that have come to him since he became adjunct professor in 1923 have amply vindicated his independence and his determination to devote his time and his talents to the matter of the Southwest. He became professor in 1933. He has lectured widely on American university campuses. He has held Rockefeller, Guggenheim, and Huntington fellowships. Perhaps his highest academic acclaim came in 1943, when he was invited to Cambridge University as visiting professor of history and awarded an M.A. degree, the citation of which reads in part, *"De bobus longicornibus quod ille non cognivit, inutile est allis cognoscere"* (What he does not know about longhorns is not worth knowing). In so far as I know, Dobie was not displeased with the words *bobus longicornibus*. Only a minority of the trail drivers of Texas would have understood their significance, but the animal they knew. He is of the matter of the Southwest.

That Dobie went to Cambridge as professor of history is not surprising. If the matter of the Southwest did not fall into conventional forms and categorical disciplines, so much the worse for the forms and disciplines. He would follow themes. His range was unfenced.

He has always insisted that "the University of Texas should be *of* Texas as well as *in* Texas; that it should express the genius of the

192

land, reflect its traditions and interpret its life," even in its physical setting. That is the reason he has found much that displeased him on the campus. The landscapists seemed determined to get rid of all native plants along with the natural contour of the land. "They planted undeviating lines of prostrate junipers, but thank God, some mesquite trees came up anyway." They also decorated the entrance to the mall with a Coppini fountain, "a conglomerate of a woman standing up, with arms and hands that look like stalks of Spanish dagger; of horses with wings on their feet, aimlessly ridden by some sad figures of the male sex, and various other inane paraphernalia. What it symbolizes probably neither God nor Coppini knows." On the other hand, the Proctor mustangs descending the hill in front of the museum delight the soul. They belong. The cattle brands that decorate Garrison Hall also belong, but not the signs of Zodiac on the old library building. No structure on the campus reflected the genius of the land better than the Home Economics building. Its architecture "suits the purposes of the building, the climate of Austin, the ground on which it is erected, and the traditions of the state." The Tower, on the other hand, "would fit any university 'of the first class' anywhere in America, that aspired to be a huge and huger factory for turning out degrees." He suggested that the tower be laid on its side. His suggestion was not acted upon, and he refused to move in along with the rest of the English department. Old B Hall remained his headquarters as long as he was on the staff.

A University of Texas and not merely in Texas would show proper respect for Texas books. It would not only acquire them, it would house them appropriately. In 1938 Dobie protested that the Texas Collection was housed and administered as an appendage to the Latin American Collection. He thought that the university should care "at least as much" for the Texas Collection "as it cares for the books of the Queen Anne reign . . . or the books on Mexico and South America." He proposed "a corner furnished in native woods, and decorated with pictures by Russell, Remington, Dunton, and other western artists. A corner eloquent, beautiful, interesting—a corner belonging to the land and expressive of it—a corner that would through its influence pervade the whole university and the whole state—a corner forever Texas." The Texas Collection is now adequately housed in the old library building, rechristened the Barker History Center. It contains collections of range paintings by Frank

193

Raugh and a Remington sculpture. Dobie's private collection of some seven thousand volumes is being acquired by the University and is being moved to the Southwestern Rooms of the New Humanities Center. But the Corner Forever Texas has not materialized.

He saw and still sees no place in a University of Texas or of anywhere else for professors of Education (written with a big E). His ingenuity in finding ways to bring these "unctuous elaborators of the obvious" into a discussion of any subject is remarkable. His experience as a high school teacher reminds him that he had to take a course in education in order to get a license to teach. All he can recall being taught in the course is that if the room is too hot, raise the windows; if it is too cold, put them down.

A University of Texas and not merely in Texas would in its courses give some attention to books pertaining to the state and region. Dobie's conviction on this point was no doubt strengthened by the fact that some time he had had to read from the works of Cotton Mather and Jonathan Edwards, and in these worthy theologians, he had found little of literary merit and little pertinent to life as he had known it. There were more significant writers of our own region. He proposed to offer a course in the "Life and Literature of the Southwest." The course was approved and first offered in the spring of 1930. In regular and summer sessions he gave it seventeen times to a total of 1596 students in classes ranging in enrollment from 54 to 196. He had to have help in reading his papers, and I was his helper in 1930 and I think again in 1932. His students came from all departments, but especially from English, history, and journalism. He welcomed the journalists, among whom he found some excellent students, but he often scolded them for their fragmentary paragraphs, and he let them know that he thought taking a multiplicity of courses in journalism was a waste of time that could better be spent on more substantial subjects.

He was not a generous giver out of A's and B's. He read every final examination paper himself. When he had read one, he would ponder a moment and put down a number expressing his judgment on the performance. The gradations were minute. He might put down 76 for one student and 77 for another.

The students who took the course were attracted by the subject and the man, one of the few great teachers I have known. I attended many but not all his lectures. He would come into the classroom with a battered briefcase stuffed with books. The class would be reading, let's say, Andy Adams' *The Log of a Cowboy*, and Dobie would be prepared to talk about stampedes. He would give accounts from oral sources, retelling incidents he had heard from George Saunders, Ab Blocker, and Sug Robertson. He would read from *Trail Drivers of Texas*, from James Cook's *Longhorn Cowboy*, and so on until all aspects of the subject had been illustrated; why the cattle stampeded, the way they ran, the way they were controlled, and the qualities and emotions of the men who followed them through thunder, lightning, hail, and rain. He talked and read with unaffected animation, making no effort to conceal his pleasure, which was enhanced by the pleasure obvious in the faces of the students.

It used to be said that the students were not taking a course in the Life and Literature of the Southwest: they were taking a course in Frank Dobie. I suppose that any course is in some sense a course in the instructor. Otherwise an impersonal teaching machine had just as well replace him. But this was true of Dobie's course to a greater extent than of some of the other popular courses. He justified the course partly on the ground that every student was entitled to his own heritage, but how deeply he considered the heritage of a student born and reared in Dallas is open to question. He selected those parts of the Texas and Southwestern heritage that he found most interesting and valuable. He paid little attention to the traditions of the Old South, either tidewater or upland, and popular urban culture bored him. He once said he regretted that automobiles had been invented. Automobiles, however, are a necessity in present-day life. Jukeboxes are wholly without justification. Once on our way to El Paso he, Frank Goodwyn, and I stopped in Sonora to eat. It is goat country, and he had his heart set on a dinner of *cabrito*. At several restaurants we found no *cabrito*. Then we drove across the tracks to a Mexican place and gave our order. We were the only Anglos in the place. Before our plates arrived, a customer put a coin in a slot, and out came not "El Toro Moro," not "El Corrido de Kansas," not even "'Home on the Range," but some such thing as "Pistol Packing Mama," or "Mr. Mississippi." I was glad that Dobie wasn't armed.

In preparation of the course Dobie mimeographed a thematically arranged reading list, for which he was soon receiving so many requests that he published it as a thin book titled *A Guide to the Life and Literature of the Southwest*. He enlarged it from time to time by

195

adding new titles and expanding his comments until it reached two hundred pages in the edition of 1956. The book sold in stores to the public who read, but one reason for the demand was that courses modeled on Dobie's were being introduced in other institutions. They are now given in practically all the senior colleges in Texas and in the universities of New Mexico and Arizona. I have no figures on the enrollment past and present in these courses, but I suspect the number would exceed ten thousand. I further suspect that the interest aroused in these students has had something to do with what Edward Weeks of the *Atlantic Monthly* has called the Texas Renaissance. When Henry Nash Smith went to Harvard to take a Ph.D. in the newly inaugurated interdisciplinary program in American studies, he reported that the only course faintly resembling the Harvard programs was Dobie's course initiated many years earlier at Texas. In each themes were pursued through whatever forms and disciplines could illuminate them.

Dobie became editor of the Texas Folklore Society in 1922 and remained in that position until 1942. He edited fifteen numbered publications and four books in the Society's Range Life Series. During his twenty years as editor he, more than any other man, shaped the policies of the Society. His interest in folklore is humanistic. Upon his retirement from the editorship in 1942 he said, "I care next to nothing for the science of folklore, which some scholars reverence and which seems to consist of the tedious process of finding out, through comparisons and analogies, that nothing new exists under the sun." He did, however, publish a number of analytical articles. Perhaps I have published more than he did, but throughout the series there is what one reviewer called "a middle course between the cold bare bones of scientific investigation sometimes identified as folklore, and the outcroppings of sentiment offered by the amateur members of folklore organizations." Undoubtedly the Texas Folklore Society is the leading state society in America, and has made its influence felt nationally. In 1962, MacEdward Leach, retiring president of the American Folklore Society, took the members to task for writing only for each other and suggested that they could profitably emulate the Texans.

But the qualities that drew praise from the humanists drew condemnation from a few of the "scientists," who found Dobie deficient in "scholarship." He himself once remarked that he did not know why

196

he took an M.A. degree. "I was just drifting," he said. "I certainly was
not inclined to be what academicians call 'scholarly'." In this context
"academicians" does not include every member of the academic community, only those, a majority no doubt, whose scholarship he found
dull or insignificant, particularly those who, he thought, murdered to
dissect. As early as 1925 he expressed a creed from which he never
deviated when he suggested that the Texas Folklore Society adopt
for a "constitutional bedrock" a statement of William Butler Yeats:

> The various collectors of Irish folklore have, from our point of view, one
> great merit, and from the point of view of others, one great fault. They have
> made their work literature rather than science, and told us of the Irish
> peasantry rather than of the primitive religion of mankind, or whatever else
> the folklorists are on the mad after. To be considered scientists they should
> have tabulated their tales in forms like grocers' bills—item the fairy king,
> item the queen. Instead of this they have caught the very voice of the
> people, the very pulse of life.

Dobie thought that "Of all forms of human expression, folklore is
the most sensitive to environment. It reflects the temperament, the
ideals in heroes and clowns, the occupations and the ways of life of
the folk who weave their lore and transmit it. It is, indeed, the autobiography, unsigned and unconscious, of a people."

There are many approaches to the study of folklore, but they all
boil down essentially to two. One is to consider the lore in relation to
its local cultural context. The other is to extract the item under consideration from its social setting and treat it in one of several ways—
as a metaphysical entity, as a psychological phenomenon, or as a
variant of an item common to several times and places.

The latter method was the one employed by L. W. Payne in an
article which Dobie published in 1930, with this editorial comment:

> He seems to be saying that the collections should lead to monographic
> disquisitions on the historical and ethnographic evolution of each particular
> song with particular attention to its borrowing from other songs. Doctor
> Payne's point of view certainly has its rights. . . . But, personally, I had
> rather hear Doctor Payne sing his famous song about 'the bust-up down in
> Bell [County]' than read his disquisition.

He wanted the Society "not only to gather and record the folklore of
the region, but to make the people of the region comprehend and

enjoy it." The presentation of folklore, then, is an art and not a science.

These statements were made with special reference to folklore, but they apply equally to all of Dobie's writing. And in all the books he has written, as distinguished from those he edited, folklore is only a part. They contain among other things history, biography, natural history, descriptions of nature, and vivid sketches of character, addressed to all intelligent readers, not merely to scholars. Dobie has never written a novel. Nevertheless Carl Van Doren felt that he should be mentioned in his book *The American Novel.* "Dobie hunted not the treasure," he says, "but the treasure-hunters, traveling anywhere to hear their fanatic proofs that legendary hoards must exist, their agile explanations why they had not come to light. Stories about buried treasure are always magical. The magic of Dobie's stories gains more than it loses from the shrewd, humorous, reasonable telling."

There is no lack of scholarship back of this art. In a buried treasure story a reader would not find motif and tale-type numbers or a discussion of the story in relation to similar stories from other times and places. He would find it related to its own cultural setting. Back of this were hours in libraries and archives, interviews with oral informants, and a look at the terrain. And the sources would be there for anybody who wanted to look them up.

When the regents of the University, all appointees of W. Lee O'Daniel and Coke Stevenson, attempted to purge the department of economics for departing from the "true" economics and initiated a series of events that led to the firing of President Rainey on November 1, 1944, the immediate resignation of three regents and the subsequent resignation of three more, and the retirement of Coke Stevenson from politics, Dobie was in England, and for this reason played a less conspicuous role in the fight for academic freedom than he would have had he been in Texas. Like Thomas Jefferson, one of his heroes, he had declared war on every form of tyranny over the human mind. Censorship of the student newspaper, the *Daily Texan,* had been a recurrent issue. If left free, student journalists are likely to publish something offensive to somebody in the power structure, and when they do, presidents and regents show concern. On every occasion Dobie spoke out in behalf of the students. He seldom wrote out-and-out political articles, but in writing about rattlesnakes he

198

could by indirection link them in an unflattering way with the governor. He could take to task a member of the legislature who proposed to introduce a bill closing the university to students from other states, on the grounds that they occupy housing needed for Texans and "in the more important place, they bring new ideas." "Yet," said Dobie, "there are few people who need ideas more than Texans do." As he was about to leave for England in 1943, he said, "When I get ready to explain homemade fascism in America, I can take my examples from the State Capitol of Texas. A politician like John Lee Smith [the lieutenant governor] is what I mean by a homemade fascist." Coke Stevenson had said that Dobie was a trouble maker and that he should be summarily dismissed. By the spring of 1947 Stevenson was no longer governor, and there had been changes in the board of regents. Factual records do not specify motives, and I do not know whether or not the regents were out to get Dobie. The rule under which his connection with the University was terminated is often called the Dobie Rule, but chronology does not indicate that it was passed specifically to dismiss him without overt violation of the tenure rule. The "Dobie Rule," the gist of which is that "except in very unusual circumstances, such as military service or prolonged illness, a leave of absence . . . will not be extended beyond two academic years," passed the first reading at a meeting of the board on November 16, 1946, and its final reading on January 10, 1947. Dobie, who had been on leave for two years, in April, 1947, applied for an extension of his leave through the fall semester of 1947–1948, giving as his reasons that he was committed to complete a book-length manuscript and that he was suffering from cedar fever which he could relieve only by a temporary residence away from Austin. The professors of English recommended that the leave be granted for reasons of health, and Dean H. T. Parlin concurred in the recommendation. On September 18 Professor L. L. Click wrote President Painter that the professors of English saw no reason to change their recommendation of April 28. On the same day, apparently after a conference with President Painter, Professor Click wrote that Dobie was unwilling to return to duty with his teaching assignment reduced to give him more time for work on his book. On September 23, Click again wrote the president, saying that Dobie had not returned to duty and that he had no intention of doing so. His name was deleted from the budget and the deletion was confirmed by the regents on

October 24. He had not reached the age of retirement, and hence under a rule drafted not by the regents but by a committee of the general faculty, he is ineligible for the status of professor emeritus. A recommendation of the professors of English that an exception be made was not approved.

His achievements since 1947 have been gratifying. Although long concerned with the matter of the Southwest, he had never been any more provincial than any writer who writes about the environment he knows best. I once said that a good regional writer deals with the universal as it is modified by the culture of a region. Dobie has done this, and those of us who have known him for a long time have noted a gradual increase in the emphasis on the universal.

At seventy-five he is still a fighter, though not an indiscriminate one. His particular enemies are self-appointed censors of textbooks and libraries and officials who listen to them; university officials who suppress plays; news media that suppress and distort the news—in short anybody whom he suspects of trying to exercise tyranny over the human mind.

HENRY NASH SMITH*

An enemy of reactionary demagogues

Frank Dobie has two widely different public personalities. One of them is a personification of the Old West, a picturesque and harmless figure out of the past. The other, belonging very much to the present, is a powerful controversialist with a zest for speaking his mind on economic and political issues. The two roles seem contradictory because the Old West as it figures in popular culture is a kind of icon of conservatism. Like the Old South of moonlight and magnolias, the legendary frontier of Santa Fe trail and cattle range offers an imaginary escape from the machines and regulations and red tape that envelop us. We like to dream of a big country with no fences where a man had room to breathe; and by some accident or alchemy of public-relations engineering, the glamor and nostalgia of this dream of the past have become linked in the public mind with the economic individualism of big business and the hatred of the federal government that is the one unifying emotion of right-wing radicals. Thus according to the stereotypes, Dobie ought to be either a non-political antiquarian or a super-patriotic defender of big business.

The truth is notoriously otherwise. For thirty years he has been a highly vocal enemy of reactionary demagogues and a defender of labor unions and of many unpopular causes. What the Western tradition means to him is totally different from what it is taken to mean in popular culture. The freedom he associates with early days in Texas and the Southwest is the freedom of men and women to resist

* Chairman of the Department of English at the University of California at Berkeley, the author of two books, and the editor of many others.

all coercive forces, including the pressures exerted by rich men and the demagogues who serve them. The kind of freedom he has celebrated, directly or indirectly, in a dozen books is not the kind of abstraction processed into slogans by public-relations experts but a quality of the experience of actual human beings in immediate contact with a sun-parched earth—its dust and heat and relentless distances, its austere plants and lean animals. This world—historical or fictive, as you will—has little place for the profit motive or the imperatives of getting ahead. Again and again Dobie's characters remind one of Whitman's lines about animals: "not one is demented with the mania of owning things." Even the obsession with buried treasure that is the unifying thread of *Coronado's Children* is curiously non-commercial. Dobie's desert dreamers wear out their lives in bondage to visions of gold and silver, minted into archaic coins or cropping out in ledges of almost pure metal, but the treasure they lust for could never be converted into digits entered on the books of a national bank in a forty-story skyscraper.

Nor does Dobie's recreation of the Old West validate the visual symbols of the past that are current in our day. His cowboys—some of them—wear ten-gallon hats and high-heeled boots, but this equipment has only a tenuous connection with the Stetsons in the checkrooms of expense-account restaurants or the ornate footwear resting on the accelerator pedals of air-conditioned sedans. It is particularly instructive to think of a book like *The Longhorns* in connection with two recent movies that draw upon vestiges of the cattle culture in contemporary life. *Hud* presents the transition from the West of saddlehorse and Winchester to the West of oil leases and Cadillac convertibles in terms almost too simple and direct, but the film brings a telling indictment against a set of attitudes often linked with the West in present-day folklore. The insolvent physical grace and masculine swagger of the protagonist in his cow-country garb are fully congruous with his indifference to all values except his own crude desires. In the memorable last scene he has in effect killed his father (representative of the integrity of older ways) and has come into possession of the ranch. But the diseased cattle are dead and buried, and Hud himself is cut off from relations with any human being. In this fable individualism, with a Western coloring, is identified with neurosis.

The other film I have in mind—*Dr. Strangelove*—makes an equally pointed but more ambiguous use of Western symbols. The pilot and commander of an eight-engine jet plane armed with an arsenal of nuclear bombs wears cowboy boots and has a vividly Southwestern accent. When he receives his radio orders to bomb a Russian missile installation, he performs a ritual act like that of a Japanese Samurai donning the white robe in preparation for hara-kiri. He takes his Stetson from the safe containing the code books and puts it on his head before issuing the orders that prepare the crew for their final mission. The film ends with the pilot riding a bomb down through the opened doors of the bomb bay, waving his hat like a bronco-buster in a rodeo. Whatever else this disturbing final sequence may mean, it makes the cowboy pilot represent a whole set of American attitudes toward the Cold War, and suggests that, wrenched from his historical contest, the protagonist of the Saga of the Saddle can become an agent executing with *élan* the orders of an insane general of the Strategic Air Command.

Dobie's West has as little relation to this cold-war hysteria as it has to "private enterprise" and influence-peddling. His vision of the past is permeated by a concern for human beings that has been leached out of the fossilized Western symbols preserved in contemporary popular culture. Let me say it again: Dobie affirms the concrete experience of human beings in physical contact with the earth and air, and with other human beings. The tradition he celebrates has nothing to contribute to contemporary ideologies of the business system. If his two public personalities conflict, the paradox lies not in his attitudes, but in the perversion of the tradition of the Old West by contemporary society.

H. MEWHINNEY

He has never been an exile

The difference between Frank Dobie and most other authors who have written during our century is simply that Dobie is a full-grown man.

In our day one of two fates has almost inevitably befallen the artist.

He may exile himself and become an intellectual and emotional alien, even though he continues to live among his fellow-tribesmen and fellow-demensmen. And here we have all those oddball doctrinaires who are now writing in France, the Americans who write for the *Nation* with the full confidence of Job's comforters that wisdom shall die with them, the others who write those airy and graceful confections of nothing in particular for the *New Yorker*. The heartiness or even the vulgarity of Fielding or of Smollett is gone. Addison, and Steele, and Dr. Johnson were sure that they were conversing with their fellowmen and even instructing them. That confidence exists no longer, unless perhaps Walter Lippmann has a little of it.

Or the artist may discover how to please the audience and proceed to do just exactly that. Consider the unctuousness of the *Saturday Evening Post* or of the *Reader's Digest*. Consider the phoniness of the *Cosmopolitan*. Or, for that matter, consider even so accomplished a story-teller as John O'Hara. Somebody said that even the scullions in Balzac have genius. Well, even the most flamboyant and expensive harlots, even the most ponderous tycoons that one finds in the pages of O'Hara somehow manage to be deplorably dull.

Or take the tally a little farther. Consider Ernest Hemingway, who won a Nobel prize. Two things are chiefly notable. The first is the marvelous narrative technique. The physical event becomes extraordinarily vivid. And yet the skill is no greater than that of Kipling in such stories as "The Drums of the Fore and Aft" or "The Undertakers." Kipling was the man who had little sense enough to exhort us solemnly to take up the white man's burden. And similarly we at last discover that Hemingway's other notable quality is that his outlook is that of an uneasy eighteen-year-old boy, trying to put up a bold front after he has read Darwin, Spencer, and very likely Jack London. Or, when he hunts antelopes in Africa or tries to catch a big fish at sea, he is merely another trophy-seeking city dude, even though an accomplished one. There is even some resemblance to that other fighting man, Cassius Clay.

This is not saying much about Dobie, is it? Well, it is saying at least that Mr. Frank is real. That he has loved the out-of-doors without trying to impress himself upon it, without trying to see how big a moose or how big a bear he could shoot, and has still roped and saddled many a horse in the early morning and smelt the smoke of many a campfire at night.

He has never been an exile. He has been as ready to speak his mind about what was going on around him as Emerson or Lowell ever was. And quite a number of people have listened, in Texas and elsewhere, too.

LON TINKLE

A writer loyal to real experience

Frank Dobie himself started the style of finding a Homeric epithet for the subjects of the *Observer* memorial issues. The one Dobie chose for Roy Bedichek was "The Natural Man." Hubert Mewhinney supplied one for Walter Prescott Webb, "The Man of Massive Common Sense." No doubt many contributors to this Dobie issue will underscore this one for Mister Frank, "The Man of Integrity." Integrity, in the modern sense of existential authenticity and of creating one's own sense of self instead of borrowing or inheriting it, characterizes Dobie's fundamental modernity of mind.

He revealed it in a rather dramatic yet spontaneous way when he concluded his speech at the last annual Texas Institute of Letters banquet, which was held in Dallas. He was taking the place, on short notice, of Katherine Anne Porter, who had arrived in Dallas with a 102-degree fever that sent her to the hospital. Dobie, who often concludes a talk by just abruptly stopping, was about to sit down; then he paused, presumably because he had thought of a good curtain line or maybe because he felt the occasion required a kind of personal testament. White-suited as usual with a red rose some lady had pinned to his lapel, he brushed back the white shock of hair with his left hand and with that familiar gesture of clearing the air in front of him, made an arc with his right arm.

"People," he said, "are always complaining nowadays that they don't know where to turn for answers to their problems. Well, they might turn to themselves. We all might turn to ourselves."

This got a standing ovation. Dobie had unconsciously and spontaneously defined the essence of himself: a courageous self-reliance

206

and a courageous willingness to be responsible. More than any man I ever knew, Dobie is haunted by a sense of responsibility to reality.

I say reality instead of truth or fact or justice, because reality is a fusion of concrete things with powerful feelings and abstract ideas —and Dobie is a man powerfully magnetized by the concrete, the rich particularity. His writing is alive with details, with striking inventories of fact—but it doesn't just "inventory." It is writing, like that of any true artist, that separates the real from the fake.

This is a harder thing to do than most people will admit; the tiring effort to make the distinction hurries most of us into dogmatic or doctrinaire thinking. The only dogma Frank Dobie respects, I believe, is the dogma to oppose all dogmatism.

Hence, his extraordinary anchoring in the concrete, the tangible, the specific example. He values the rich particularity over the empty universal, and in this sense he is a "regionalist." He is a relativist, not an absolutist. People in the East often suppose he is absorbed in the past, in the local. Far from it; but his instinctive wisdom does relate everything to time and to space. Time is history and space is region and you can have both anywhere. They constitute most of our daily experience. Dobie is a man loyal to real experience, whether of the past or present.

This, as we shall see, is what his work records, and with resonance. And not just his work, but his behavior as a man.

A dozen memories come to mind in verification. During the great drouth that ended in 1957, some of us were talking under the giant elm in his backyard. After a good deal of abstract discussion of economic effects and the future of Texas, Dobie suddenly said: "What makes me suffer the most is to go out to Cherry Springs [a country place he had then] and see the trees thirsting for a drink. I feel with them. I share their agony." He was making us see a concrete side of reality. He was vindicating, no doubt, the natural man's view, just as real, if not as important, as that of the social man.

As much as it fitted Bedichek, the epithet "Natural Man" fits Dobie. I think of the time he was in Brackettville to watch John Wayne's filming of a longhorn sequence in the movie *The Alamo*. Dobie was enchanted with a gnarled and magnificent old mesquite growing just outside the building used as commissary. After breakfast that morning, he communed a while with the mesquite. A photographer importuned him to hurry; John Wayne was waiting out on location to

207

have some "still" shots made of the Duke and Dobie inspecting the Alamo "replica" on Happy Shahan's ranch.

"Here's the thing to photograph," Dobie rebuked him. "Get some pictures of that old mesquite. It has survived wind and weather for, I guess, several hundred years. You never saw such a big trunk on a mesquite. Now there's something noble. And send me some of the pictures. I'll pay for them."

The mesquite was photographed, casual and natural in its pose. The drive out to location began, scriptwriter Jimmy Grant at the wheel. Dobie was identifying every thing that grew along the road. Suddenly he told Grant to stop. Dobie got out of the car and beckoned us all to follow. I thought of the thousand extras waiting for our arrival before shooting began, and tried to recall the figure I had heard about the hourly cost of this movie, not remembering whether it was thirty dollars or three hundred or even three thousand.

"Look, Jimmy," Dobie called, his face as bright as any wildcatter just bringing in a strike, "here's a juajillo bush. This explains that honey you liked so much at breakfast. It's the best honey in the world and all because the bees suck these 'wahee' bushes ..."

A dozen cars back of us, carrying actors and crew, stopped to see the phenomenon. We started again and at last came to a rise where we looked down on Hollywood's re-creation of Old San Antonio. Parking there, Jimmy Grant pridefully turned to Frank and began:

"How do you like that, Mr. Dobie? We got a Spanish architect who studied old documents and—"

Dobie had turned to lean over a bush beside the dirt road. He hadn't yet directed one glance to the counterfeit set.

"Look, Jimmy," he interrupted, "here's another juajillo bush."

John Wayne came over and Dobie was feted the rest of the day. The big scene to be filmed was the herding of longhorns into the Alamo by the Texans. Bill Daniel had assembled for Wayne, with much ingenuity, a magnificent herd of two hundred longhorns, powerful monsters unlike the captives you see in Brackenridge Park.

Dobie was elated. To stars and extras and on-lookers he explained about the breed. Wayne put him in a director's chair, marked "The Duke." Ken Curtis and Chill Wills were summoned to sing for Mr. Dobie some of the songs Dimitri Tiomkin had composed for the movie. Frank seemed to listen, but on that brilliant sunlit morning he kept an eye on the movements of the longhorns as they milled around under the control of Bill Daniel and some Mexican riders.

Like the mesquite and the juajillo, the longhorns were part of the real thing. The music wasn't.

"No, Duke," Frank told Wayne, "what you need is some of the songs the Mexicans really sang. I think you ought to make 'La Paloma' your theme song."

It was a typical Dobie performance, always bluntly battling for the real and the authentic and the natural, usually losing to the world of prefabricated images and emotions and ideas.

When we left a day or so later, I saw him look with long affection at that old mesquite. He did not find the flora and fauna more interesting than the Hollywood people, just more real. But with his immense gusto and zest for living, with his ever-present curiosity about the new, he thoroughly enjoyed the experience of this alien world. He was full of reactions and steadily amused. He liked the warm friendliness and unpretentiouness of John Wayne; he understood, while spurning, the super-sophistication and incomparable cleverness of Jimmy Grant, who could not possibly have believed in the reality of the ideas or scenes he improvised with such commercial knowingness. Frank noted all the toadying, the struggle for power, the obviousness of starlets on the make, the Grand Panjandrum behavior of imperious director John Ford, legendary for his "westerns." Frank was even amused by the regal snubbings we got on several occasions from British actor Lawrence Harvey, who treated us in the way he thought fitting for the "natives." ("Damned two-bit snob," muttered Dobie.)

In this storm of hectic and interesting activity, Frank's shelter of integrity was sure. We had been flown over by General Motors to take brief part in a TV "Spectacular" the company was making about the production. Frank was to be in an outdoor shot, seated on an old wagon in front of the herd of longhorns, whose history he was to suggest in three or four minutes. Hopefully, the TV men handed him a "suggested" script. He glanced at it, then said, "Give me a piece of paper. I couldn't possibly say this stuff." He thought and wrote. "This is what I'll say," he said. And he did.

We were shown, along with some bigshot financiers who had flown in for the weekend, "rushes" of the movie, perhaps three-fourths of the final film. Frank's running commentary, made in a low tone to me, was perhaps too audible. The film was not made for the likes of us and we could only say so, while supposing that experts spending twelve million dollars on a commercial entertainment knew what they were doing. We were not invited back for the Grand Finale, although hundreds of other Texans were.

When Dobie's own achievements are assessed by that last arbiter, time, I imagine the scoreboard will look like this: (1) he will be judged the Great Mentor of Texans of all time, teaching them more about their time and space than any other single mind; (2) he will be judged truly an exemplary "type of excellence" organic to his region but meaningful anywhere; (3) he will be judged as one of the three "durable" and unforgettable writers Texas has thus far contributed to the English language, the other two being Walter Prescott Webb and Katherine Anne Porter.

Personally, I think Dobie will rank as a memorable creative artist, though this word must be explained in this context.

Contrary to historical usage, the term "artist" in our century has come to be reserved for, or at least appropriated by, writers of "creative imagination." That is to say, only novelists and short story writers, poets and playwrights. This is perhaps due to the fact that both Flaubert and Edgar Allan Poe in the nineteenth century fixed an esthetic form for prose fiction. After Flaubert's *Madame Bovary*, the art-novel was a separate genre. Such earlier "novels" as *Don Quixote* and *Gil Blas* and *Tristram Shandy* were excluded from the domain of the true novel. Similarly, Poe organized the poetics of the tale into the "short story," also an exclusive genre.

More importantly, perhaps, with the great development of printing and therefore journalism and article writing, artists of the "creative imagination" quite legitimately stressed the differences between their goals and those of mere reporting. This became all the more necessary when the mass audience, thanks to universal education, made commercial writing a profitable profession. A distinction had to be made between an "artist" and a "writer." For reasons of taste and critical integrity, "literature" had to be defined. It came to mean only the products of creative imagination.

In this limited sense, then, the famous interview that Katherine Anne Porter gave the *Texas Observer* in the autumn of 1958 was semantically correct. Miss Porter said, in essence, that she was the first

210

and the only Texas-born writer to achieve international fame as an artist in the European sense of the term. Miss Porter, an eminently sensible woman, was careful to point out that she was not referring to herself as a "genius," as the careless would assume. She is a novelist and a short-story writer of flawless craft, admired and appreciated all over the world. Neither Dobie nor Webb is famous for "art-form" fiction.*

Nonetheless, Dobie qualifies as an artist, and he is a great story teller. In the anthologies of "World Literature" that I teach at Southern Methodist University, the selections are by no means limited to the modern twentieth-century limited definition of the "artist." There are historians such as, inevitably, Herodotus and Thucydides, essayists such as Montaigne and Matthew Arnold, letter-writers such as Cicero and Mme. de Sevigne, autobiographical writers such as Saint Augustine and Rousseau, just as there are tale-tellers from the anonymous masters of "The Arabian Nights" on down, just as there are thinkers and philosophers and literary critics and some impossible to classify, notably Voltaire. This larger meaning of "literature" is historically correct.

In this wide sense, Dobie has made literature. His main themes are the staples of Western writing: the enlargement of individual free-

---

* R. Henderson Shuffler wrote in October, 1964, that when he asked Dobie, in reference to "Midas on a Goatskin" in *Coronado's Children*, why a man who could write so beautifully didn't do it all the time, Dobie said: "That kind of writing takes too much time. Right now I'm not trying to be that kind of writer; I'm a collector and preserver. The old tales must be put into print before they're lost for all time. They are the stuff from which future Texans will produce great writing" (*Texas Parade*, October, 1964).

After President Johnson gave Dobie the Presidential Medal of Freedom, Dobie wrote:

"As for the Presidential Medal of Freedom, I do not place myself on a plane with T. S. Eliot (whom I do not care to read), Helen Keller, Walter Lippman, Carl Sandburg and certain other individuals nominated for the award. At the same time, I have for years known that my writing considerably on Southwestern and Western subjects has in certain quarters lowered my reputation for literary achievement. That regard has never bothered me. I have written the best I could on what I wanted to write about. In my own judgment, I have in several books written with more power, precision of diction, vividness and continually cultivated use of the English language than quite a few of the literati have achieved" (Column in the *Houston Post*, July 26, 1964)—Ed.

dom, the celebration of life even in its tragedies, the love of nature, the courage to endure, the compulsion to discover the nature of reality and report it with fidelity.

All this he has done using the raw materials at hand. It isn't a literature made out of other literature, but out of authentic experience. And yet it has its mythic worth.

Who can read Dobie's masterpiece, *The Mustangs*, without seeing that he has made of their experience a mythic pattern of the human condition, without seeing that the book incorporates the Greek sense of evanescence (the short life of the individual measured against the long duration of the race) and the Vergilian sense of "tears in the nature of things," or without seeing that this work is the testament of a poet?

I often turn to it and recall Paul Valery's definition of art: "Art is whatever arouses your sense of despair . . . and gives you succour." (The three dots are Valery's.) On almost any page, Dobie's controlling intelligence makes points that metamorphose, that transmute, the news-reel of events and behavior into mythic meanings, into Songs of Mankind.

A few examples. Casually, after destroying the legend or "rumors" that "wild-running mustangs of the plains sprang from seed lost by the Coronado and De Soto expeditions," he notes reflectively: "Rumor delights in maligning good men while they are still alive and in romanticizing bad ones after they are dead." Everywhere in the book the artist's presence is felt, not only in chiseled sentences and structure but in the thought.

Thus:

Of all the notabilities of the True Faith who explored into the unknown vastness of America—to inform the natives of their fealty to Europe and Pope, to clarify their minds on the identity of the Holy Ghost, to sack their gold and silver, if they had any, and to make them dig for more if veins could be located—Hernando de Soto had the best horses and suffered the worst disasters.

The irony continues for several more pages but becomes the irony of fate rather than the author's. Along the way, Dobie tells a little vignette, a love story of a conquistador and an Indian princess, that subtly and superlatively underlines the irony that governs the whole chapter. I sometimes wonder, in talking with friends, if they have ever really read Dobie with close attention. In his writing he does not semaphore his effects.

Consider the opening of the chapter, "Wild and Free":

No one who conceives him as only a potential servant to man can apprehend the mustang. The true conceiver must be a lover of freedom—a person who yearns to extend freedom to all of life. Halted in animated expectancy or running in abandoned freedom, the mustang was the most beautiful, the most spirited and the most inspiriting creature ever to print foot on the grasses of America . . . Only the spirited are beautiful.

It could not be put better, or indeed more spiritedly. Dobie claims writing is difficult for him and he slaves over his sentences. In this regard, he demands of himself the most exacting craftsmanship. He doesn't stop at demanding it of himself. On many occasions, in print and in talk, he has paid tribute to Bertha Dobie for her critical scrutiny of his manuscripts. One suspects he urges her to make him do his best. My own suspicion is that he doesn't find writing difficult but fears facility.

It must have cost him something to compose the last page of *The Mustangs* in free-verse form. Every reader will be glad he did. It is a poem that will be often anthologized. I say "cost him" because he must have realized that he could have been doing this all his writing life. And no one, then, would have doubted that he is a myth-maker, an authentic poet.

The pains Dobie takes to carve his sentences into perfection have rarely been noticed. Bill Bedell, reviewing *I'll Tell You a Tale* for the *Houston Post*, gave an example of how fruitful such an investigation can be. Bedell was the first among reviewers to compare what changes from original versions Dobie had made in preparing the final form for this sort of "Dobie Reader." Then, Margaret Hartley gave an ampler treatment in the *Southwest Review*. Their articles were a revelation of Dobie's dedication to craft.

Of course, anyone who heard Dobie's magnificent speech to the Texas Institute of Letters at the Houston meeting of 1959 should have been alerted to his concern for form and structure. He spoke memorably of pace and tempo in writing, above all of the importance of cadence, of rhythm. He said that often while riding horseback as a young man he made up sentences to shout aloud and to match his mount's movement. But he said his feeling for rhythm in prose came

213

first of all from his reading of the King James version of the Bible. He said for him writing was a matter of re-writing, that he worried a manuscript up to the last minute of a deadline. (I knew that he had left a council meeting of the Institute that afternoon early in order to keep on polishing the text of his speech. He had the manuscript at the meeting; I saw pages on which the typed script was barely visible in all the re-shaping added with pen and ink.)

But if anyone else dares make a change in one of his manuscripts, Frank can have a fit. Having handled shorter Dobie articles for the past thirty-five years, first on the *Southwest Review* and then on the book page of the *Dallas News*, I can report that in the early days many a hot letter greeted bungling editing. Frank is still capable of rage, and to cross him occasionally is still worth risking just for the pleasure of seeing such fighting rapture. I have never known any other writer who took his craft so seriously.

If you think Dobie is not dedicated to craft, compare his two versions of the best longhorn story ever told, "Sancho's Return." Here is the first paragraph, given first in the 1941 form in *The Longhorns*, then in the revision for *I'll Tell You a Tale* (1960):

To begin with, a man by the name of Kerr had a little ranch on Esperanza Creek in Frio County, in the mesquite lands south of San Antonio. He owned several good cow ponies, a few cattle, and a little bunch of goats that a dog guarded by day. At night they were shut up in a brush corral near the house. Three or four acres of land, fenced in with brush and poles, grew corn, watermelons and "kershaws"—except when the season was too drouthy. A hand-dug well equipped with pulley wheel, rope and bucket furnished water for the establishment.

This is how he re-writes it:

In the mesquite and whitebrush country southward from San Antonio, Kerr had a little ranch on Esperanza Creek. He owned several cow ponies and maybe forty cows and their offspring. His *pastor* (shepherd) dog, a mongrel, guarded a small flock of goats, bringing them about sundown to a brush corral near the house, where Kerr's wife barred them inside. Three or four acres of land, fenced with brush and poles, grew corn, frijoles, watermelons and calabazas—except when a drouth was on. A hand-dug well equipped with pulley wheel, rope and bucket furnished water for the establishment.

214

The second version paints pictures, replaces the passive voice with active agents, enriches the detail, and stresses verbs. Above all, Dobie has varied the rhythm and made it prance. The thought groups match the needs of respiration. I am sure he tried that second version out loud. The entire story is a lesson for anybody interested in the architecture of prose.

Sometimes in this anthology of his work, *I'll Tell You a Tale*, Dobie seems content with the first minting. That little gem, "The Marques de Aguayo's Vengeance," which seems to me one of the best short stories in the world, remains entirely unchanged.

Dobie was the first first-rate writer to appear in Texas of the three generations now living. His *Vaquero of the Brush Country* (1929) was a revelation. All the university lads wanting to be writers saw that a man could keep on living in Texas and write about Texas material and still achieve national acclaim. When *Coronado's Children* was published the next year, this truth was evident. It was published by the Southwest Press in Dallas (of which I became general handyman when it was founded in 1927) and two years later was published in New York as a Literary Guild selection.

This was an omen for young talents such as Fred Gipson and Tom Lea and Paul Crume; Dobie's career remained so for the next generation, too. Meantime, in 1930 Katherine Anne Porter had published her first volume, *Flowering Judas*, and in 1931 Walter Prescott Webb published *The Great Plains*. In New Mexico, Oliver LaFarge in 1929 had written "Laughing Boy," which won the Pulitzer Prize. In Oklahoma, Stanley Vestal was producing his memorable biographies of Kit Carson and Sitting Bull. In 1933, Paul Horgan, then living in Roswell, won the Harper $10,000 Novel Prize with his *The Fault of Angels*.

National magazines announced that a Southern and Southwestern Renaissance was in full swing, ending Mencken's slur on the South as a "Sahara of the Bozart." Mary Austin and Witter Bynner came over from Santa Fe to visit the Texas writers centering around the *Southwest Review,* bringing recollections of D. H. Lawrence, who had written in 1929 that "I think New Mexico was the greatest experience from the outside world that I ever had."

Dobie of course had been compiling Texas legends and editing the publications of the Texas Folklore Society ever since 1922. He was in the thick of this regional ferment and has remained the central figure in it ever since. But he was never narrowly provincial and always stoutly maintained that although a writer must be anchored in the concrete, in his own time and flesh and space, he must also view this realm or region with enlightened perspective. No wonder, however, that many critics still wrongly think of him as a mere "regionalist." In the national context of this "renaissance" of the late twenties and the thirties, Dobie began his career. This lingering faulty "image" may explain what I, at least, regard as a scandal in the literary world, the fact that his *I'll Tell You a Tale* was the most neglected superior book published in 1960. (That was the year the Pulitzer fiction prize went to Allen Drury's second-rate novel *Advise and Consent*. Dobie's "tales," of course, could not be classified in the fiction category.)

This man of integrity, this artist, is also an exemplary type of excellence for our times. Frank Dobie is ferociously independent but he is not thorny or spiky. He probably has more loyal friends than any living Texan, and perhaps half of these disagree with his ideas. Anybody who has seen him in any large gathering has been struck by the variety of personalities eager to shake his hand and to enjoy a moment in his presence—from politicians who abominate his forthrightness to business moguls, from youngsters to old ladies, from booksellers to ranchers and newspapermen. Even his enemies, and a man with so many friends is bound to have plenty of enemies, brighten in his presence and regard him with resigned affection.

I have had Dallas businessmen who met him by accident, in the Menger bar, say, or on a plane, speak to me time after time, savoring the recollection, of a moment of magic talk with Dobie.

I think this is because he is the easiest man in the world to be with. We once drove to Corpus Christi for Austin and after an hour of good talk relaxed into silence. An hour later, Frank started talking again. "There is a kind of silence that is a sign of friendship," he commented.

But he is not only easy, he does have a magic of presence. Somehow around Frank, everybody feels intelligent and life seems good. Many famous men leave you feeling diminished (a few of my own examples: William Faulkner, W. H. Auden, Thomas Mann), but Dobie leaves you feeling ampler than you are.

The amazing thing is that he has found time to keep alive literally hundreds of friendships. Perhaps this is because he is fundamentally a too generous man. His willingness to help other writers is legendary —writing forewords for books of friends, handing over long-accumulated documentations from his own files, reading manuscript for critical correction, helping find a publisher, simply lending moral support. Any annual meeting of the Texas Institute of Letters becomes a sort of Dobie Tribute, with principal speaker and prize-winners gratefully acknowledging some sort of debt to Mister Frank. On at least two occasions, afternoon speeches have consisted primarily of some Texas writer's reading aloud advice sent by Dobie in letters. From looking over files at the *Southwest Review* and at the *News*, I can testify that he has been joyfully promoting this sort of intellectual ferment since at least 1922. Unlike most writers, he is neither jealous-hearted nor egocentric.

An exemplary man is one whom it strengthens you to think upon. I am sure I speak with the voice of nearly every Texas writer alive today when I say that Dobie's work and his existence have been the most important source of strength that we have found outside ourselves in our time. In moments when it is hard to cope, the mere thought of that granite-like face on which experience has carved its map, that face whose muscles tense at folly or relax into that life-warming grin, is healing and salutary. He belongs to the life-enhancers.

"I wasted my golden youth on lost causes," Dobie told a reporter in Dallas in 1960, no doubt speaking casually but perhaps going deeper than he had realized. It is true that he has made so many public appearances, is such a congenital defender of "underdogs," has been such profitable newspaper "copy" for most of his life, has given so much time to editing and helping other writers' work, he has become a "celebrity" these days more than a "writer" in the public mind. Dobie as a "character" has obscured Dobie the artist. Too many Texans, listening to him, reading reports of his pronouncement on "politics" and "educationists" and "super-patriots" and "typical Texans," feel they know Dobie without having taken the trouble to read him. Too many who have read him have not read between the lines.

He is our Robert Frost; he is an institution.

If he lends his presence to an occasion, it takes on extra shine. But that same presence presides in his books; that same presence and his craft are what makes them literature. Dobie is a whole man, giving proper proportion to literal fact, to scientific observation, to the transforming power of imagination, to human and individual meaning. What he ultimately stands for is the legitimacy and the value of poetic truth. His mustangs belong to verifiable fact, but they also symbolize a new breed in a new world, doomed to disappear but destined to endure in the ideal of freedom. His home-haunted longhorn Sancho bespeaks man's yearning for a life that is not rootless, a loyalty to the sense of place. Without using modern techniques of introspection in his works, he nonetheless knows who he is. He has incorporated into his writing the self-knowledge of a wise man who believes that mere literal chronicle cannot exhaust the amplitude of reality.

In short, Dobie is a man of creative imagination. Posterity will, I believe, take him much more seriously than he has been taken in his lifetime. It will keep his books alive as long as any written by Texans or about Texas since Cabeza de Vaca's *Relacion* of 1542, not alive just as history or folklore but as the work of a unique artist, bearing witness to reality. So long as individual sufficiency is reckoned a virtue in the understanding and the structuring of life, Frank Dobie will be proudly remembered. So long as story patterns convey meanings, as they have since the dawn of literature, in a way unlike that of other forms of expressing truth, Dobie will remain one of the few Texas "immortals."

CHARLES RAMSDELL

Dobie revisited

The yellow daffodils, in an arc following the bend of the creek, glowed in the shade and burst into glory where a shaft of late sunlight struck them as they curved with an effect of infinity beyond the trees and the house.

Frank and Bertha Dobie had led me and the young student who had come with me to the bridge over the creek by their house to show us the most pleasing view of her daffodils. And the vision seemed to me a good sign, coming at the start of the quest I had set out on, which was, for one thing, an attempt to renew old satisfactions. We all know how disappointing such an attempt can be, but, weepy poetizing to the contrary, there are times when you can come home again, if you want to. On this short visit to a place that awakened long memories, I found what I was seeking, and something else besides.

Bertha Dobie's flowers—ranunculus, candytuft, and others that made harmony with them—looked as exultant this spring as I could remember they ever looked in any spring of my youth. And at last I got up the nerve to ask her, "Is it true, what envious female gardeners used to say: that you plant one bulb or one seed on top of another, so as to keep your garden in continuous bloom?" Her reply was an amused and enigmatic smile.

Frank Dobie had lost none of his pervasive warmth. He entertained me and the half dozen university students I had invited— when they finally showed up—with anecdotes from his new book on cattlemen and with salty remarks on all sorts of matters, as he used

to do with other young people, and these kids too were plainly enchanted. They were also plainly a little bit high on beer. But the
Dobies, if they noticed, never let on. They didn't even appear to
notice the resounding clatter in the kitchen when the poet among us,
a big shambling bear-like blond, who had gone in there on the absurd
pretext of setting his highball glass down, dropped or bumped into
some utensil, making his friends acutely aware that he was filching a
few extra swallows of Scotch.

The idea of bringing these youngsters here had been mine, and I
was just a trifle nervous about them. I had discovered, quite casually,
that admirers of Dobie's work are a whole lot more frequent in this
new generation of students than in the previous ones I had known,
and several of these youthful admirers, when they found out I had
been acquainted with him nearly all my life, asked me for an introduction. So I called him on the phone.

"Bring them over," Frank said. "When I was young I preferred to
be around old people, because I felt I could learn most from them.
But now I feel I can learn most from the young."

That Dobie learned anything from these crew-cut, beshorted boys
and one handsome, beshorted girl, I doubt. They were overflowing
with enthusiasm, among other things—at one moment they begged,
almost in chorus, to be shown the "restroom"—but they were not very
coherent. For a while before they finally got there I didn't think any
of them (except the solitary youth who happened to come with me
and saw the daffodils) would ever make it to the Dobies' on a lovely
festive Saturday afternoon in early spring. Already half an hour
late, they phoned to report, amidst bubbling laughter, that they were
on the lakeside, and had left their car keys on the opposite shore, and
would have to go back for them in a motorboat, but they were coming. And they came.

That they appreciated and, each according to his capacity, understood Frank Dobie, I am certain.

"What I liked best," said one boy as we drove off, "was the way his
eyes lighted up when he told a story. The way he loves all of life,
everything about it."

"What impressed me," said the big blond bear, poet, and whiskey-
snitcher, "was the way his wife took pleasure in talking about him
and his work. Marriage is a sacred institution! When I get married,

believe it or not, I'm going to be faithful to my wife. [Cheers.] How wonderful to have a wife so loyal and devoted! Marriage is a sacred institution!"

"You tell Mr. Dobie for me," said a third youth a little later, while soaking up a clearly superfluous beer, "I think he's the most wonderful son of a bitch in the world." He had tears of deep feeling in his eyes when he said it. But, reading this statement back in his mind, and deciding it was not a message that elder generations would understand, unaccustomed as we are to the modern college boy's transmutation of fighting words into highest praise, he said, "Pardon me. I don't know how to express myself." And then went on to express himself so eloquently, in such torrents of words, it would be impossible for me to set them down. But his essential thought was this: by interpreting the background of life in Texas and the whole region of the Southwest in terms of literature, he has given us dignity, something solid underfoot that was not there before, the foundations of a culture.

From where I stood it seemed to me the golden arc was infinite.

The visit to the Dobies and the experiment on the younger generation concluded a phase of my quest entirely to my satisfaction. But I still wanted to renew my acquaintance with the Dobie books, not having read some of them for many years. I read them, and then remembered I had written reviews of several when they first came out. But I have been able to dig up only one of these pieces. It appeared in the *Southwest Review* for October, 1935, and I was twenty-four at the time. I am astonished to find that it sums up nearly perfectly my final judgment, not on this particular book alone, but on Dobie's work as a whole.

The book was *Tongues of the Monte*, which has been re-issued lately as *The Mexico I Like*, and here is what I said about it:

I feel that Mr. Dobie has found his richest vein in this book. He writes about Mexican ranching-folk, how they live and what they believe. But the whole account, a personal narrative, owes its real distinction to his warm understanding of people and their ways. It is written with a zest and a freedom that only now and then were apparent in *Coronado's Children* and his other work. And though he is rigorously classified by the academic as a gatherer of folklore, and even called himself, at least once, a "social historian," it is when he lets himself go and refuses to behave like any sort of

221

professor at all that his writing is often as pungent and fresh as the smell of brush country early some morning in April.

This book, so far as I know, is the first full-length description of life on the cattle ranges in that vast rugged desert of Northern Mexico, a land as ruthless and magnificent as its cougars or its rattlesnakes. Mr. Dobie is careful with his details, but he also paints vividly. I doubt if any reader of this book will ever feel again that the Mexican and his customs are entirely alien to him. And surely it will be good for us to have this much solid truth—solid earth, I started to say: the stories, the songs, and the people are all so close to the soil—after so many stacks of volumes by ladies who have had breathless adventures in some of the better-class hotels.

And still, the best parts of the book are not merely faithful descriptions. They are rather avowals of Mr. Dobie's affection for simple people and robust ways: for straightforward men, warm-hearted women, and fine horses; for comradeship and easy, footloose living. And when he writes about such things, his prose, which at times is deliberate and factual, takes on a glow, becomes elated, and sings.

The rare power of sympathy, which raises the best of Mr. Dobie's writing to a dignity far above any that the treatises of other specialists in Southwestern culture have attained to, is more abundantly revealed in this new book than in his others. Surely no reader of *Coronado's Children* has forgotten the picture of the "second sorriest white man in Sabinal," the town scavenger, seated on his goatskin in a patio bright with zinnias and morning glories, and dreaming of treasure buried in a certain place he knew of, where he would go and dig it up some day. Perhaps there is nothing in *Tongues of the Monte* better than that epitome of all human desire, but there is still Inocencio, the author's outspoken companion, and Toribio, the goatherd, who, employed in the rudest of occupations, turns out to be anything but a fool. I do not know another writer whose sympathy has less of the egocentric in it, less of pity or of patronizing. Mr. Dobie is not moved to commiseration by the goatherd's deplorable standard of living, nor is he indignant at meeting with an almost naked victim of the System. He seems, rather, to think that there may be something in the fellow worth finding out. What is more, he actually takes a liking to him, smell and all. And one suspects that he envies him a little.

The book is a rendering of simple—and sometimes opulent—natures, as seen by a very generous one.

Amen. I am not sure that this book is better than all the rest. I happen to be a Mexico buff, and I know there are other readers who are more interested than I am in longhorns, mustangs, even Englishmen. I still think "Midas on a Goatskin" is a short masterpiece. But the point is, the same golden generosity flows through all of Dobie's best work, giving it warm life and making us return to it with pleasure again and again.

RONNIE DUGGER

Down a bytrail

I seldom see Mr. Dobie—he might be working, over there in the white house on Park Place by the creek, and I feel I would presume going over there often. Once over there, though, along in the late fifties, on the porch where we had gone to get some wood, I told him I wished he had written more about these times and out of himself, perhaps in novels. I knew this was audacious and probably unwise, but I had begun to feel dishonest with him for not having said it. I mentioned his *Tongues of the Monte*, which appeared in 1935. He said sometimes he thought his work was futile—he had been contemporary just since the Second World War. "The world is going to hell," he said, "and I can't do anything about it."

During the time of *Tongues of the Monte*, Dobie said in his introduction to it, he made various trips on horse and mule with pack and *mozo*, "wandering through the vast, unpopulated mountains of Mexico, lingering at ranches and mining camps, living the freest times of my life." In the book itself he said, "I was a free being, absolutely untethered." In mysterious ways *Tongues of the Monte* disembodied itself from his chronicling of stories of the past on the frontier and expressed talents that had been lying in him unplied, suggested directions his work might have taken if he had not returned to The University of Texas and the course he had set for himself.

Neither folktale nor novel, fact nor fiction, *Tongues of the Monte* is a blend of these that draws body from its loyalty to truth about people and mystery from the fictions Dobie worked into this truth. Which part is true, which made up? Dobie never says, letting the true and the imagined interenchant each other. "The characters are inventions, patched up from realities," he explained later. "I invented

224

a slight string of experiences on which to thread tales and people. I tried to weave the life of the Mexican earth into a pattern. It is truer, I think, than a literal chronicle of what I saw, whom I heard, and where I rode or slept would have been." He let the tongues of the book play softly back and forth between the truth that is true and the truth that is made up, as one supposes Pasternak did in the novel from his own life in Russia. As well, in Dobie's book, as much concise and some magical story-telling, there is a kind of writing that surprises one's idea of him.

At this instant [he wrote] I happened to glance towards the mountains to the east, and, although dusk was approaching, the sun having disappeared, I saw one of them aglow with a soft yet brilliant blanket of light, rose and amethyst and golden, misty like a veil and at the same time pellucid, surpassing in beauty and strangeness and effect upon the imagination any light my eyes have ever beheld. . . . The light kept shifting and changing with unbelievable rapidity. Now it was a spectral red, like the lips of the woman-mate to Death in "The Rime of the Ancient Mariner"; now a smouldering luster of copper like the un-natured and ominous hue of a full moon in midnight eclipse; now, again, all misty loveliness, and at the last a dying blush as soft as the half-caught aroma of honeysuckle hidden in the dusk.

He had seen this at the Hacienda of the Five Wounds, where also—

As I learned upon arising, it was Dolores's saint's day, and according to custom, it had been inaugurated with the dawn serenade. She was seventeen years old, and now somehow she suddenly appeared to me as fresh and lovely as the morning of the first day. It is not often that in a Mexican home a strange man more than glimpses the unmarried daughters, except at meals. I was ceasing to be a stranger in the house. Anyhow, on the evening of this day Dolores was present when somebody told a story of a young lover who rescued a girl from the Comanches and carried her to safety on his horse. That made me remember a story I once heard in Chihuahua, and as I told it I could feel Dolores listening. Through it I meant —partly meant at least—to tell her how fateful it is for a maiden to fall in love; at the same time I know now that I was conscious of the "mighty magic" almost any tale of love and fierceness would have upon this maiden, a solitary rosebud that, whether she knew it or not, all the winds and sunshine in a garden yet pristine to her were calling, pulling, drawing to open into a flower with petals as red as the blood of the heart and stamens lush with golden pollen.

225

Snaking slowly across the desert of Northern Mexico—

And so we rode. If not in time, then in distance covered, the *jornadas* had to be short, for with pack mule and without grain or other forage travelers cannot rush barrenness that stretches away and away into other barrenness. It was as if I had never known any other land, any other life, any other beings but Inocencio, the mule, and the two horses.

If he imagined that he was beloved in Dolores at the Hacienda of the Five Wounds, or if he really was, and if his *mozo* told him, I am yours, and crossed his hand with his blood, why this is something like the love of now, finding a form. It is one of the charms, for me, of Turgenev's *Hunting Sketches* that while they were surely in a large sense true, there was too much magic in them for all those things really to have happened in the obvious sense to this literary lord, striding the Russian countryside in search of game and life. In Northern Mexico Dobie was also a kind of lord—a writer from a college, whose *mozo* told him that after God, he was next—and he was wandering the *monte* in search of stories in the lives of the people, but also, I think, in search of himself. As *Hunting Sketches* was Turgenev's preparation for his novels, so might *Tongues of the Monte* have been Dobie's, but for his turn back.

Returning from this bytrail of his life, he became our fiercely honest elder. When I was a freshman at the University in Austin, his was the first cause that inspired me—the regents had fired him, as we all well understood, for being openly and boldly for the liberal, Homer P. Rainey, for governor. Dobie has been stronger and more honest than the state university has, and the irony of the institution now buying his library that spurned having him living and working within itself is not lost upon us—nor is the University's failure, for all its glomming onto the celebrations of him, to make personal amends to him, commensurate to the wrong it did him and continues in force against him.

Although he stood up for "the people," with Jefferson he believed in the natural aristocracy. Seated, one evening in the summer of 1959, at the head of the dinner table, he spoke of a senator from another state who, quoting Edmund Burke, had declared that, rather than merely represent the people, he would conduct himself in accordance with his conscience. Dobie wrote the senator that he had left out a key word, "enlightened," in Burke's reference to conscience. "Any damn nincompoop can vote his conscience!" Dobie growled. "It's got to be *enlightened* conscience."

Irascible about sentimentality, occasionally he has let me know of his wearying with what he sees to be an attitude of charity toward the underprivileged, and of unrealistic egalitarianism, in the *Observer*. Again, speaking of the movie about the Alamo, I believe he was, he said, "You can't have intellectual integrity and slop—appeal to slop!—conscious appeal to slop!" In May, 1960, in his downstairs work room, I admired a photograph of Pasternak he had there. The Russian is sitting at a table, a cup of something hot and a bottle and cut-glass wine glasses there before him; he is gazing, lost in loneliness, thinking something deep and tired. Later Mr. Dobie sent the picture to me having written on the back of it, "in the name of one of the holiest of the holy ghosts—a man who saw into things and would not fool himself."

Once he paused in the *Observer* office complaining of the details that had been keeping him in town, away from the country where he could work. To get a book done, he said, a man has to "associate with himself." Bill Brammer said the other day, in Austin where he is writing again, "It never occurred to me—ever—until I read Frank Dobie, that I could be a writer. There simply were no writers in Texas." Dobie has been personal proof that a writer can work here when things of this kind have seemed strange and beyond us. He, and Bedichek and Webb also, have been our modern frontiersmen, showing us the possibilities of our own place.

More information on Dobie's relationship to The University of Texas late in his life became known to the Texas Institute of Letters after his death, and I passed it along to Observer *readers in this note in the April 2, 1965, issue:*

Dobie and the University

Having been one of the students who protested in 1947 because The University of Texas had dropped J. Frank Dobie from its faculty, I have resented the fact that even as the University celebrated him in his venerable old age, it neglected to correct the wrong it had done him. Specifically the question was, why wasn't he made professor emeritus before he died? Dr. Harry Ransom, the chancellor under whom the University has become a place where academic freedom is flourishing, provided, in his recent address to the Texas Institute of Letters banquet in Houston, the fact that is the answer.

Ransom reminisced improvisationally about his old friend and fellow English teacher—about how this Texas iconoclast had "succeeded admirably in disturbing . . . received opinion, accustomed ease, and very easy conformity." Dobie's running fights, literary, artistic, academic, economic, social, never became personal, Ransom said.

He remembered a meeting with Dobie at Scholz', a place about which the chancellor said, "Those of you who are not Austinites might be told that Scholz garten is a very wholesome family center." He remembered a time he and Dobie went up in the University Tower Dobie had so many times maligned: Dobie conceded that while he still hated to look *at* it, it was a pretty place to look *from.* Dobie's attitude toward profanity, Ransom said, was "both profound and informative." Once a man in their company told a lot of dirty jokes, and Dobie said after the card was gone, "That man is an utter bore. He thinks he can rescue his mindlessness by middle class cussing." Who, Ransom asked, but Frank Dobie would consider some kinds of cussing middle class?

Ransom became chancellor—"a job I knew Frank disapproved of"—and Dobie came calling on him in his office, only to notice what Ransom called "the elegant little wastebasket." Dobie told him, "It isn't big enough. It's the most important piece of furniture a chancellor should have." When crises arose at the University Ransom would get little notes from Dobie, and, Ransom said, "I knew that he was still among us."

On one occasion, Ransom then said, he and Dobie were on the sixteenth floor of the University Tower. At this time "the board of regents were actually all Dobie enthusiasts." Ransom recalled proposing to Dobie that he become professor emeritus—the English department, leading professors, and the regents would approve, he told him. Ransom continued:

He said to me, "If my books are going to be at the University, I will keep teaching here, and I don't want to be emeritus anything," and turned the talk to some other subject. But before he left, he said "I want you to promise me that you will never raise this subject again," and I said, "All right," and until tonight I've never mentioned this to a soul.

HERBERT FAULKNER WEST*

Many of his books will endure

When I was asked to write a short piece on J. Frank Dobie, I decided that I must see my old friend once again before I tried to put anything on paper. When I flew the necessary nineteen hundred miles I had not been in Texas for three years. Since my last visit Frank had had a serious automobile accident that had incapacitated and weakened him for some months. However, I had been told by friends he was in fine fettle.

He still flashed his warm and famous smile and spoke with the wisdom of a sage raised on the plains and hills of Texas. This time his barbs were directed against crooked politicians, unintellectual regents, and people who love only money. I had a feeling that the Dallas episode, if such a word may be used for the killing of a president, had really shaken him.

He is most happy, it seems to me, when he is on his ranch. The first one I visited with him was at Cherry Springs, and being a Yankee used to the lush greens of the New Hampshire hills, I was amazed by the bareness, the aridity, the dead trees of the country around Marble Falls. As a matter of fact there had been a couple of years of drouth, and the time was early spring. To me it was like a landscape on the moon; the rivers had dried up and it looked as if very little could survive. But to Frank, who had know the state since birth, it was Texas, and it was a refuge where he could relax and work on his writing.

* Professor of comparative literature at Dartmouth College for forty-two years, also a book reviewer and a book seller.

Soon after this visit he sold this ranch and bought one nearer Austin which he calls Paisano; I have visited him there a couple of times. He grew up on a ranch, and the academic life, although congenial, was never his proper environment. Within it he inspired many students and wrote many books, but I think he was happier when he was riding over his acres and supervising his Mexican help keeping the ranch in good order.

When I saw him last, he had just completed, after a determined effort, his latest book, *Cow People*. Wherever he is, Frank is obviously happy only when he is working on a book, and he has written eighteen. He is a painstaking craftsman, and many of his books, I feel confident, will endure. When R. B. Cunninghame Graham wrote of W. H. Hudson that he was a man of the plains, simple and direct, with a natural style "as the green grass grows," he might have also been writing about J. Frank Dobie. There is in all of his books a kind of massive simplicity. They are saturated with honesty, with facts, and with a complete understanding of what he is writing about.

One of my jobs at Dartmouth College as director of the Friends of the Library has been to get rare books for the Dartmouth Library. We have a reasonably good Dobie collection, and we hope as time goes on to make it better.

In my copy of *Apache Gold and Yaqui Silver*, which is handsomely illustrated by Tom Lea, Mr. Dobie wrote in June 1951: "These people had nothing but hope. They were rich in it. As I grow older I wonder if any other form of wealth is more enriching to lives. At the same time I grow stronger against blindfolds. Damned if I know what I believe, but always I believe in fairies. And I hope will always have hope."

Another book of his, which I suspect he likes as much as any, is the one he has called *Tongues of the Monte*. After we had toured the hill country together in March, 1957, he wrote in my copy:

I think there were two printings of this book by Doubleday, this being the first. I went to Little, Brown and Company and Doubleday let the book die, transferring the plates to me. I thought it might sell better if tagged by the title; I wrote an introduction to it and let the Southern Methodist University Press [then called University Press in Dallas] have it for nothing under the title *The Mexico I Like*. After a printing of only one thousand copies had been sold—this was during World War II—this press could get no more paper. After the war ended, Little, Brown took it and still has it in

230

print under original title. It has more of strangeness than any other book I have written. I mean to read it someday.

Another book I would recommend to anyone wanting to know something about the true Texas would be Mr. Dobie's *Tales of Old-Time Texas*. These stories, such as "The Panther's Scream," "Not a Drouth Crack," "Guarded by Rattlesnakes," "Jim Bowie's Knife," seem to spring from the very soil of the state.

I have three Dobie books which are favorites of mine because no one else could have written them and because they reflect best the real life of Texas. The first is *The Voice of the Coyote* (1949). Thirty years of research, thousands of miles of travel, and talking to hundreds of men produced this truly great book. "The coyote," Dobie says, "is extraordinary as a character, quite aside from economic, political and like importances. He has something in common with Abraham Lincoln, Robin Hood, Joan of Arc, Br'er Rabbit and other personalities—something that sets popular imagination to creating."

With the coyote, Mr. Dobie has immortalized in *The Longhorns* the famous Texas steers—"gaunt, wiry, intractable . . . pioneers in a hard, strange land." This book, illustrated with photographs and magnificent drawings by Tom Lea, really tells all there is to be told about this famous animal of the Spanish conquistadores, the terrible excitement of the stampede, the tremendous bull fights on the range, and "ghost" steers.

In *The Mustangs* Mr. Dobie has told with great artistry and myriads of facts the old stories of the mustangs, once the glory of the Western range.

Well, the wild ones—the coyote duns, the smokes, the blues, the blue roans, the snip-nosed pintos, the flea-bitten grays and blue-skinned whites, the shining blacks and rusty browns, the red roans, the toasted sorrels and the stockinged bays, the splotched appaloosas and the cream-maned palominos, and all the others in shadings of color as various as the hues that show and fade on the clouds at sunset—they are all gone now, gone as completely as the free grass they vivified.

A magnificent book!

I salute J. Frank Dobie as a great writer and a great Texan.

HART STILWELL

Listening with the third ear

Several years ago a psychiatrist named Theodore Reik wrote a book he called *Listening with the Third Ear*. It didn't exactly set the psychiatric world afire, but it did put down in moderately good English (for a social scientist) the thesis that listening should be more than a momentary pause while waiting for your turn to talk again.

Psychiatrists must listen with the third ear in order to fill in the personality gaps left out, deliberately or subconsciously, by the patient. Most people don't even listen with the first two ears, much less the third. And for that reason anyone who really listens is almost an oddball.

Well, J. Frank Dobie listens.

And during the countless hours that I have watched him in the process of listening, I was forced to conclude that all the talk about the lost art of conversation is bunk—what we have lost is the art of listening.

For quite a few years I lived within two blocks of Pancho Dobie's home. It was real nice dropping by in the afternoon and shading (as he put it) under the big trees in his back yard and drinking his whisky and taking part in a conversational—and listening—binge.

Quite often the triumvirate was there—Dobie and Bedi and Webb.

Webb listened—or at least remained silent—to a fault. He would talk only when there was a spell of quiet and it became obvious that he would not have to compete for the platform.

Bedi was much more of a talker—and, of course, his talk was always good to hear.

232

Dobie has always been in between. He will not fight for the floor, but he will not wait for an unspoken invitation to move in.

Above all he listens—certainly with two ears, sometimes with the third ear, also.

When he talks he frames his sentences slowly and carefully—probably a habit acquired while wallowing in academic freedom—and the sentences always have a sort of magic in that they convey a touch of personality, that of Dobie and that of the person he talks about.

There are dozens of people in Texas who are far better craftsmen than Frank Dobie when it comes to putting down one word after another in the construction of a piece of writing. There are few who can get the touch, the flavor, the mood that Pancho can.

And when you shift from what he writes to what he says, and watch the play of emotions as reflected by his face, then the impact is far greater.

The manner in which Dobie listens may be more restricted than that of the professional listening of a psychiatrist, for Dobie, when he listens, is not probing for the abnormal, the hidden traumas, the suppressed hostilities which the psychiatrist must search out and then analyze. But Dobie catches the flavor of what is said—the personality of the talker as that individual wants to present his personality.

And, of course, we all have a dual personality, one built for public presentation, one reserved for ourselves, so that it can contribute to our confusion and misunderstanding.

I have seen the results of this careful listening by Pancho in many charming little things he has written.

Many years ago, out at Joe Small's cottage on Lake Travis, I introduced an old friend of mine, the late Captain Billy Molesworth, to Dobie.

Captain Billy was a truly great talker. In all the years I hunted and fished with him, not once did he tell a really corny story—and the air we breathe is full of corny stories.

At that little gathering Captain Billy told a story he had told me before—about the preacher out in the Uvalde country who prayed for rain and brought forth a gullywasher.

Well, not long ago I saw that story in print, as told by Pancho. It

233

seemed that Captain Billy was telling it to me. I caught the rich flavor of the old man's personality in reading Dobie's account of what he said.

Dobie was listening with two ears—but with only part of the third ear. It was clear that he wanted to take Cap as Cap presented himself—not as a sort of skeleton that would be left after a pack of psychiatrists picked all that was good out of the way and left only the bones.

So I got the feel of Cap again. And I realized that Pancho Dobie had done what I never could do in the dozens of stories I wrote about Cap—get the real flavor.

So I wonder if Pancho isn't a whole lot more valuable to us than people who listen with the third ear and lay bare our souls—a procedure not many are strong enough to accept.

Sure, Pancho Dobie listens—but he hears the music and the poetry and the beauty. He is a selective third ear.

I hear the H-Bomb and corruption in office and viciousness.

JOSEPH C. GOULDEN*

Handling the "insult approach"

Somebody once said, and I'll agree of my own experience, that a good measure of a man is how he deals with a brash, unlearned cub reporter. Mrs. Richard Nixon once frowned at me when I warned her she was about to step in a cow paddy at a Dallas fair grounds stock barn. It's ridiculous, of course, but of such trivialities are opinions made, even of presidential candidates.

As a general assignments reporter for the *Dallas News* I often used an "insult approach" in interviews with visiting celebrities. A nasty question at the outset provokes spirited replies; a mad subject is more apt to speak freely. So we come to Mr. Dobie, who in the fall of 1960 was in town for a book and author luncheon.

On the phone the night before Mr. Dobie said yes indeed he'd be happy to meet me in his room, and yes indeed I could bring along my father, a Dobie admirer.

He was alone, in house shoes and shirt sleeves; Mrs. Dobie, he said, was shopping.

"Mr. Dobie," I said as he played with his pipe, "last night I read all the clips about you in the *Dallas News* morgue. During the 1940's you had something to say about everything, and strong things. Then you disappear, there are no more stories, no more fire. Whatever happened to Dobie the Iconoclast?"

(Translated: Whatever happened to you, old man? Lost your spirit?)

* A reporter for the *Philadelphia Inquirer,* previously for the *Dallas Morning News* and the *Los Angeles Times.*

Dobie got interested in the pipe, and his eyes crinkled and I think maybe he chuckled. He grinned at my dad. "I tell you what I'll do," he said. "I'll be happy to start writing a column again, like I did for the *News* before Ted Dealey stopped it. You get them to agree to publish it, and I'll put some fire back in that newspaper."

We all laughed, and I told Mr. Dobie I'd write Ted Dealey a note (I did, he didn't answer), and after that, it wasn't a newspaper interview, it was mostly a conversation between Mr. Dobie and my dad. When Mr. Dobie saw me writing a note he'd slow down, and here are some of the things he said during the next hour:

Progress.—"My definition of progress is 'a state in which nobody in particular wants to run, but everybody has to run to keep from being run over'."

Public Life.—"I wasted my golden youth on causes. The only salvation for the human race is for people to arrive at a just sense of values. And a just sense of values is not implanted by a political victory in an election. The mob might be right once in awhile. But if the majority always had a just sense of values, we'd always elect a good man, a wise man, a strong man, and turn things over to him. If you work for causes, you've got to be leading society around every two or four years. Enlightenment is the only answer."

The Press.—"The press, like everything else in Texas, is conformist. I don't think the newspaper owners are eager for divergence, and they call the tunes. They, like the magazines, want brightness, but in a vacuum. You can't have that and thinking, too. You can get brightness in a vacuum in a lightbulb, but not in a human being."

Charity.—"I'd rather give my dollars to the liberation of the human mind than for curing sore eyes in poor people who are going to maintain closed minds."

Dobie.—"I consider myself something of an artist, a conscious craftsman. I have tried to write well. My idea of life is not to win an argument, an election; it's producing something useful and interesting."

I apologized in print again the next morning: "If J. Frank Dobie has mellowed with age, it is an aging like that of whiskey, not of an apple stored in a cellar for the winter. The fruit loses its crispness. J. Frank Dobie has lost none of his."

EDMUND HEINSOHN

A question of implications

A mutual friend asked, "Is there any feeling of constraint when Frank Dobie and a man of the cloth are together?" Not when Dr. Dobie and this man of the cloth are together. With the consent of Dr. Dobie the following two conversations are recalled. While he was suffering from a heart attack and pneumonia, I found him in an oxygen tent at St. David's Hospital. To the question, "What in the world are you doing here?" he replied: "Not a thing, just lying here, no ambition, no aspirations, no anything, just reflecting." After he left the hospital, I visited him at his home. As I was about to take my leave, he said: "You seem to be a pretty intelligent sort of fellow. That being the case, how can you preach the kind of stuff you preach?" To this question I made answer in thiswise: "Dr. Dobie, there isn't much difference between the two of us. The principal difference is that I think more highly of Frank Dobie than he does himself, and that I simply cannot believe that an oxygen tent is big enough to hold Frank Dobie." He enjoyed the compliment, but did not accede to the implications.

It is possible to stretch an umbrella so large that the man who disagrees with you is forced to get under the umbrella with you. In like manner, religious terms can be so defined that the man who makes no profession of religion is made to appear as a man of religion. I am trying to avoid doing this to Frank Dobie. Some concepts of God he has made the targets of his barbs, and in some instances his shots have been devastating. But the Frank Dobie whom I know in the presence of life has a sense of awe and reverence and mystery and wonder and meaning and purpose. In my book he is a religious man.

In the presence of human injustices he has the passion of the Old Testament prophets. He is a man of great ethical concerns, and these are not without their religious roots. A few years ago Southwestern University at Georgetown, Texas, celebrated "Frank Dobie Day." Southwestern University chorus was giving a program in his honor, and he was seated on the platform with the chorus. When asked if he had any special preferences he suggested that some of the old revival hymns be sung. One of the most beautiful passages to come from his pen was the description of Gonzales, the newsboy, on his knees at the foot of Dobie's bed in St. David's Hospital, praying for him. Soon after the assassination of President Kennedy Dr. Dobie wrote with appreciation of the way in which his father always closed his evening prayer: "Lord, bless all who are in authority over us." Because of his spirit of compassion I sometimes wonder if he has not unwittingly embraced the flower and fruit of the Old Testament as portrayed in the New Testament.

I have enjoyed chiseling around on Frank Dobie, but I have not tried to trim him down to size. To me he remains my dear friend, a man of great stature and one of God's obstreperous sons.

SAVOIE LOTTINVILLE

The universality of Mr. Dobie

Character has been variously described. It is an ambivalent word. We are sometimes uncertain whether it is meant to convey strength or merely to serve as a descriptive phrase. But when I think of J. Frank Dobie, whom I first saw in action nearly thirty years ago, I think of the strength which comes from firmly held conviction and from something perhaps even greater, the gift of friendship.

With few people I have known has the commitment of friendship been so complete and inspiring as with this man from the Brush Country. There is a special quality to it that goes far beyond loyalty. It is a line of confidence extending from a finely critical consciousness of character itself, and once given, it is known by the receiver to be fourteen-carat.

In a sense, it was a curious place to meet, but we did meet on the Battlefield of San Jacinto. There, he and perhaps another hundred of us were to witness what we subsequently referred to as the Second Battle of San Jacinto. Mr. Dobie was the principal speaker that evening in the early nineteen-thirties at a meeting of the Southwestern Library Association. For some reason unknown to us, the public place chosen for our banquet had not been reserved entirely to our staid but interested group: at a corner table some outsiders were whooping it up. As the time arrived for the preliminary speaking, those at the corner table became restive and there was muttering about talking when there was good drinking to be done.

After a brief introduction by Carl Milam, the secretary of the

American Library Association, Mr. Dobie rose to speak. Putting down his bulldog pipe and resting his notes on the stand before him, he looked out over his audience. From the corner table a woman's voice broke the silence, almost profanely: "Who is that old buzzard?"

Undeterred, Mr. Dobie smiled and began his address. The unconvinced in the corner listened a while, occasionally allowing a loosely held fork or knife to clatter against china. Their neutrality gradually changed to hostility, and four voices swelled against the speaker's. Still Mr. Dobie remained unabashed, but out at the fringes of his audience were men who, even though of the academic cloth, could be pushed only so far. A battle was about to take place.

Suddenly Carl Milam, sensing imminent danger, rose and asked for adjournment of the entire meeting to another room. There, a smiling Frank Dobie began over again an address which none who was present was likely to forget. Closing it, he said sagely, "I've known people to win battles but nobody wins a brawl."

I still think we could have. There were more of us.

As a great many people know, the Dobie speaking style is unique. The rough-hewn head, so much like Charley Russell's; the twinkling eyes looking out from craggy brows; the voice with a touch of sandpaper to it; and the massive resources of literary learning and wit— these are the characteristics of one of the best thinkers-on-his-feet of our times. And in an age which has all but forgotten the uses of metaphor, here is a man who enriches the language with figures of speech every time he gets to his feet.

The Dobie writing style was summed up in Vergilian crispness and wit by the Public Orator of Cambridge University, who said, as Mr. Dobie was presented an honorary M.A., "He knows more and writes better about the longhorn (*longicornibus*) than any other man living."

It was appropriate that Cambridge should do something about the man who had just completed a year as a visiting professor. But the recognition this senior English university gave to our Southwesterner is only a measure of the regard in which he is held by English-speaking peoples everywhere. It said what many had long since concluded, that Mr. Dobie has written from sure knowledge and with great charm about a set of dimensions in Western history, life, and folklore which no one else has attempted with his degree of success.

In the doing, he has demonstrated how happily the talents of a student of English and American letters could be applied to one's own environment.

There are analogies, to be sure: the familiar one of Charley Russell in painting and sculpture (far abler than is Frederic Remington, who had a possible finer technique but with a less convincing result); Eugene Manlove Rhodes in the short story and the novelette; and Walter Prescott Webb, the master conceptualist among the historians of the Great Plains. Mr. Dobie and these creative spirits have many characteristics in common: a thorough familiarity with their subjects, a reverence for artistic and historical truth, and a deceptively easy style.

The Dobie insights, informed by a thorough grounding in literary character, drawn from a lifetime of critical study, are conveyed with quickly chiseled strokes. No less can be said of the life which has passed before his eyes. I think the closest parallel I can draw is from Charley Russell's small line drawing of two cowboys saddling a pair of horses in the rain. Only a man who has seen and felt such an incident could get such superb results with so few strokes of the pen.

It has been said that only a man with a good heart can be a good humorist. Dobie's wit is by now a firm part of the contemporary scene. But there is also a Dobie gift for irony (some, on the receiving end, have called it sarcasm) which has the power to curdle milk. Somehow one gets the impression that agreement, which has become a national disease in the last thirty-five or forty years, is not a part of Mr. Dobie's Decalogue. If it were, the strength and integrity he has so solidly exhibited would have given way long since to a dull and lifeless conformity, which for the critically oriented is another word for intellectual cowardice.

I should like to remind Mr. Dobie's friends and admirers that Oklahoma (which toots a small horn softly) claims the man, just as it has certain claims on Sam Houston. Mr. Dobie taught at Oklahoma State University early in his academic career, and he was invited to join the faculty of the University of Oklahoma just as he was closing his association with The University of Texas. It is an old kinship of the spirit, and a very old friendship. We of the north bank of the Red River are part of the horse culture too, and if he had chosen to come once more among us, this is the subject on which we would have honed to hear Mr. Dobie lecture, as he had done so effectively at Austin, Cambridge, and elsewhere.

What I am saying is that the best test of both character and ability is that they should be insistently shared by localities other than one's own. This, after all, is the measure of universality. If there is any doubt about the universality of Mr. Dobie at this late date, I think it is limited to places where television is an overriding habit and books are seldom seen.

FRANK H. WARDLAW*

"J have that honor"

What shall I say about my friend Frank Dobie?

It is an assignment fraught with danger, for I tend to be sentimental about people with whom my affections are deeply engaged, and Frank regards sentimentalists almost as highly as he does Professors of Education.

I should be able to write about him easily today, for I am sitting on the gallery of his ranch house at Paisano looking across the dry bed where Barton Creek ought to be flowing toward the rugged bluffs and the tree-studded hills beyond. A fresh wind is whipping across the gallery and there are no noises except the sounds of the country. I spent last evening in Frank's room, with longhorns and mustangs and paisanos and coyotes and skunks and a ragged old buzzard peering down at me from the walls. In the corner was a beat-up pair of handmade shoes from England, each with a thirty-degree inward angle; Frank's feet are non-conformists too.

I cooked a steak last night over an open fire outdoors, and while I was eating it three deer ran lightly and without fear across the rock-strewn hillside above the house, an armadillo rustled here and there through the yard poking his snout into anything that seemed promising, and a skunk passed within five feet of me (I remained quite still) and made his leisurely way around the house.

The doctors have got Frank Dobie hobbled in town right now, but this isn't the first time and he will soon be back at Paisano. In the meantime his friends Tomás and Gomez are taking good care of the

* Director of the University of Texas Press.

243

place. Yesterday afternoon they were here setting out trees along the creek bank. When they finished they came up to the house to put away their tools and joined me in the kitchen in a glass of *cerveza*. Tomás had just seen a large snake and, while he was looking for something to kill it with, encountered a bobcat, which caused him to forget all about the snake. Tomás and Gomez said they would have to watch "Meester Dobie" very carefully when first he comes back to Paisano. "Last time after he was so sick," Tomás said, "we would bring him up to the house and leave him in his room and go to our work, and then we would see him way over yonder across the creek or coming over the hill back of the house."

They told me to tell him that all of the little trees which he had planted early this year were responding well to constant watering and looked as if they would live, and that the copperas he had prescribed for the ailing pear tree beside the shed apparently had been exactly what it needed.

At Paisano I have spent some of the truly memorable evenings of my life—good food, good drinks, good talk. Usually there were just a few men there—Walter Webb, Roy Bedichek, Mody Boatright, Wilson Hudson, and (when we were lucky) Glen Evans or Johnny Faulk. Sometimes there would be other friends from Austin or visitors from other parts—men like George Fuermann, Lon Tinkle, Walter Whitehill, Lyman Butterfield, Alfred Knopf, Bertram Rota, and J. B. Priestley (the "beeg hombre," Gomez called him). The night before Priestley was here he attended a dinner with a number of young faculty members from the university and he was in a jaundiced, overbearing mood, but at Paisano he mellowed and added richly to the good talk which flowed through the evening.

Webb and Bedichek and Dobie wrangled endlessly on those occasions about all sorts of things—religion, politics, education, history, literature, grass, the habits of wild animals and cattle, everything under the sun and beyond it. A favorite topic was death, which they discussed with great geniality, and funerals, concerning which each had strikingly non-conformist views. Dobie and Bedichek had a compact that whenever either should detect signs of senility in the other he would let him know immediately. In the heat of argument this privilege was sometimes invoked.

Bedichek and Webb still attended our occasional sessions at Paisano. Bedi was planning to go to Paisano with Frank Dobie and Wil-

son Hudson to grub up stumps for firewood that afternoon of the day
he died in the kitchen while waiting for the cornbread to get done,
and Walter Webb was on his way back to Austin to have dinner with
some of us (not at Paisano) when he was killed instantly in an automobile wreck. They left us so suddenly that it still doesn't seem that
they are gone; and whenever we sit on the gallery at Paisano or around
the "philosopher fire" inside they still enter into the conversation as
naturally as though they were present, and their opinions are invoked on all topics. Soon after Bedi's death Frank called for a party
at Paisano "at which we shall pour a libation to his ghost." He pre-
dicted that we would eat sometime before midnight. No more cheerful
memorial service was ever held. It rained hard that night and Barton
Creek roared out of its banks. Dobie and George Fuermann drove out
the next morning with Glen Evans walking ahead of the car over the
lowwater bridge to make sure that the creek wasn't high enough to
drown the engine. The rain added to the cheerfulness of the occasion.
Frank's spirits soar every time Paisano gets a good rain. He loves Paisano more than any place on earth and he suffers when it suffers.

Every place, every institution, every man in whom Frank Dobie
has invested his affections—from Tomás and Gomez to the President
of the United States, from Paisano to Cambridge University—has
never been quite the same again. I visited Cambridge ten years after
Frank Dobie spent a year there talking about American history and
loosely related subjects. Nearly everybody I met, when they learned
that I was from Texas, asked me immediately and with affection
about Frank Dobie (one man came up to me and asked me about
him on the strength of my hat alone). They all said that no American
who has visited Cambridge had left behind him such good feeling
for the United States, such understanding.

The University of Texas is a prime example of the lasting quality
of Frank Dobie's influence. It was seventeen years ago that the Board
of Regents ended his official connection with the university, but during all of those years he has remained a vital force on the campus.
The regents could remove him from the payroll, but they could no
more extirpate his influence than one can kill an idea by removing a
book from a library. By insisting on his right to say what he damned
please on any topic no matter how sensitive, Frank Dobie strengthened for all time the hand of every Texas professor who believes in
liberty of thought and of every administrator and regent who seeks

to protect that liberty for the faculty. Many people have contributed to the present firm dedication of The University of Texas to the principle of academic freedom, but none more importantly than Frank Dobie.

The day may come when people forget that Frank Dobie went to jail rather than pay a parking fine (it seemed like a good idea at the time), but the Dobie legend and the Dobie spirit will live on at The University of Texas, not only in his fine library with thousands of pages enlivened and illuminated by his pithy marginal comments, but in the principles of enlightened non-conformity and uncompromising courage and amplitude of spirit.

That word "amplitude," a favorite of Dobie's, possibly sums up more accurately than any other the principle which has guided his career as a writer, particularly in recent years. It explains how a man most of whose writing has been devoted to regional topics has at the same time been the most effective foe of provincialism in thought that this region has yet produced—and God knows Texas has needed him. In his *Guide to Life and Literature of the Southwest,* first published in 1942, Frank Dobie wrote: "I have never had any idea of writing about my section of country merely as a patriotic duty. . . . I would interpret it because I love it, because it interests me, talks to me, appeals to my imagination, warms my emotions."

To a later edition of this same book, Dobie added "A Preface with Some Revised Ideas." In it he said:

It has been ten years since I wrote the prefatory "Declaration" to this enlarged and altered book. Not to my generation alone have many things receded during that decade. To the intelligent young as well as the intelligent elderly, efforts in the present atmosphere to opiate a public with mere pictures of frontier enterprise have a ghastly unreality. The Texas Rangers have come to seem as remote as the Foreign Legion in France fighting against the Kaiser . . . If during a decade a man does not change his mind on some things and develop new points of view, it is a pretty good sign that his mind is petrified and that he need no longer be counted among the living.

Frank Dobie cares about as much for consistency as Emerson did, and he is constantly changing his mind about people and issues. He told me once that the reason he didn't get further along with the autobiography which everyone was pressuring him to write was that

246

"it is depressing to me to think about what a damned fool I have been in the past." The record of his life—whether or not he ever gets around to writing it up—and of his writing is that of ever-increasing amplitude, ever-increasing awareness of the oneness of the world, of the subservience which all lesser loyalties must bear to those which are due to "the damned human race," a phrase of Mark Twain's which he has often quoted.

> There are no substitutes for nobility, beauty, and wisdom [he wrote]. One of the chief impediments to amplitude and intellectual freedom is provincial inbreeding. . . . I'd like to make a book on *Emancipators of the Human Mind*—Emerson, Jefferson, Thoreau, Tom Paine, Voltaire, Arnold, Goethe . . . When I reflect how few writings connected with the wide open spaces of the West and the Southwest are wide enough to enter into such a volume, I realize acutely how desirable is perspective in patriotism.

Not only has Frank Dobie's thought grown in amplitude throughout the years but his skill in the craft of writing has likewise grown. His last major book *The Mustangs* is likewise his finest, to my way of thinking; his autobiography, of course, may exceed it.

It is impossible to estimate what Frank Dobie has meant to the literature and to the writers of the Southwest, or to calculate the thousands of hours which he has spent talking to and reading the writing of would-be authors. But as he has grown older his standards have grown more rigorous and he has become increasingly impatient with writing which reveals the limited mind, the restricted outlook.

He has read many manuscripts for the University of Texas Press. All of his comments on them bristle with his insistence on integrity and breadth of view. Witness the following:

> I don't regard this manuscript as worthy of your imprint. The writer maintains a provincial point of view. As you perhaps know, one of my later tenets is that no matter how provincial the subject, a modern writer must transcend the provincial point of view. This writer doesn't have enough outlook. . . . He is too concerned about himself. We do not give half a damn when and where he drank a Coca Cola or if he drank one at all. His car, on which he spends so many words, is less than consequential. He seems to have an idea that his personal experiences illuminate the subject.
>
> He uses far too many adjectives. If all the "olds" in his manuscript were cut out, it would be shortened by several pages. He speaks of "the world-famous 6666 Ranch" and "the world-famous Pitchfork Ranch." His world is no bigger than the Texas Panhandle. He shows consciousness of some-

thing that happened before 1876, but a very dim consciousness. His time limit for antiquity is too meagre for a historian. He does not know the meaning of words and is wordy throughout. "The unique little village of Guthrie, Texas" is an illustration. Guthrie is not unique and "little" is redundant.

The style is juvenile. The writer lacks maturity of mind. . . . Going back to diction, I don't see anything "mysterious" about a cow and her calf knowing each other. If they didn't know each other, anybody who knows b from bullfoot would be puzzled. There is no at easeness with either cattle or men.

About another book, Dobie commented: "The author is a damned egotistic Philistine."

About another: "The opening chapter is inane. Some of the writing is interesting, most of it concerns events that just happened to happen in the Big Bend. . . . Every statement in the first paragraph page 3 is a lie."

About a book concerning a certain section of West Texas: "Chamber of Commerce baloney. . . . The author dares not bring up the dearth of water; he never mentions wind and sand."

On manuscripts which he reads for us, Frank Dobie can seldom refrain from writing marginal comments in his unmistakable scrawl. Once before returning a manuscript to its author I had to erase from the margins three times a certain earthy expression, first cousin to the one which Hemingway's "Author" had to explain to the Old Lady in *Death in the Afternoon* (just substitute "horse" for "bull" and the terms will be identical). "Madam," the Author said, "we apply that term now to describe unsoundness in abstract conversation or, indeed, any over-metaphysical tendency in speech." If there is any tendency in speech or in writing which Frank Dobie detests it is an over-metaphysical tendency.

I don't mean to imply that Frank Dobie is always harsh in his criticism of others. Nothing excites or pleases him more than unexpectedly to encounter genuine quality in writing. The first book which he recommended to the University of Texas Press was J. Mason Brewer's manuscript, to which the author had given the impossible title "Negro Preacher Tales from the Brazos Bottoms of Texas." Frank not only recommended it unequivocally but he wrote a discerning preface to it and re-christened it in a moment of inspiration *The Word on the Brazos*.

One day Frank called and told me about an unusual book which had just been brought to him—for forty-odd years Texans have been thrusting their manuscripts on him to read. This was the work of a seventeen-year-old high school senior from Beaumont who for two years had been engaged in editing his grandfather's memoirs without the knowledge of his parents. "Most Ph.D. dissertations aren't nearly so good," he told me. And so we published Johnny Jenkins' *Recollections of Early Texas*.

And then there was the time when he called and told me flatly that "I've got a book here that you are going to publish." The late Ralph Jackson of Beeville, who had recorded the story of his family for his children without thought of publication, had sent a copy to Frank Dobie because he thought it might interest him. The result was that gem of a book *Home on the Double Bayou*.

Frank's judgment is not, of course, infallible, and he has blind spots where certain kinds of books are concerned (haven't we all?), but his mind separates the genuine from the spurious almost unerringly and he never hesitates to express his opinions forthrightly. "Hell," he said in a letter once, "when I want to say anything I say it out, and I don't go around behind tree stumps to get it suggested."

A whole article could be written about Frank Dobie's contempt for censors. He will take up the cudgels against them anywhere, any time. It is largely because of him that the Texas Institute of Letters has in the past made its influence felt powerfully in support of freedom to write and to read—and will again some day. "I rate censors as low as I rate character assassins," he wrote once; "they often run together."

Once I drove to Fort Worth with Frank Dobie to attend an autographing party for *The Mustangs*. I fell into conversation with a well-dressed man who had brought over a number of books for Frank to autograph. He explained to me rather apologetically that he liked Frank Dobie's books although he didn't like his politics. "However," he said, "when my friends tell me he is a communist, I tell them that I don't really believe it." And then he asked, "Are you a friend of Mr. Dobie's?"

"I have that honor," I replied instinctively.

Jane and I had met Frank Dobie through his books long before we came to Texas in 1950, and I met him in person at the Southwest Writers' Conference in Corpus Christi a month before we loaded our

249

family and livestock in the Chevrolet and headed out for the great adventure of organizing a new press at The University of Texas. We arrived hot and tired and a bit dispirited (few motels and fewer cars were air-conditioned in 1950 and traveling with four young children isn't exactly recreational at best). In our mailbox when we arrived was an invitation from the Dobies to have dinner two nights later in their backyard with the Bedicheks and with Tom and Sarah Lea from El Paso. It was the finest introduction to Texas which any couple could have received. We have had the honor of the Dobies' friendship ever since, as have our children.

Every now and then Frank calls me at the office and suggests that I come by to see him—"but make it the right time of day"—and every now and then I invite myself. We sit out in the backyard by Waller Creek, Frank with his shoes off and his hat on, surrounded by Bertha's wonderful flowers, and talk about everything under the sun, usually in the company of our mutual friend Jack Daniel. We differ sharply on many issues (I am a shade more conservative than he is, and still have some formal religion, and believe that the public schools our children attend are much better than those I went to), but Frank has never exacted agreement from anyone as a price of friendship or respect. He is as good a listener as he is a talker.

Once George Fuermann sent to Austin by me a remarkable pint bottle of rye whiskey which had been twenty-two years old when it was bottled during Prohibition "for medicinal use only." He instructed me to share it equally with Frank Dobie, Walter Webb, and Jim Hart. Roy Bedichek, who never drank anything stronger than beer, was to do the pouring. Miraculously I made it back to Austin with the bottle unopened, and so one evening before the Town and Gown meeting the elect gathered by Waller Creek to claim their portions of this noble rye. Bedi figured out that there would be four ounces apiece for the topers and we decided to take our shares in two two-ounce drinks. We had just about finished the first drink when a young man with a pack on his back—a birder friend of Bertha's nephew Edgar Kincaid—came around the side of the house in search of Edgar. Frank introduced us and invited the boy to sit. Then he leaned forward and peered keenly at the stranger from beneath bushy brows. "You don't drink, do you, young man?" he asked.

"No, sir," the boy replied.

"Thank God!" Frank said fervently.

Jane says that she wishes there were room enough in this piece for me to talk about Bertha, whom we both specially admire, and not just because she has had the simple courage to go through life as Mrs. J. Frank Dobie. But there isn't room, and anyhow she deserves a piece of her own. A woman of intelligence, humor, great good sense, and quiet loveliness, she is as remarkable a person in her own right as Frank is in his.

As you can see, this has turned out to be a rather personal piece about my relationship with Frank Dobie, and I am afraid that I haven't been altogether successful in avoiding a display of sentiment. Today I asked myself what his friendship has meant to me personally. It has, of course, meant the best of comradeship, and stimulation of ideas, and broadening of horizons. But, perhaps most of all, it has brought heightened courage to me, just as it has to The University of Texas—not as much as his own, of course, but some anyhow. And I know that if I ever do something which I know I shouldn't or fail to do something which I know I should simply because I am afraid, I may still "have that honor" but I will no longer deserve it.

WALTER PRESCOTT WEBB

I have known Frank Dobie for about thirty-five years

Walter Prescott Webb spoke of his friend Dobie in connection with the Texas Folklore Society meeting on April 23, 1955 in the Driskill Hotel in Austin. Webb said:

I have known Frank Dobie for about thirty-five years, maybe a little longer. There are many sides to him, more facets than I know, and I suspect more than he knows or suspects. He can not be confined, and is not subject to definition. All I can do is to describe some of his attributes as I have known them. Some of them may surprise you, but if they do, that will only illustrate how impossible it is to understand.

The first thing to which I call your attention is that Frank Dobie dislikes Texas. He is never happy when he is here; he is never miserable when he is away. The happiest years of his life he spent in an Oklahoma agricultural college where he said he felt completely at home. The thing he likes best about Texans is their boastfulness. He said that the only thing he disliked about Oklahomans was their modesty. He never quite got used to it.

A second characteristic is his unfailing spirit of obedience, his submissiveness to authority. He likes all the people in high places, and he is especially fond of regents. He is always anxious to please them, and they never gave an order that he did not obey with alacrity. There is not any instance where they said come, that he did not come running. He can anticipate their wishes. He was never known to keep galloping around on the prairie when he was ordered in to the campus. The regents often cite him as an example of what a university would be like made up entirely of Dobies. A thing of undisturbed beauty and a joy forever. A very quiet place it would be.

Mr. Dobie is a great defender of architects and sculptors. He is particularly fond of the architects who designed the University buildings, those who put all the windows on the west side so as to incubate the heat, make life in them intolerable for seven months in the year, and make expensive air conditioning imperative. He once expressed his unstinted admiration for the Tower on the Main Building. Dobie said that Texas had plenty of length and breadth, and that it should also have height in proportion. No sense in spreading out over all this space, with shaded walks to fend off the sun. What we need, he said, is buildings imported from other regions, and that are comfortable only when they have snow on the roof. Dobie said you did not need a porch, that the only use for a porch was to put saddles on and provide shade for dogs. He is not the critic who said of the University Tower that it would look better laid down on its side with a porch around it. That was another fellow who is to Dobie as Bacon to the English Bard.

His admiration of Texas sculptors surpasses that for the architects. He thinks the cenotaph on Alamo Plaza in San Antonio is the very embodiment of the artistic spirit of Texas, and that the sculptor who made it should be proclaimed an honorary Texas Ranger. He might add a few horses, but otherwise he approves of all the best Texas art.

Dobie is the best camp cook I know, excepting one. He does not want any of the conveniences. He would prefer to build the fire out of cow chips, but since the drouth has burned them up, he will compromise with green brush, and the harder it is to gather the better he likes it. He will grudgingly use wood that others have gathered, but I have never known him to set the woodpile on fire rather than drag off a few chunks. He will not use a griddle to broil a steak. He wants a green stick with the steak speared on it. He likes the fire so hot that he can burn the steak up on the outside and have it raw on the inside. If he can drop it a time or two in the ashes, he considers the flavor improved. Some of his customers have said it didn't hurt.

Dobie is a total abstainer. He never drinks whiskey except on social occasions, and Dobie is really socially inclined. He does not know the difference between good whiskey and bad whiskey, and really shows a strong preference for the more vicious brands. He can not tolerate Jack Daniel's or Old Forrester.

Dobie is quite fastidious in his tastes. He believes that everybody ought to dress for dinner, and he never misses a chance to put on tails or a dinner jacket. This is the influence of a year in England. You can tell by his stiff formality that he has departed far from his Texas heritage.

Dobie is one of the famous gardeners of Austin. His home on Waller Creek is set in grounds that are the envy of all his many visitors. He does all the planning himself, and any time you go there after five o'clock you will find him working near a table that is well equipped with what it takes to stimulate the artistic imagination of a gardener. It is generally assumed that Mrs. Dobie contributes something to this beautiful garden, but this is an error. Frank does it all.

There he is, ladies and gentlemen, and with all those simple virtues it is no wonder that we love him as much as we misunderstand him.

ROY BEDICHEK

J have been associated with him a good deal since 1914

On the same occasion, the late Roy Bedichek said of Dobie:

In the five to seven minutes which the totalitarian dictator of this otherwise pleasant occasion has allowed me, I must undertake the compression of an inconveniently expansive subject.

I have wanted for a long time to try to clarify in my own mind the personality which provides the theme for this gathering of folklore folks. I have been associated with him a good deal since 1914. I have observed him at long-range addressing the public in speech and in print, and at short-range in man-to-man conversation. For twenty-five years we have both attended a bi-weekly discussion club where opinions are kicked about in free-for-all and sometimes more or less heated disputation.

Again, I have listened as he has turned on the charm with audiences, retailing the folkways, folk-wisdom, or the folk-tales of an environment in which we were both brought up. I have been received time and again into the tree-shaded, flower-bordered home, nestled in a crook of Waller Creek, and experienced, as many of you have, the lift which genuine hospitality gives the flagging spirits of man.

Moreover, I have read his books and magazine and newspaper articles and have been surprised now and then into guttural gurgles by a pregnant phrase or turn of homely wit, or by the quaint humor of situation, pleasantly contrived. I have envied the ingenuity with which he extracts considerations of startling significance from the

255

ordinary and the commonplace. I have talked often with his friends about him and occasionally with his enemies.

Surely I should know something worth telling about Dobie.

Therefore, when commissioned by the aforesaid dictator, I lost no time in taking to my typewriter to do up in a seven-minute package the quintessence of Dobieism. Presently, I had twelve pages. Then it occurred to me that I was not the only person on the program. My egotism had undertaken an unnecessary responsibility. Others will have their say. Had we gotten together beforehand and parceled out the victim, there would be less duplication, better coverage, and more thorough dissection. Realizing at last that I was not to sit in solitary grandeur at the speaker's table, I crossed out all except what's left on the next two pages. I find that it deals with only one characteristic; but at that, one which more than any other seems to me to illume what is dark in Dobie while perhaps rationalizing actions and pronouncements often misunderstood by his nearest friends.

Dobie is sincere. His well-known, because outspoken, abomination of pretense in life and art is only the reverse side of his passion for sincerity in his own life, personal and public, and in his own art.

The other day a charming woman, a famed hostess, was inviting Dobie and me to dinner, after which she engagingly promised to show us some slides she had made of her trip last summer. "I'd like to come for the company but I sure as hell hate pictures," drawled Dobie in reply. Later this lady with a lovely tolerance said to me, "Now wasn't that just like Dobie."

To an invitation to join a literary club, Dobie replied, "Dear Bill, I can't work up any enthusiasm about a literary club. I wouldn't want to hear *anyone* read his writing for an hour or two." Just like that— no weasel-words, no cushioning phrases. Still, I suppose in the last thirty years, he has read sympathetically and criticized with the patience and tenderness of a skilled surgeon doing an operation hundreds of manuscripts of young, unpracticed, but aspiring writers. This comes of his sincerity as a teacher. Many forget that Dobie is first and last a teacher, and one who takes his teaching seriously.

They say he is a rebel, at least, a nonconformist. He is a "controversial figure," which means during the present hysteria to keep your mouth shut *or else* if that which you think is in any way critical of the status quo. A few years ago a managing editor told me that the Big Boss made him drop Dobie's column because he continually

256

flouted the policy of the paper. Yet he has the art, should he choose to exercise it, of glossing over his real convictions and exhibiting them in a diorama of protective coloring. But again his sincerity interferes. I heard an old friend of his boyhood apply an epithet to him which signified the worst of the worst, the damndest of the damned, in those circles where the bigotry of race-prejudice reaches fanatical intensity. Dobie knows how his freely expressed opinions on race-relations are received among some of his oldest and dearest friends. But he disdains compromise and camouflage. Dobie is sincere. His refusal to conform has deprived him not only of friends and position, but has affected deleteriously the market for his literary output. We shall all have to admit it. He is a "controversial" figure, and *homo gregarius* loves conformity because it provides pleasant dozing in comfortable inertia.

But, I ask you, do we sufficiently realize the blight put upon art by this present-day mania for orthodoxy? Does even a culture-group such as this realize keenly enough the importance to the maintenance of our traditionally American way of life of an individual whose sincerity forces him to speak out in defense of it?

A hundred years ago John Stuart Mill saw the paralyzing strictures which an industrialized society was throwing about the individual to restrain in him every impulse of a spiritual nature likely to thwart the so-called "march of industrial progress." Listen to the words of England's greatest social philosopher of the last century, addressing himself to this very theme:

In our times from the highest class of society down to the lowest, everyone lives as under the eye of a hostile and dreaded censorship. . . . Thus the mind itself is bowed to the yoke. . . . In this age the very example of nonconformity, the mere refusal to bend the knee of custom, is itself a service. Precisely because the tyranny of opinion is such as to make eccentricity a reproach, it is desirable, in order to break through that tyranny, that people should be eccentric. . . . That so few now dare to be eccentric marks the chief danger of the time.

And, I may add, a danger grown vastly more menacing in our own land and time.

TOM SUTHERLAND

Acrostic

Freedom is food for people who
Range big pastures, hunting stock . . .
And wake alone, in grass and dew,
Near a nickering horse or two . . .
Kin to the earth and natural rock.

Death of a thousand cows in drouth
Ought to wear out the restless drover,
But the lonely man straightens his mouth:
"I'll head out west for a while—ride south—
Eat later—look the country over."

ARCHER FULLINGIM*

But the children know

The first time I ever heard of J. Frank Dobie, the No. 1 Texas writer, was when my sister, Virginia, was attending The University of Texas back in the 1920's. She had a class under him. He was the top English teacher at the University at the time. She would write me letters in high praise of him. When Dobie published his first book *A Vaquero of the Brush Country,* I bought an autographed copy; it had an imitation rattlesnake skin cover and was finely printed on fine paper and in big, beautiful type. After that, every time Dobie published a book, which was every two or three years, I bought it.

Along in the 1950's, Dobie wrote a book called *The Mustangs* that was more than a documented history of those horses of the plains and prairies. In it one discovered about freedom, not the kind of freedom the John Birchers rant about, but the kind of freedom the mustangs knew, and Dobie throughout the book managed to teach the meaning of true freedom. . . . It was the kind of a book to live by and live with, and I have not known many books like that in my lifetime.

So in 1953, when I moved into this tin building, there were these twelve-foot high walls on each side and the white ceiling, and the walls are of sheetrock over two inch boards, and I prevailed upon my brother-in-law, Tom K. Simms, to paint me a mural about Dobie's mustangs, which he has always liked to paint and to sculpt. I told Tom I wanted him to illustrate Dobie's mustangs in the mural, but he

* Editor of the estimable East Texas weekly, the *Kountze News,* who wrote this column after the special issue of the *Observer* on Dobie appeared.

wouldn't read the book, but he did look at the drawings which were all right, but not half as good as the murals on the walls of the *Kountze News*. Tom wouldn't read the book, and for weeks I told him about it and read portions of it to him, but I doubt if he listened, for Tom knows about horses of all kinds. He has spent much of his life drawing horses and the rest drawing pictures of Jesus and he never gets the two mixed, but before he began painting the mural he seemed to get the feeling of freedom that Dobie taught so unobtrusively in the book. Tom Simms painted the mural, 4½ feet high and 50 feet long, and it took him three months. That mural may be the most important single thing in Kountze, and Tom Simms may be the most important man, so don't put too much emphasis on that wild look he has, and the wild way his hair waves, but you had better believe those hell-fire sermons he preaches. I have never met Frank Dobie, but Bertha Dobie his wife was here one day last year, and she saw the mural, but I had a feeling that she was not too much impressed, but I know what I know: That if I can spot greatness in Mozart, in Faulkner, in Dobie, in Conrad, surely I can know when I see it on a wall. Now what do you say, Bertha Dobie?

Anyway, I have Dobie's mustangs under my eyes all the time. I cannot tell you how much they have meant to me, not because they are just paintings, but because they are connected with the mustangs. I know they can stand alone without the Dobie connection by the way children look at them. They have been on the wall for eleven years, and I consider they are there for my edification. I'll admit that at first, I thought that I had it here for the enjoyment of the public. I figured it would be an asset to the shop and I wanted all to see the mural. Finally, I became aware that other painters and children, only, would raise their eyes to the mural. Children know what it's about. It is the first thing they see when they come into the shop, and they don't want to leave until they have seen it all. Children are always concerned with freedom and they recognize what's in the mustangs' manes, eyes, nostrils, feet, hooves, tails, and marvelous muscles; they know what it has to do with. Some adults don't care about the true freedom which they have shaped into something else that passes for freedom; you hear it in the big talk of bosses and also in the big talk of union bosses, and you hear it from the Birchers, too. Some of these people have been forced to adopt current prejudices that pass for freedom. But the children know. After a while you get used to a mural and for days it's just there; then all of a sudden you look at it, and Dobie's mustangs come back.

The reason Dobie is the subject of this column today is that the current issue of the *Texas Observer*, published at Austin, is devoted solely to Dobie. The articles are by many noted writers—Walter Prescott Webb and Mody Boatright, Roy Bedichek, now dead, Lon Tinkle; also articles by critics and editors and one I analyzed carefully only because it was written by a man I have met, Angus Cameron, an editor for Knopf Publishing Co.

Altogether they present a picture of Dobie I have taken for granted, although I have never met the man. I have sent him mayhaw jelly and he has sent me books and pamphlets, and he has written about me in his Sunday column published in daily newspapers, including the *Houston Post*. Still I know a lot about Frank Dobie because I live with his books and I live every day with his horses, and I know about the kind of freedom he writes about. It will be with me to the day I die. I believe that in learning about mustangs, Dobie learned more about the earth they trod and about their pursuers and about the function of all creatures with calcium bones and water-soaked bodies that came out of the sea billions of eons ago and finally walked on the land.

When Frank Dobie walks down that lonesome valley, he will have become aware that like the mustangs and the grass, he must become a part of the earth again, something we all must become reconciled to.

J. FRANK DOBIE DIED IN HIS SLEEP

ON FRIDAY, SEPTEMBER 18, 1964

J. E. REYNOLDS*

Impressions of a friendship

I doubt that any friendship can be so easily explained as Montaigne's "Because it was he, because it was I." If my friendship with Frank Dobie had depended solely on the few days we spent together, there would not have been many hours on which to base the respect and affection I held for him. Frank's books were my introduction to him; the written word, in the form of letters between us over a period of eleven years, strengthened my feeling toward him.

I had been addicted to Frank's books for years before we met. In 1950 Frank wrote an essay for the *Southwest Review* entitled "Books and Christmas." It was not until 1952 that I came upon a copy. There is a statement in this delightful essay that reads, "I have made use of thousands of library books, but any book that really talks to me I want to own." I am a bookseller, specializing in the history of the American West. Always on the lookout for a potential customer, I mailed Frank my next catalogue. He ordered, and his name was placed on our permanent mailing list.

My first letter from Frank was dated February 6, 1953. I had sent him an article I had written for the *Antiquarian Bookman* and had asked him for a photograph of himself to place in my shop. He wrote that he had read my article with interest and that he was sending the photograph, adding, "I hope to see it hanging in your shop sometime." This was my introduction to Frank's good will toward sellers of books, his outgoing generosity with his time and his creative energies.

---

* A bookseller in Van Nuys, California.

One of the prime tools of the bookselling trade is Frank's *Guide to Life and Literature of the Southwest*. Every bookseller dealing in Western Americana quotes J. Frank Dobie. Frank declined his privilege of copyright in 1942 and the *Guide* has remained in public domain ever since. On the copyright page are these words: "Anybody is welcome to help himself to any of it in any way." This was Frank's way of tipping his hat to booksellers. He once wrote me, "I don't understand any collector of books and searcher for knowledge who fails to appreciate book dealers. I've often felt myself to be in a kind of partnership with them."

Possibly we exchanged four letters before our first meeting in Los Angeles in December of 1954. Lawrence Clark Powell, an enthusiastic admirer of Frank and his writings, had, as head librarian of the University of California at Los Angeles, arranged for Frank to make a talk before the Friends of the UCLA Library. I wrote to Frank about his coming visit to say that my wife, Rosalie, and I would like to have him out to our place for lunch. The day after Frank's talk at UCLA I called for him in Westwood and we drove to our home in San Fernando Valley. The few hours Frank had free passed too quickly; I would have wished for much more time to enjoy the range of his conversation, from current world problems to Picasso to the way a *vaquero* rolls his shuck cigarette.

Our second meeting was in March, 1956, when Frank came to Los Angeles to participate in a symposium on the literature and art of the Southwest and Mexico, held at Occidental College. The symposium ended on a Saturday afternoon, and Frank came to stay with us overnight. That evening and the next day we lived the hours together up to the hilt. It seemed as if Frank were a member of the family; he fitted. A continuum of thought had been established during our brief visit in 1954, and deepened through correspondence. It is said that nothing contributes more to the felicity of friendship than agreement on politics and religion. We found ourselves agreed as to the apparent necessity of the former, and we remained uncommitted to the latter.

It was during this second visit that I came to appreciate Frank, the physical man. There was not the slightest affectation in the way he moved his body, unguarded, natural. His walk gave evidence of the time he spent in the saddle. His was a face lined by many past experiences and goodwill and compassion, a face made for laughter and good times. His eyes reflected a keen sensitivity, their intensity quickly changing in response to objects, sounds, and silences. On occasion, something not easily forgotten, his eyes could become piercingly cold.

Nothing incited Frank's indignation quicker than the violation of truth. Lon Tinkle, book critic of the *Dallas Morning News,* once commented on Frank's belief in "the moral obligation not to deceive oneself." That Frank could be hard on self-deceivers is testified to in a letter he sent me, describing a "certain Texan" who posed as a "survivor of the Old West." Frank wrote:

I met him once at a meeting of the oldtime Texas Trail Drivers at San Antonio. He invited me to come up to his room in the St. Anthony Hotel. There he pulled off his coat and revealed a six-shooter he was wearing. There was no more point in his wearing a six-shooter in San Antonio than there would be in my wearing one to your house. He didn't wear it as if he were used to it. He was a four-flusher. He never talked the language of range people at all. He had no look, no gesture, no accent, no suggestion of the West.

Had Frank been capable of hate, which I doubt, it would have been directed toward any despot or censor. In a letter he wrote, "The more I contemplate Jefferson, the greater he looms for me. If there is a more far-ringing sentence than this one of his, I don't know it: *I have sworn upon the altar of God eternal hostility against every form of tyranny over the mind of man.* God, it makes you shiver with admiration!"

We continued our exchange of letters, sometimes a few lines and, on occasion, Frank wrote long, wonderful letters. An April, 1956, letter had this line, "I'm rushed and dogged to the ground," and in June, "My steam is down and eating does not raise it." Something was aggravating Frank and I suspected it was the lack of rain. The Southwest was in the grip of a drought. A merciless sun was drying up water courses, withering vegetation, killing the hundred-year-old oaks on Frank's country place, Cherry Springs. The entire Southwest was athirst. In July he wrote, "I seem like the characters in the play 'Waiting for Godot.' Godot never comes. Godot is not defined. Some people take Godot to be God, but I don't think so at all. I believe the Godot I'm waiting for is rain. This drought is drying me up like the dying oaks over the country."

In the fall of that year I began preparing a Christmas catalogue that was dedicated to Frank. Larry Powell consented to write an introduction for it. "Christmas, the Southwest, and J. Frank Dobie," Larry called it. He disregarded Mark Twain's admonition that "It is best to read the weather forecast before we pray for rain" by asking, "in the name of the river gods," for an end to the drought, a gift to Frank Dobie "for his gifts to us." The catalogue was mailed out early in December. On December 18 the rains came to Texas. In a letter to Larry the following spring, Frank wrote:

It has rained 23 inches this year out at Cherry Springs. The foreground and the backgrounds are so green and the trees that did not die are so burgeoning that one has to look twice to see the skeletons. The tanks are full and running over. The weeds are so rank that the grass can't grow under them, but since very little was left to grow in most places, the weeds are a great blessing. Probably I have seen another wild flower season as riotous and various in color, as vigorous in plants, and as extensive as this, but if so, I have forgotten it. I ride along or look out and Wordsworth's "jocund company"—of daffodils—sings in my consciousness and I am jocund. If you and Jack Reynolds could be here, we'd go over the hills to Cherry Springs and all be as jocund as the Mexican primroses and the black-eyed Susans.

Early in 1957 I corresponded with Carl Hertzog in regard to his designing and printing a book written by Larry Powell, which Carl later printed for me. One August day Carl telephoned to invite Rosalie and me to El Paso as his guests at a testimonial dinner to honor Tom Lea, scheduled for the evening of September 14. When Carl said that Frank would be there, that news set our course for El Paso.

On the night of the dinner it was not difficult to spot Frank among the hundreds of people at the El Paso Country Club. Most of us are nameless in a crowd, but Frank Dobie stood out; he had magnetism. We were able to talk only briefly, but arranged to have breakfast together the next morning.

Sunday morning Rosalie and I met Frank at the Paso del Norte Hotel for a mid-morning breakfast. Ordinarily Frank was an early riser, but the previous night's festivities had kept him up until a late hour. We had a fine breakfast of ham, eggs, and hotcakes, with plenty of coffee. Frank was a great advocate of abundant breakfasts and had chided me for my usual toast and coffee eye-opener. He

268

once said, for my benefit, that the old-time ranch foreman never hired a cowhand who ate a skimpy breakfast, as he would not have staying power.

That afternoon a group of us was to attend a bullfight in Juarez's Plaza Monumental, where six La Laguna bulls were to be fought in honor of Tom Lea. Frank, however, was returning to Austin on the noon plane; he had not planned to attend the *corrida*. If I had known what Frank was to write a year later, I would not have asked his opinion of bullfighting on that Sunday morning. What he wrote was, "I'm constantly struck with how close man is to the beasts of the field rather than how close to man the beasts of the field are." His answer to my question that Sunday morning was worded differently, but it had the same impact: "Beauty is not justified through violence."

The next day Rosalie and I headed for a three-thousand-mile automobile trip into Mexico. We temporarily lost contact with home and did not know until later that within a few days after Frank's return to Austin he was struck down with virus pneumonia. The world nearly lost one of its most humane, air-cleansing voices.

Frank's recovery was slow and he had a long convalescence. He wrote that he now subscribed to the Spanish-Mexican *dicho*: "Isn't it beautiful to do nothing and then after that to rest?" Temporarily he had to forego the use of a typewriter and had to use a dictating machine. "When a man gets too old to adapt," he wrote, "he had just as well quit, and I'm going to have to adapt." Frank's years of observation in preparation for the writing of *The Voice of the Coyote* now paid dividends. He had learned well the lessons of Señor Coyote on how to accommodate to circumstances.

Frank's reservoir of energy never dropped so low that he failed to write his regular Sunday column for the *San Antonio Light* and three other Texas newspapers, a deadline he had not missed since the column's first appearance in 1939. By September, 1958, he was working on an introduction to the Limited Editions Club reprint of *Ramona*, and during that month he wrote an introduction to one of my catalogues. After he sent me the manuscript he wrote, "Well, I've sold the place out in the hills, Cherry Springs. It got so I had to get somebody to drive me to it, and I couldn't take care of it. I feel lost without it."

A letter from Bertha Dobie in December contained good news.

Frank had bought a new country place less than 18 miles from Austin, which "he means to call Wild Gobbler. He says that already he has more feeling for Wild Gobbler than he ever had for Cherry Springs. But I don't know about that."

The desire to make medicine with Frank was strong within me. Frank encouraged this desire, and it was decided that we visit him in July, 1959. By June, Frank had changed the name of Wild Gobbler to Paisano.

I call the place Paisano [he wrote]. It's on Barton Creek. The creek will be running if we can get two or three rains through summer. The house belongs to the land, and the two together have charm. It can be as hot as the hinges of hell here in July and August. If you will risk the hinges, in lieu of air conditioned hotels or motels, you and Rosalie will stay out at Paisano while in Austin. I expect to stay out there with you, part of the time anyway. The house has all modern conveniences, including a refrigerator that makes beer and watermelons cold.

A July that might be hot enough to make us "take off our flesh and sit on our bones" couldn't stop us!

Our route to Austin was via El Paso and San Antonio. Out of El Paso we sped eastward through the high rolling plains and rough plateaus of the great Trans-Pecos, a land of ephemeral vegetation that miraculously supports great numbers of cattle. This is a region whose vastness Frank described as being "altogether out of proportion to the size of the Pecos River." Once we made a roadside stop for Rosalie to pick a bouquet of what she thought was "purple sage," remembered because Frank later told her that what she had brought to show him was *cenizo*, neither purple nor sage, but a gray bush sometimes covered with pink flowers. Frank held Zane Grey and his *Riders of the Purple Sage* responsible for the perpetration of this misinformation; it was just one more reason why Frank was no admirer of the dentist-turned-western-novelist.

What tricks memory plays! It "confounds us" with its emphasis and erasures. My recollection of the area around the Dobie home in Austin is dim, but how vivid are the smiling faces of Frank and Bertha as they greeted us at the door of 702 Park Place. As we sat in Frank's downstairs bedroom-study I was conscious of books, paintings, bronze sculptures and Indian pottery, but my interest was not so much in them as in the man who had collected them.

270

Soon after we arrived, Frank asked me to go with him on an errand, the first of two stops that afternoon to stock provisions to sustain us during our stay at Paisano. Throughout our visit, Frank was host in the grand manner; any suggestion of sharing food and drink expenses was vigorously refused.

I drove Frank to a meat market which was just that. They specialized. Frank said that he had traded there so long he could not recall buying meat anywhere else. The butcher, his white apron stained with sanguine evidence of the day's work, seemed to read Frank's mind, for within a moment he had a loin placed on the well-worn chopping block. There was a twinkle in Frank's eye as he asked, "Is that calf meat?" The butcher, acting as if he had not heard Frank's question, made his cut, resulting in the most finely marbled thick sirloin steak I had ever seen. As we waited for it to be wrapped, I asked Frank to explain his jest on calf meat. "Calf meat is not conducive to virility," he said. "The *viejo* eats bull meat and rides a stallion."

When we returned to Park Place, Bertha had everything ready for Paisano. Edgar Kincaid, Bertha's nephew and a well-known Texas ornithologist, and Gomez, the houseman, accompanied Bertha in one car. Rosalie drove our Chevy, and I drove Frank in his Ford. We made our second stop at a supermarket. Frank and I staggered out, burdened with a wide variety of comestibles. I recall the big watermelon, Frank's favorite fruit. One of Frank's prescriptions, a kind of Texas penicillin, was iced watermelon, interspersed with the sipping of Jack Daniel's.

It was not long before we outdistanced Austin's urbanity and turned west onto a country road. The tranquility of the surroundings pleased the eye; it was a quiet landscape. This was the time of day to scare up wildlife. Frank's trained eyes spotted something. He shouted, "See him! Slow down!" A few yards ahead stood a ring-tail cat. A moment later he was off into the brush. Before we had driven another hundred yards a half-dozen wild turkeys scurried off to the right of the road. I was amazed at their speed; Frank remarked that a turkey hunt was a real test of marksmanship. My anxieties, born of the city "where we are elbowed out of enjoyment," were rapidly disappearing. A relaxed, yet vibrant, contentment came over me.

Soon we passed through a section of road framed by high growth, and I sighted Paisano on a slight rise. Trees in full foliage stood

271

within the fenced grounds. We drove through the gate, parking under a large oak. After carrying in our baggage, I left Rosalie the job of unpacking and wandered out on the front porch. Frank called it the "gallery." In front of the gallery, looking like a giant slingshot, was a dead oak, its naked, mutilated trunk standing in melancholy testimony to the years of drought. Edgar was watching a pair of vermilion flycatchers through the largest binoculars I'd ever seen. Frank told me they were World War I German Army issue. During the coming days we spent many hours on the gallery, cooled by gentle afternoon breezes, looking through the German binoculars, or gazing off into the distance across Barton Creek, to the high truncated escarpment that frames Paisano to the south.

It was twilight when we all sat down to dinner. What a feast Bertha served that evening!—cold turkey and ham brought from Park Place, corn on the cob freshly picked from Paisano's garden, and hot biscuits with natural honey and homemade mustang grape jelly. The table was set outdoors on the west side of the house, near the kitchen door. During our stay, Frank, Rosalie and I ate all our meals, except breakfast, at this outdoor table.

Soon after the table was cleared and the kitchen put in order, Bertha, Edgar and Gomez bade us goodnight and drove back to Austin. We three were left to a comradeship rich in memories.

On that first night Frank handed me a key and pointed to his locked bedroom closet. He said, "That closet isn't meant for clothes." Inside was an assortment of bottled warmth. Above my desk as I write are two tokens of remembrance brought home from Paisano, two empty bottles whose labels read, "John Begg, Superior Blended Scotch Whiskey. By Appointment to the late King George V." Now drained are the golden pegs of liquid from Royal Lochnagar, but the bottles remain to evoke pleasant memories of those summer evenings on Paisano's gallery.

Frank's prodigality extended to food as well as drink. I have mentioned the sirloin steak purchased the first afternoon in Austin. This we relished, broiled to perfection, after our first day at Paisano. I recall that Frank asked Rosalie to bring out the broiler pan so he could mop up the drippings with his bread. Another day we drove our two cars to Austin; Frank was to stay at Park Place overnight to catch up on mail. We were to return that afternoon to Paisano. Unknown to us,

Frank again went shopping at the meat market. When Rosalie and I were ready to leave, Frank handed Rosalie two large packages, asking, "Do you know how to cook stew?" She does. One package contained porterhouse steaks for Rosalie and me for that evening, the other a large quantity of stew meat. Rosalie cooked the stew for Frank's return to Paisano the next night. Along with the usual stew vegetables, provided from Frank's garden, she included string beans, also from the garden. This fascinated Frank, for he said he had never had string beans in stew before. He set a grueling pace at dinner that night, insisting that Rosalie save the leftovers for the next day's lunch. He did not want the stew reheated; he ate it cold. That in turn fascinated Rosalie, and it pleased her. Stew that is palatable cold has to be good!

Our first morning at Paisano I awakened early. The warm morning sun, the call of the bobwhite, and the buzzing of the bees in the lantana growing outside our bedroom window all conspired to activate what Frank called "rejuvenated life juices." I went out to explore on my own. At the barn, the door resisted on unwilling hinges. Inside were evidences of the former owner's workday tasks: old automobile license plates helping to date the age of cans of rusted nails, half-used coils of wire, an array of worse-for-wear handtools, some carelessly-closed cans of paint, and a couple of nearly used-up brushes. I had spotted an old cultivator seat, made into a garden chair, which was so rusty that it was no good for clean pants. By the time I heard Frank talking to Rosalie in the kitchen, I had scraped off most of the rust and had painted the cultivator seat a forest green. When Frank surveyed my handiwork he recommended that I repeat my artistry in the near future on another cultivator seat located in the tomato patch, which was Frank's favorite spot to sit and survey the surroundings. One afternoon while Frank was napping I did paint it. Soon after our return to California, Frank sent a letter in which he remarked, "I believe you did the best job on those cultivator seats that I've noticed anywhere."

The house had a spare room, a utility room, where, among mounted deer heads and other baggage of the past, was a large sack of coarsely chopped grain. Upon rising, Frank would go to this room and scoop out a tin cupful of grain, taking it out to scatter near the barn. The bobwhites, for whom it was meant, were usually there waiting for their benefactor. If they were late for breakfast, Frank whistled a very good facsimile of their call. This brought them running.

Each morning, for about half an hour before breakfast, Frank and I hoed weeds. Rosalie commented that we seemed to do more talking and leaning on handles than hoeing. During these pre-breakfast weedings Frank often talked about the disposition of nature. He was offended by man's "damnable habit" of disturbing what he called "the orderly disorder of nature." The pair of abandoned wagon wheels near the compost pit, still resting on their rusted axle, with vines and weeds growing between the spokes, was natural and met with his approval—but not wagon wheels neatly nailed to fence posts, not an ox yoke hanging from the crossbar of an entry gate. He disliked the "do-daddy pretenses" that make otherwise pleasing abodes look like "two-bit California tourist courts."

The downward thrust of Frank's hoe had resolution, cutting deep into the root systems of what he called "the invaders of productive soils." Once, while piling up the result of a morning's weeding, he remarked, "They are the bandits, the delinquents of the flora. They gang up in the power of numbers and expropriate the land, choking out the nutrient grasses." The human parallel was obvious. During another hoeing session Frank said, "I guess I'm a lot like Ben Lilly when it comes to lonesomeness. It has never overtaken me when alone. You are never alone in experiencing the pulse of nature around you. Nature is not a Pollyannish better-than-all-possible-worlds where there is love, non-violent and utopian equilibrium—no, there is dominance, dictatorship, exploitation, brutish and unthinking."

It was not merely the recognition of, but the cognition of, nature's "unwearied power" that was important to Frank Dobie. The lessons to be learned from the observation of natural things are available to all. In speaking of the reading of books as sources of knowledge, Frank wrote, "I should probably have been a wiser and better informed man had I spent more time out with the grasshoppers, horned toads, and coyotes."

The essence of Frank's cognition of nature is made manifest in these words of his, to me one of the most powerful declarations of faith I have ever read:

No hymn lifts my heart higher than the morning call of the bobwhites or the long fluting cry of sandhill cranes out of the sky at dusk. I have never

seen a painting of the Crucifixion more spiritual than "rosy-fingered dawn."
I have never smelled incense in a church as refining to the spirit as a spring
laden with aroma from a field of those wild lupins called bluebonnets. Not
all hard truths are beautiful, but "beauty is truth." It incorporates love and
is incorporated by love. It is the great translator and transfigurator of the
world. The sense for it distinguishes mundane coarseness from divine re-
finement. It is the goal of all great art. Its presence everywhere makes it
free to all. It is not so abstract or difficult as freedom and justice, but beauty
and freedom and justice, all incorporating truth and goodness, are to me
unshakable poles of faith and sustainers to mind and spirit.

Frank had expressed a desire that we three visit his beloved
Cherry Springs together. We made the trip the day before we left
Paisano to head home for California. During the years that Frank
owned Cherry Springs he had expended considerable time and
money recovering its potential. He was concerned that the new
owners might allow the land to be overgrazed; he said, "That would
be like an artist having his painting mutilated." When we were within
a quarter of a mile from the white frame house he asked me to stop
the car. He got out and inspected the grass, taking in the entire landscape with expert eyes. He concluded his painting had not been
mutilated.

We toured Cherry Springs for over an hour, Frank pointing out the
landmarks. Once we stopped and took a short walk off the road where
we picked leaves from a pleasantly aromatic, low-growing bush that
Frank called "San Nicolas." Frank asked Rosalie to brew a tea from
the leaves that evening, which she did. He told how, a number of
years before, he was packing out of the Big Bend country in the dark
of night with his Mexican guide when he smelled a perfume in the
air that he could not identify. He asked the guide the source of the
pleasant aroma, and the guide answered, "San Nicolas, Señor."

As we walked over the grounds near the house, Frank retrieved a
discarded blue graniteware coffee pot that showed the marks of long
use. He put it in the car with what I considered, at the time, unusual
care. Upon our return to Paisano the first thing Frank did was to
take that pot into the house and carefully place it at the side of the
stone fireplace in the parlor. Then he turned to me and said, "That
coffee pot has been my companion over thousands of miles of Mexico.
I've cooked beans and boiled coffee in it. It brings back memories of
many a pack trip in which it served me well."

We tried not to let the next morning's parting dampen our spirits that last night at Paisano. We sat in the twilight on the gallery, tall glasses in hand. We talked late and arose early. We packed the car in silence. The reality of our departure was upon us; we knew that there is "no joy so great but runneth to an end."

We said our goodbyes hurriedly. I remember when Rosalie was getting in the car Frank remarked how nice she looked in her blue gingham dress. As we drove off we waved until Paisano was out of sight, Frank standing on the gallery waving back. On the margin of a newspaper clipping Frank sent us with his first letter after we returned home is written, "For Rosalie and Jack, whose tracks at Paisano will always be there for me."

On my desk is a paper weight in the likeness of a sea shell, formed from the limy deposits of the Mesozoic age, originating in the limestone stratum of Texas' Edwards Plateau. Frank gave it to me at Paisano. Its appearance belies its toughness, its resistance to the tyranny of time. It symbolizes, for me, J. Frank Dobie and his literary legacy, recalling Whitman's

> My foothold is tenon'd and mortis'd in granite,
> I laugh at what you call dissolution,
> And I know the amplitude of time.

HARRY RANSOM*

"J am busy becoming contemporary with myself"

J. Frank Dobie and his literary career have been described in many generalizations. Each is true in part—but only in part. Each will deserve restatement as Dobie, the writer and the man, becomes a permanent figure in the history which he helped to make.

Dobie's earliest public and academic reputation acquired the misleading label of "folklorist." As a matter of fact, "folklore"—which he constantly re-defined for himself and his readers—was only a point of departure. Among sundry intellectual specialities and academic moated towers, the term gave him a small, habitable fort. From its hand-hewn battlements he took occasional potshots at the stiff educational formalities, empty ceremonies, and stuffed vanities of the academic world. Within its walls (which opened wide gates of access to him by all kinds of unarmed honest folk) he maintained the essence of his selfhood. He refused to form a troop of little admiring defenders within this free stockade. The only "Dobie School" which appeared from 1920 to 1964 was a wide and friendly company of all sorts of estates, ages and attitudes who in fact or in spirit were schooled by his example. About one of the University's proudest and most ambiguous mottoes, he once said, "Truth can't be institutional-

* Chancellor of The University of Texas System, who knew Dobie thirty years, beginning when they were colleagues on the English faculty at Austin.

ized. It can be learned and it can be spread, but there is no curriculum for intellectual honesty."

In his lifetime, Dobie became one of the Legends of Texas. Yet his is a legend too large to fit into future editions of his early book by that title.

As an author of books, essays, and stories, as editor, talker, teacher, newspaper columnist, letter writer, epigrammatist, and genius in the rare art of eloquent silence, Dobie was an individualist. On occasion, his individualism appeared to be Texan and sounded American. Its purely literary origins, however, were in the purest idiom of the English language. More than once he said that the piece of writing which had influenced him most was Hazlitt's "On the Feeling of Immortality in Youth." His work shows the influence of no "Western" writer. He "collected" Hudson. He adapted John Stuart Mill. He admired White of Selborne (and every other man who not only looked into nature but really saw it and felt it and joined it to living belief).

In the formal sense, Dobie was never a student of literary classics; but he had a profound knowledge of Biblical and Shakespearean text and remembered words of men as different as Walton, Burton, Lamb, Carlyle, and Thoreau. He taught literature not according to period, theme, circle, or critical theory. He simply laid open for his students a wealth of durable ideas, transient attitudes and fleeting impressions with great clarity and deep conviction, but without dogmatism. His literal summary of his pedagogy: Every teacher should have many saddle bags crammed with facts, fancies, impressions, and opinions for his own campfires and his own forced marches. But no student should be harnessed in the trappings of any teacher.

As a stylist, Dobie developed his own ways of writing. The process was less deliberate than that of most authors and less conscious, except for the long and profound influence of Bertha Dobie. His memory resorted constantly to the melodies of the best English and American writers. Yet his tongue and his pen were often tuned to the Texas range, the Mexican tale-maker, and rhythms in his own head. By these means he brought sense and substance into what might otherwise have been pages of borrowed provincialism smeared with local color.

A reader of Dobie's "bibliography" will find both depth and breadth. Concerning plans for the volume, he was highly dubious and only reluctantly cooperative. He kept saying: "Let's wait until something better comes. I don't want a bibliography deposited until I'm deposited."

Future scholars must arrange and keep rearranging the categories of his writing. Despite his own disclaimers and those of his most attentive readers, one section will surely be "Folklore"—the lore of the Southwest and Mexico, which he recorded after immeasurable travel, wide reading, wider correspondence, and careful listening. Among his earlier works are legendary treasure, folk custom, folk language, tales and anecdotes in motion and lost anecdotes and tales to which he gave new impetus. His earliest devotion was to the range as part of American history, an unspoiled and undefensive loyalty to the ranch, ranch life, and to the people, animals, plants, seasons—a calendar which cannot be turned back and a compass of hard times, good times, courage, failure, joy, companionship in an unstaked, unfenced world.

Dobie's earliest impact upon academic study and writing (and the periodic shock waves which he generated in academic circles) have caused many of his strongest admirers to forget one of his great intellectual strengths. There are those who cherish the Dobie "position" only because of the intransigence with which he invariably confronted the organized intransigence of regulations on which he thought the regulators set too much stock. When such a regulation (from traffic law to academic administration) seemed to him to be a device—even a reasonable device—he refused to erect it into a philosophy or a way of life.

Among many shifting positions in these external matters, Dobie never hesitated on any given day to proclaim, "Here I stand." Yet he was never satisfied with merely standing pat or staying put. Unlike many writers and teachers who discover a good thing and convert it into an insurance policy or a security guarantee, Dobie kept changing his points of view, his willing exceptions, his keen interests. In a dozen ways, he wrote and said, "I am busy becoming contemporary with myself." His joy in that process is a sensation which no close-minded writer—radical, liberal, conservative, reactionary, or narcissistic—can ever share.

In the future of criticism now beginning, Dobie's volumes on the longhorn, the coyote, and the mustang are likely to attract most attention and gain highest praise. His lyrical passage on "The Mustang" will probably be quoted more often—at least in classrooms and on official occasions—than anything else he wrote.

The likelihood is double irony, good and bad. Good because in the broadest sense, Dobie was a poet. Bad because this memorable manifesto on freedom may be mistaken for sentimental devotion, nostalgia or prescriptive doctrine. The real mind and spirit of Frank Dobie as a man are reflected better in *The Mustangs* as a whole, in the companion books, and throughout a life of talk and written words not yet in print. By all of these Dobie expressed his aspiration to freedom for himself and for every other human being. He attained that freedom in his thinking, maintained it—sometimes against formidable odds—in his living, and defended it unforgettably as the essential condition of all men who would stay fully alive.

MARTIN SHOCKLEY*

When I heard of Frank Dobie's death

When I heard of Frank Dobie's death, I thought of the death of the old poet in "Night of the Iguana." Nobody said, "Please, God, now"; but even those of us who sometimes think we might manage things better must approve. Mr. Dobie read his special issue of the *Texas Observer*, received his Presidential award, saw the first copy of his last book, and went quietly to sleep. Well done, God.

It may be regretted that The University of Texas, only now recovering from the Rainey scandal and the Painter shame, never accorded him the full measure of honor which is his due. He was awarded honorary degrees by Southwestern University and Cambridge. His name will be honored among authors and scholars while the names of the regents who drove him out will live, if at all, in infamy.

Among many fond memories, I recall the amusing irony of introducing him to the Texas Folklore Society. I was toastmaster that year when he was main speaker and honored guest. I remember my introduction:

A Texan not by birth but by choice, I came to Texas with about average ignorance and prejudice. I had always considered the coyote a pesky varmint, a cunning chicken thief, a sneaky villain best seen over the sights of a 30-30; then I read a book by Frank Dobie and learned that the coyote is a noble creature with a proud and independent spirit and a fierce love of

* Professor of English at North Texas State University, secretary-treasurer of the Texas Institute of Letters, and past president of the Texas Conference of the American Association of University Professors.

freedom. I had always considered the longhorn a stupid cow critter, all bone, gristle, and stringy meat, mean, vicious, and hard to handle; then I read a book by Frank Dobie and learned that the longhorn is a noble creature with a proud and independent spirit and a fierce love of freedom. I had always considered the mustang the sorriest specimen of horseflesh, hammer-headed, wall-eyed, ewe-necked, sway-backed, broom-tailed, ornery and dangerous; then I read a book by Frank Dobie and learned that the mustang is a noble creature with a proud and independent spirit and a fierce love of freedom. Now, they tell me Mr. Dobie is writing about rattlesnakes, and I anticipate an agonizing reappraisal.

Frank enjoyed it as much as I did.

Never a narrow regionalist, he found among the mustangs and the longhorns significant symbols of universal human values. I have sometimes felt that Texans lack the perspective to appreciate Frank Dobie, a greater man in Cambridge than in Austin. Texans tend to think of him as a mossy-horned maverick, the symbol of intransigent individualism. This he was, but he was far more. I identify in his career five of the major concerns of my time. First, he loved and understood his land and his people; his career was based upon the interpretation of his own Southwestern heritage. Second, as a professor he forcefully repudiated the popular cult of educational mediocrity, always demanding quality, always urging toward that excellence which we have not yet achieved. Third, he spoke for equal justice for all races even before the Supreme Court, the United States Congress, and the Christian Churches came to join him. Fourth, among isolationists and Dixiecrats he constantly affirmed his faith in an international society based upon law, justice, and universal human rights. Fifth, among Birchites and bigots he stood always and uncompromisingly for intellectual freedom. I know no man with whom I can more closely identify in intellectual interests and moral values. In all five, the Dobie position, once maverick, is now majority.

Addressing the Texas Institute of Letters, Harry Ransom said that he had tried hard to understand Frank Dobie, and had decided that the fundamental principle of Dobie's life had been to pitch in on the side of the underdog. I thought then, and have not changed my opinion, that I know no more honorable principle for a good man's life.

Now that he is gone, each of us bears a larger responsibility for the support of those ideals which were more ably supported while he

282

lived: to stand up taller on the side of decency; to speak out more courageously for the cause of justice; to extend more generously to others those rights which we most cherish for ourselves. A man who fights for his rights is a brave man, and I respect him; but a man who fights for the rights of others is a noble man, and I honor him.

Frank Dobie never held office, yet by proclamation of the governor of Texas he was buried in the state cemetery. In the heart of Texas, he lies deep.

EDMUND HEINSOHN

He brought a free man

The Reverend Heinsohn said, in part, at Dobie's funeral:

J. Frank Dobie's active connection with The University of Texas faculty covered a third of a century. Some of us find it difficult to remember the University as ever having been without this man and his influence. Such has been the impact of his life upon the institution and upon us.

What was it then that he brought to the University? He brought a free man. Again and again he declared his independence of those things he thought would restrict his freedom. He realized that in order to be really free a man must be able to say to the position he occupies that he does not have to stay in that position, but is free to go to something else. He knew the freedom that a man knows when he is not the prisoner of his financial income, that he could make less and still be free, and that he could make more and possibly lose his freedom.

We have a way of giving lip service to free enterprise. And usually we are talking about free enterprise in economics, and stop short of free enterprise in thought, in speech, in press, and in religion. Quite frequently we do not have confidence in the operation of the open market-place of ideas. Frank Dobie was always with his ideas moving into the open market there to do battle with others and their ideas.

His was the kind of freedom that made it possible for him to stand in the presence of royalty and not feel inferior, and stand in the presence of the lowly and not feel superior. In Texas, in Oklahoma, in

New York, in the nation's capital, in Cambridge, his voice was lifted not only in defense of freedom for himself, but also in the defense of freedom for all. He used his freedom to stand up for justice in the presence of injustice, and in a spirit of compassion to come to the help of those in need.

His shaggy head was always a little ahead of his body. Those of us who had the privilege of knowing him well could always say: There freedom walks, there freedom thinks, there freedom talks, there freedom teaches, there freedom acts, there freedom hopes.